SHAPING TEXT

…because there is nothing on it. The title of the book, set small, that's all. 'Half-title' or 'bastard title' is what this page is called. The French say 'false title' (*faux-titre*) and the Germans call it 'dirt title' (*Schmutztitel*). The actual presentation of the book – including its subtitle, author, publisher and perhaps the place and year of publication – happens on the title page, which comes right after this one. The half-title is a bit of a throwaway page. Its original function was to protect the book block on its way from the printing office to the binder or buyer. Some bookbinders used to cut off the half-title, to resell the paper. Then as now, it is not a good idea to discard the half-title and begin the book block with the title page, as the book cover or binding will be glued to it (with or without the use of endpapers) and the page will not open elegantly. And so this page will forever be a non-page: a false start, a leaf with no contents. Except in this book.

Everyone who picks up a newspaper, takes a walk in the city, watches television, receives an email, reads a letter, fills in a form or visits a website, uses a product made by somebody who, consciously or not, has been

SHaPing

text.

Shaping text is our term for how communicators choreograph content in order to guide and influence readers. This book is about the choices that are made while doing so, both intentionally or unwittingly. It provides the necessary apparatus to make decisions more consciously and to be a better and more expressive judge of other people's designs. It is also a richly illustrated tour of the wondrous world of typography and type design. This book was written by **Jan Middendorp** in Berlin and first published in 2012 by **BIS Publishers** in Amsterdam.

→ **Marian Bantjes critiques the alphabet**
(From her book *I Wonder*, Thames & Hudson /
The Monacelli Press, 2010)

BIS Publishers
Building Het Sieraad
Postjesweg 1
1057 DT Amsterdam
The Netherlands
T +31 (0)20 515 0230
F +31 (0)20 515 0239

bis@bispublishers.nl
www.bispublishers.nl

ISBN 978 90 6369 223 0

Copyright © 2012 BIS Publishers
and Jan Middendorp

Image research and design
Jan Middendorp

Editorial and production assistance
Catherine Dal, Anthony Noel, Florian Hardwig
and Christine Gertsch. Florian Hardwig contributed texts to pages 110–115 and 138–139.

Drawings
Christine Gertsch, Christin Huber, Edgar Walthert

Photography
Eva Czaya, Christine Gertsch, JM

Typefaces
Agile (Edgar Walthert, Incubator/Village), Rooney
(Jan Fromm), the Shire Types (Jeremy Tankard)

THIS is a very nice pair. Whoever
did this was really thinking about
the relationship between the upper-
and lower-case. I like the way the
capital **B** has some variation in the
proportions from top to bottom.
It has muscle; it has fat.
    Obviously designed by a man,
the ball and stick of the lower-case
b is simple and, appropriately, half
of the capital **B**. Talk about male
and female! That buxom, pregnant
capital together with the excitable
lower-case. *Bbbbeautiful.*

UNSUPERVISED junior
designers. This is just lazy
design, in my humble
opinion. It is a curve, and
a smaller curve. What's
up with that? Think
outside the circle.

126

Preceding pages: 'M' from Raffia Initials,
a 1952 typeface designed by Henk Krijger
for the Amsterdam Typefoundry. This
unpublished digital version, drawn by
Canada Type's Patrick Griffin in dialogue
with Peter Enneson and the author, has
separate fonts for the three or four
strands in each letter.

The typeface family used for the title is
The Shire Types by Jeremy Tankard: six
fonts that mix upper- and lowercase
letterforms and that can be combined
freely. Hence the different appearances
of the title on the back and font cover
and title page.

contents

7 Introduction: Culture, communication, typography

11 Ways of reading

These words don't mean a thing... **12**
Legibility: design versus science **14**
Typography and the designer's role **16**
Visual rhetoric **18**
Modes of reading **20**
Stream of ideas: immersed in a text **22**
Navigation: guiding the reader **24**
Staging the reader's experience **26**
Seducing with type: packaging **28**
Seducing with type: book covers **30**
Corporate identity **32**
Information design, at your service **34**
Designing for the web **36**
Type for type's sake: products for typophiles **38**

41 Organising and planning

Controlling the canvas **42**
Modularity and efficiency **44**
Divine proportions **46**
Secret formulas of book design **48**
Looking into grid systems **50**
Types of grid **52**
The grid exposed **54**
Grids on the web **56**

59 Knowing and selecting type

Thinking about type selection **60**
Text and display: bread and butter **62**
Typeface, font, family, font format **64**
Family members **66**
Italics true and false **68**
Typeface anatomy **70**
Comparing fonts **72**
Type classification **74**
Classifying by writing tools **76**
Old letterforms, new fonts **78**
'Type' before Gutenberg **80**
Broken script (blackletter) **82**
The renaissance oldstyle **84**
Royal contrasts **86**
Typographic noise **88**
Dominant type: Modernism, Art Deco **90**
Modularity in type and lettering **92**
That Swiss feeling **94**
The emancipation of the sans-serif **96**
Text typefaces: an update **98**
Optical size: tailor-made type **100**
Choosing typefaces **102**
Combining typefaces **104**
'Type' without a font **106**
Scripts: fonts or lettering? **108**
Finding and buying fonts **110**
Type on the screen: the facts **112**
The year of webfonts **114**

117 Typographic detail

Making text look right **118**
Formatting the paragraph **120**
Alignment **122**
Hyphenation & justification **123**
Distinguishing sections, paragraphs **124**
Initials **125**
Letter and word, black and white **126**
Fine-tuning headlines **127**
Spacing: tracking and kerning **128**
Adjusting optical alignment **129**
OpenType functions and features **130**
Small capitals **132**
Ligatures &c. **134**
Swashes, flourishes, beginnings and endings **135**
Punctuation at home and abroad **136**
Hyphens, dashes, spaces – ¡and more! **137**
Numerals, figures, digits, numbers **138**
Adjusting to circumstances **140**
Small and narrow type **141**

143 Design strategies and concepts

Typography and good ideas **144**
Style and statement **146**
Reference, pastiche, parody **148**
Logo strategies **150**
Corporate typeface **152**
Materiality & the third dimension **154**
Spatial illusions **156**
The fourth dimension **158**
The allure of the hand-made **160**

163 Type and technology

History of typographic technology **164**
Five centuries of typesetting **166**
Lithography **167**
Speeding things up **168**
Typesetting with light **170**
Display type for everyone **171**
Pros and cons of progress **172**
Type in the digital age **173**
Further reading **174**
Image index by designer **176**

das gesicht unserer zeit ist klare sachlichkeit
die neuen **bauformen** sind nicht mehr architektur im alten sinne: konstruktion plus fassade

das neue **kleid** ist nicht mehr kostüm

die neue **schrift** ist keine kalligraphie

häuser, kleider, schriften werden in ihrer form durch die einfachsten elemente bestimmt

Culture, communication, typography

← Page from the type specimen launching the Erbar typeface, Ludwig & Mayer, Frankfurt am Main, 1930. The text reads, with lowercase modesty (or pretence): 'the face of our time is crisp and business-like. the new forms of building are no longer architecture in the old sense: construction plus façade. the new garment is not a costume. the new letter is not calligraphy. the shapes of houses, clothing and letters are determined by the simplest basic elements.'

↓ Leaflet for 'Polish handyman team' in the Netherlands. A typical example of vernacular desktop design, set centered in Times New Roman. Martijn Oostra collection.

POOLS
KLUSSENTEAM
RENO-POL

BIEDT ZICH AAN

-SCHILDERWERK BINNEN EN BUITEN
-STUKADOREN , TEGELEN
-BEHANGEN
-PARKET LEGGEN , LAMINAAT
-VERBOUWEN , ONDERHOUD
-LOODGIETERS , DAKBEDEKKERS
-VERWARMING VAN GEBOUWEN

NU VANAF

€ 12.50 PER UUR !!!

helemaal legaal , goede referenties

Neem contact op met RENO-POL in Nederland:
Tel. 0900 040 11 02
(0.10 € cent per minuut)
of
070 514 00 19

www.reno-pol.pl

A good way to gain an understanding of an era is by exploring the writing and printing of the time. The period around 1930 was a time of change, of sharp contrasts between the old and the new. The page from the Erbar type specimen shown here sums that up quite nicely. The ornaments of Baroque architecture (a strong presence in 1930s German cities, not yet bombed), rococo clothing and Gothic typefaces are not only portrayed as hopelessly outdated, there's also something decadent about them. The Erbar typeface advertised here seems, like other business-like types from the era, Futura being the forerunner, to be part of a major cleanup. Beneath the call for the simplification of form slumbers restlessness and thirst for action – a yearning for new values.

Everything is possible

In our own time too, typography – the shaping of texts – gives interesting indications about how our culture is doing. For starters, a brief glance over the typographic landscape does not give any decisive clue about a dominant tendency, about common desires and dreams. Just like in former times, designers are looking for new forms that somehow express the technique with which they have been made – and yet these very same designers hark back to just about every style and letterform that has been handed to us from the past. Anything goes, and it has become a rare thing for anyone to get worked up about other people's choices. This can be interpreted positively – the world is an infinite reservoir of possibilities of expression, and nothing is 'forbidden' – but it can also be interpreted as indifference: who still *cares*?

Moreover, there is considerable confusion about the status of the graphic designer's craft, not to mention activities that used to be rated as highly specialised skills, but have virtually disappeared: typesetter, proofreader, lithographer. There are typesetters in the digital world, but they are few and they are dying out. Their tasks have tacitly been divided between authors and editors on the one hand, and designers and DTP specialists on the other. These people are not necessarily trained to carefully handle text, with the result that text often looks worse than it used too. Not many people notice, because you get used to everything.

In addition, pieces of visual communication are increasingly being designed by people who have little time to worry about design and composition, because they have other things on their minds: their real job is being a manager, secretary or organiser. Yet a report that a laser printer spits out twelve copies of is also a publication. A PowerPoint presentation is a form of typography. A blog is a piece of graphic design, even though bloggers may hardly realise which formal choices are being made for them and how they can influence that. In short, the advent of the computer has led to a plethora of non-professional design. One way graphic designers have found to respond to this is by incorporating elements of vernacular digital design in their work – by setting centred text in Arial, Times or Courier, by using italicised capitals, heavy underlining, black print on yellow, pink or light blue offset paper; often it is not clear whether this is irony or if this self-consciously 'undesigned' style is now simply regarded as cool. The stylistic confusion is complete.

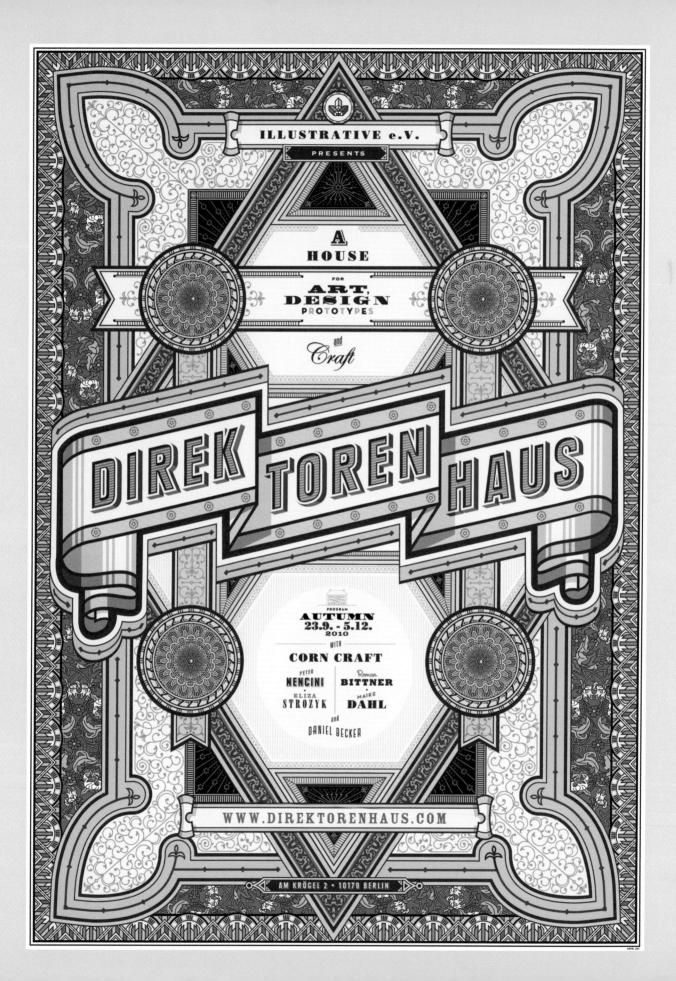

The good news is that more and more nonprofessional users are getting interested in lettering and typography. A new Windows or Apple computer comes with a larger collection of fonts than an average composing room had in stock fifty years ago. Today's secretaries, teachers or shop owners have tools for design and typesetting at their disposal that are about as sophisticated as the equipment available to professionals back then. It is only natural that some of those users want to know more about design, type and images. The massive success of specialised websites and blogs proves that. Nearly 70,000 people have subscribed to the RSS feed of *I love typography*, the typographic blog of Japan-based Brit John Boardley. The newsletters this writer edits for MyFonts go out twice a month to over 950,000 opted-in users. No trade journal has ever achieved such large audiences. Many readers are designers and publishers, but many others work in a completely different sector, are students of art, journalism or economics, or retired managers.

What kind of book is this?

This brings us to this book's target group – which is quite broad. This book is about the shaping and multiplication of written language, whether that's on paper, in the environment or on screens. It is intended as a guide for font users, for designers, writers or editors. Type, as a basic building block, is central to the contents but this is not a book about type design. Typefaces operate in a context – a book or magazine, an advertising campaign, a branding or signage project. Therefore, this book reverses the usual order: instead of starting by discussing the bricks – type – we first examine some of the structures that are built with them and the tasks they perform.

Next, ample attention is given to the development and particularities of letterforms, but mostly as part of the tasks they are to perform. We will also be zooming in on the details and discussing typographic 'etiquette'. Designers have more freedom than before, but there is still some agreement on what constitutes a good or a not-so-good typographic solution; there even is a certain consensus about typographic 'crimes' and 'sins'. These are mentioned, but without being moralistic about them. There is much sinning going on in today's typography, and it is often done on purpose. But in order to do this accurately, the designer needs to make conscious choices, and that requires some know-how about the alternatives. This is perhaps the book's chief task: to lay down a foundation which, if desired, offers a basis for more licentious behaviour.

Acknowledgements

This book took surprisingly long to make, and I'd like to extend my thanks first and foremost to Rudolf van Wezel of BIS publishers for his patience and encouragement. Thanks, also, to a few friends in the Dutch design world who have offered editorial advice: Vincent van Baar, Huug Schipper and Jan Willem Stas. Thanks to Laurence Penney for the English title. And special thanks to those who have lent editorial and design assistance during the final phase of the project: Catherine Dal, Christine Gertsch, Florian Hardwig and Anthony Noel. Thanks, finally and most importantly, to the many designers who made available such impressive examples of their personal approach to shaping text.

← Roman Bittner and his fellow members of the Berlin design studio ApfelZet ('Command-Z') were trained in the functionalist tradition of German modernism. Under the influence of, among other things, the turn-of-the-century romantic architecture of the old suburbs they developed a distinctive graphic style in which illustration and ornament play a major role. This poster for an art and design event mimics the exuberant cover designs of typeface catalogues from the last decades of the nineteenth century.

↓ In the same year – 2010 – and the same city, this poster was created by xplicit design. This, too, is contemporary, postmodern graphic design using a centred arrangement as a tongue-in-cheek rhetorical device; yet it could not look more different.

Playing with scale: Freitag

In 1993 graphic designer brothers
Markus and Daniel Freitag from Zurich,
Switzerland, needed a heavy-duty,
functional, water-repellent bag to carry
their designs. Inspired by the cheerfully
coloured lorries rumbling along the
highway just in front of their flat, they
cut a messenger bag out of an old truck
tarpaulin. As the carry belt they used
second-hand car seat-belt webbing,
while an old bicycle inner tube provided
the edging. Besides the original messenger bag the Freitag brothers have
since created and marketed over forty
types of ladies' and men's bags. When
the tarpaulin canvases are cut down to
size, the truck typography, designed on
a highway scale, acquires an unintended abstraction and at times a monumental beauty.
Photos: Noë Flum, courtesy of Freitag.

Ways of reading

These words don't mean a thing…

…if you cannot read them. This may sound like stating the obvious; yet it's worth dwelling upon the miracle of reading for a minute. Imagine that this page contained only characters from a script you don't know: Arabic, Chinese, Thai. You can look at such a page, admiring the shapes and colours, but there cannot be any question of reading. The text is a collection of abstract signs and the page will remain a sealed book to you.

If you're dealing with a script you do know – in this case: the Latin script – and if the text is written in a language you understand, then the opposite happens. You're not seeing signs, but words. You are reading. You jump from sentence to sentence at breakneck speed: your mouth wouldn't be able to keep up. And something curious is happening. 'The printed letters dissolve in your mind like an effervescent pill in a glass of water. For a short moment, all those black signs disappear off the stage, change their outfits, and return as ideas, as representations, and sometimes even as real images and sounds.' Thus Gerard Unger, the Netherlands' best known type designer, captures the essence of reading in his book *While you are reading*.

Not only is reading one of the most fascinating human skills, in our society it is also a vital one. People who have difficulty reading – a newspaper, a warning sign, a letter from the tax authorities – are socially vulnerable and more likely to get into trouble.

Learning to see

Moreover, 'reading' is more than just deciphering letters and words. From childhood we learn to see connections between the various elements that we are offered on a page. We learn to select what is important to us; we learn, if only on a basic level, to draw conclusions from the interplay between text and images. We learn to interpret the way a text is shaped – its position, contrasts, size, colour and even its choice of typeface – as part of its message.

Not every reader understands the contents of a text in his or her language equally well. There are varying levels of literacy, relating to a person's talent but more importantly to his or her background and education. The same goes for 'visual literacy'. It, too, is not so much a question of aptitude but of learning to see. However lucidly an insurance form or internet page may have been designed, it means little to someone who has never been faced with one before. It's probably a fallacy to think that there is such a thing as an interface from which anyone can grasp the workings 'intuitively' without previous knowledge. In the same way that a language needs to be learned, so too does a language of form.

Those engaged in shaping text – designers, art directors, printers, publishers, editors – need to deal with the visual literacy of their reading public. In each of these roles, one is likely to encounter a wide array of users and readers, from clueless to sophisticated and demanding. In order to communicate with such diverse audiences, content and form must be handled in a conscious and reflective way.

↓ Fragment of the front page of a Japanese-speaking newspaper in San Francisco. If you do not know Japanese, your attention is involuntarily drawn to the phrases, 'Bay Area' and 'Club Jazz Nouveau', the only words we can read.

'Rules' and 'laws'

This does not imply that to be a good designer or editor you need to abide by some guidebook full of rules and regulations. There certainly exists an impressive array of typographic 'laws' and conventions, but as we will see those rules are being bent on a daily basis, and quite consciously so, since time immemorial. Most designers have invented their own exceptions. What is crucial, though, is to know that these conventions exist in order to obey or reject them consciously – not out of ignorance.

A convention is, quite literally, an agreement – something which people have agreed to do in a certain way. A convention can be arbitrary (like driving on the right or the left) but also functional (like building in the steering wheel on the left side in cars made for right-hand driving). The discipline known as typography – the shaping of texts – has countless conventions, some of which are very reasonable and functional while others are remnants of old habits and traditions, and many are at some point between these two. As many of your users may be aware of those conventions, or dependent on them to make some sense of what they see and read, it is a good idea to learn something about typographic 'rules' and possible exceptions. And more importantly: to learn to see better than your users.

↑ Monthly calendar for the Amsterdam theatre De Balie by the Lava studio. De Balie's versatility and multiculturalism were translated into a visual identity with a multitude of typefaces and colourful ornaments. The house style displays a relaxed attitude towards typographic rules: underlined texts or bold italic capitals are not forbidden.

← Another rule-breaker: 'Cheap Aesthetics' designed by Alex Scholing, was part of a series of ads for FontShop Benelux. Deliberately ugly, the series won a mention for Typographic Excellence in the annual TDC Awards.

→ Legibility 14

→ Typographic detail 117

→ Concept and style 144–146

Legibility: design versus science

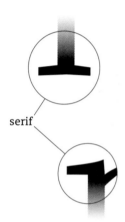

serif

Reading is a virtually unfathomable interplay between the eyes and the brain. Within fractions of seconds letters, words and pieces of sentences are recognised, connections are found, conclusions drawn. It is hard to prove what factors exactly influence the efficiency of that process. For many decades, psychologists, physiologists and typographers have conducted research on the optical, physical and psychological aspects of reading. With sophisticated machinery they have investigated the ways in which our eyes perceive the text and the brain processes it. There have been attempts to find out what kind of letters we read best by measuring reading times and questioning test subjects about their understanding of the text.

A recurring question in this context has been whether reading letters with or without serifs is easier or more agreeable. Scientists and typographers have never reached an agreement about this issue. In many essays and text books on typography it is said that classic serif types are by far the best choice for the *body text*, text masses usually set in body sizes between c. 8pt and 12pt. Supposedly, the serifs optically connect the single letters of words and lines and thus guarantee a horizontal, forward movement of the eye. This

typographers' theory is hardly supported by evidence from academic legibility research. At best, they prove that people have a slight preference for serif type in printed text and for sans-serif when reading on-screen.

It is highly likely that the typographers' theory is, at least in part, a rationalisation of personal preferences relating to traditionalism and habits. But the academics also deserve some of the blame. Undeterred by any typographic knowledge they often compared any old sans-serif (i.e. Helvetica) to the nearest oldstyle book type (usually Times), without taking into account essential variables such as size, leading, weight, contrast style, and so on. Comparing Gill Sans to, say, Goudy Oldstyle, might have yielded a totally different outcome – let alone the inclusion of contemporary sans-serifs designed for legibility, such as TheSans, FF Kievit or Shaker.

The cloud has a silver lining, though. For the past five years a new generation of typographic experts of disparate academic backgrounds has been questioning the findings of the past, trying to tackle the problem of reading with an open mind and new research techniques.

Reading: it's all in the mind

If you're lucky, this little test will show you that reading requires complex teamwork between the eyes and the brain. Try counting how often the letter 'f' appears in the text below:

finished files are the
result of years of scientific
study combined with the
experience of years.

Test!

Did you see six 'f's? That means you are very alert. Even four or five is considered a good score. Many guinea-pigs overlook three of the instances of 'f' because their brains register the word 'of', as one single shape.

How exactly do we read?

The physics of reading has been the subject of academic research for over a hundred years. Towards 1900, the French eye doctor and engineer Louis Émile Javal was the first to develop a method to measure eye movements when reading. Javal's pioneering research still forms the basis of what doctors, psychologists and typographers are trying to learn about reading today.

Reading in jumps

Javal discovered that we don't read letter by letter, but in wisps. The eye glimpses across the text, getting stuck a few times in the process: the so-called *fixations*. This way of looking-in-motion is related to a discovery made 500 years ago by Leonardo da Vinci: he found that the lenses of our eyes can see only a small section from our field of vision with total acuity – everything beyond that sharply defined centre is peripheral, 'fringe'. The nearer we approach the object we are looking at, the narrower the part we can focus on. Thus, our eyes can record only a few letters at a time. As soon as a group of letters – not necessarily coinciding with a complete word – has been recognised, they jump to the next group: this is called a *saccade*. Meanwhile the brain is not only processing the data provided by the eyes, it is also searching our internal database for words corresponding to what the eye thinks it has seen. In a way, the brain *guesses* the word or word group after a split-second-glimpse; often the eye appears to quickly jump back to check if that guess makes sense.

Some researchers attach great importance to the *word silhouette*: they are convinced that clusters of letters with a prominent outline are easier to recognise. Hence the idea that texts set in all-caps (i.e. without lowercase letters) are less legible. Unfortunately, other tests show no significant differences. It is, however, a fact of daily experience that a long text set in all-caps is not very inviting. While such a text is perfectly *legibile* – letters and words can be recognized – its *readability* – the degree to which reading is comfortable – is limited, which discourages the reader to begin or continue the reading process.

fixation point

Around the fixation point only four to five letters are seen with 100% acuity.

Around the fixation point only four to five letters are seen with 100% acuity.

32–35%   45% 75% 100% 75% 45%   32–35%

acuity

↑ A simulation of visual acuity when reading. We can discern fine details only when looking at something with the central part of the retina, the *fovea* – hence the term 'foveal vision'. Everything outside this narrow centre is out of focus. The lower line of text simulates the acuity of vision during one fixation. Although the largest part of the line is optically out of focus, you never have the impression of a blurred text. This

is because the brain assumes that the upper line is not blurred; in other words, our perception is the result of a series of sophisticated corrections.

↓ Visualization of saccadic jumps, based on the article 'The Science of Word Recognition', by Microsoft's legibility specialist Kevin Larson. Note that the eye sometimes jumps back to verify.

Roadside joggers endure sweat, pain and angry drivers in the name of fitness. A healthy body may seem reward...

the top half of the letters is most recognizable the bottom half often leaves you guessing.

↑ Our Latin alphabet has a number of peculiarities that type designers and typographers need to take into account when making and using type. For instance, in the lowercase alphabet, the upper half of most letters is more important to recognition than the lower half.

→ A text set in a combination of upper- and lowercase is supposed to be more legible because its word silhouettes show greater individuality.

FABEL
PAREL
fabel
parel

→ **Typeface anatomy 70**
→ **Sans and serif 96-99**
→ **Optical size 100**

Typography and the designer's role

Anyone involved in written communication – from an email, a book, packaging, to an entire advertising campaign – is competing for the attention of readers or viewers with thousands of other manifestations of content. Information overload has turned us into impatient and sloppy readers. Even a personal e-mail is often not read to the end. Magazines and websites are scanned, not gone through from start to finish.

In an ocean of visual messages, smart design can help to attract, hold and direct attention. In older texts on typography and graphic design the word 'arranging' often is used to describe what graphic designers do. I like to speak of 'staging' because there is more to designing than giving things their proper place. By arranging elements in two or three dimensions, designers also play with the fourth dimension: time. The eye and brain of the reader are invited to watch and read now here, now there. A good designer succeeds in effectively directing and manipulating the reader's attention.

Only in very specific cases is the designer's task to offer the text in a 'neutral' form – to create 'invisible' typography. Neutral or invisible typography is useful for texts that tell a linear story that will be read in their entirety, like a novel or essay (→ p. 22) . In most other cases, *reading* is also *looking* – and therefore a process of scanning, searching, selecting, browsing, roaming. A trained designer uses all sorts of tools to influence that process. The typography itself – the style, size and colour of letters, the placement of text on the page – often contributes to the meaning (or interpretation) of the text.

Terminology
Here's a concise definition of the terms used in this book to denote the main tasks of the trade:

- *Graphic design* is the staging of texts and images in space and time to direct and hold the reader's attention.
- *Typography* originally referred to letterpress printing using metal or wood type. Its most widespread use in English today is to describe those aspects of graphic design that focus on text and type. The word can also be used to describe the way a specific text is organised: 'the typography of this book …'. Purists prefer to reserve the word 'typography' for texts made with fonts, and use *lettering* for all custom-designed texts.
- *Type design* is designing printing types or fonts. In many French- and Spanish-language publications typography and type design are happily confused; yet in English, German and many other languages typography only means designing *with* type, not the design *of* type. A *typographer* may design books, brochures, stationery, texts in exhibitions or time tables, among many other things. But a person who designs fonts is a *type designer*.

← A book is more than just a collection of flat pages: it is also an object. If the client is willing to take the extra step, the designer can get to work on the third dimension. The book shown is about the communicative power of packaging. Designer Alex Scholing visualised and commented on the strategies of packaging design by having seductive messages printed on the book's edge such as 'Take me', 'Love me'.

Directing attention

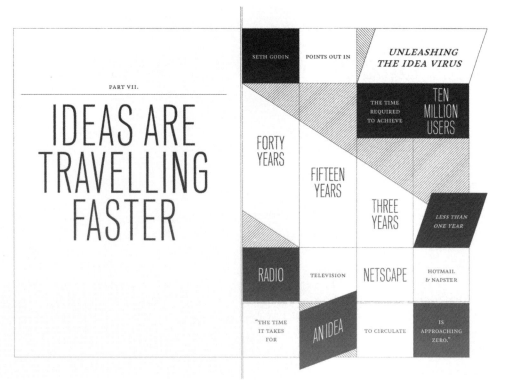

Making reading less smooth

It would be a mistake to think the text that can be read easiest and fastest is automatically the text that is read and understood best. Quite the contrary: sometimes the content is read with more attention when the reading is delayed by obstacles deliberately created for that purpose. *Hard Times* is a text by the London DJ, producer and author Matt Mason about the challenges of the new age. Inspired by Charles Dickens' 1854 novel of the same title, *Hard Times* was published on the Penguin Books website as part of the series *We Tell Stories*. The design by Nicholas Felton (New York) doesn't make the reading easier but consciously builds in handicaps. The reader is slowed down and becomes more focussed. At times, he/she is led astray and forced to re-read a certain passage.

→ **Modes of reading 20**
→ **Book covers 30**
→ **Design strategies 142**

Visual rhetoric

Rhetoric (from Greek: *rhetor* – orator) is the art of communicating effectively. In Greek and Roman antiquity philosophers and politicians developed sophisticated techniques to persuade and even manipulate an audience by means of the spoken and written word. Thus rhetoric became *a set of principles for a well-structured argument and effective presentation*, which over the centuries was further developed and is still reflected in many a management guidebook today.

We live in an era in which the use of spoken and written language is perhaps more subject to erosion than ever: even among 'intellectuals' it is handled quite nonchalantly. At the visual level, we are getting more agile. We manage to effortlessly follow the storyline of a rapidly edited film or television programme; young people read comics (or 'graphic novels') that their parents have a hard time following; we get how a website or video game works almost immediately; and we understand visual rhyming, cross references and irony.

So it pays to think about visual form-giving as consciously as orators and writers have thought about language for centuries. What works? Why does it work, and for whom? What could possibly lead to misunderstandings or unintended reactions? What is clarity, and do we always want clarity in the first place? The answers to these and other questions form a technique of persuasion with visual resources: a visual rhetoric.

Many (typo-)graphic designers have rhetorical talent, but most use it in purely intuitive ways. It may help to look beyond the familiar patterns of defining and solving problems, of functionality and aesthetics. The designs that communicate most convincingly are often the work of designers who are much more than picture makers – who are also, to some extent, writers, psychologists, sociologists, directors, philosophers or politicians.

Propaganda for books

↑ Two examples of engaging advertising for books. Left is the classic Constructivist poster for the Moscow bookstore Lenghiz by Alexander Rodchenko, produced in 1925. The young woman (the actress Lilya Brik) calls out *Knighi*, or 'Books'. The smaller text on the right reads '… in all fields of knowledge.' The letters are hand drawn, as was usual at that time.
The design on the right is the work of

Gert Dooreman of Ghent, Belgium, advertising the 2006 edition of the Antwerp Book Fair, a yearly event where the Flemish publishing world presents its offerings to the general public. The typeface is similar to the Rodchenko alphabet: sans-serif capitals (uppercase letters) with a simple geometric structure. But there is a world of difference between the two posters: Rodchenko seduces the viewer with striking visual

tools (such as a dynamic outlined photo, which was then virtually unknown); Dooreman assumes that the viewer is an attentive, visually educated reader and builds in a typographic puzzle. Inside the word *Boekenbeurs* there's a question: *En u?* – 'And you?'. Those who get it will feel they are being addressed.

Target group: you

Relax theatre

Le Nouveau Relax is the city theatre of Chaumont, France, housed in a former cinema. Its identity and posters were designed by Annette Lenz and Vincent Perrottet. In its design brief the theatre's management asked the designers to avoid any elitist graphic language. Lenz and Perrottet proposed a series based on photos by the city photographer of 'normal' inhabitants of Chaumont, lettered in intriguing perspective text blocks, silkscreened in two spot colours. The logo was based on the old cinema's sign. In a small city like Chaumont, posters that show relatives, neighbours or friends immediately grab the attention of passers-by; the series soon became popular. The message 'Nouveau Relax is for you, too' was heard by a broad section of the population and helped improve the theatre's accessibility.

← The designer's role   16

→ Modes of reading   20

→ Concept and style   144–146

Modes of reading

We read all day. Newspapers, websites, advertising, business cards, text messages, logos, street names, wayfinding, fines. Occasionally we even read a book. A text can be huge or tiny, nearby or far away, it can be a single word or a series of densely printed pages. Consequently, there is not one single way of shaping text, but many different ones. What works well or looks good is not the same for all types of text. How about trying to classify our various ways of reading into categories – a classification of reading modes? This could help us to understand why one text is designed in a certain way, and another very differently. It can also help the designer in making choices. The German typographer and teacher Hans Peter Willberg has tried to invent such a classification. He deliberately limited himself to book design, leaving aside many forms of text that are not available in libraries or printed on paper – from advertising and signage to subtitles, forms and information leaflets for medicines. Nevertheless his typology of reading modes provides a good start for a more diversified view of why a certain kind of work is better designed in this way and another in that way. The following, personally coloured representation of the Willberg scheme may provide some insight into the diversity of the challenges both the reader and the designer face on a daily basis.

On the subsequent pages we take a closer look at ways of shaping text to address different modes of reading.

	What, where?	**How?**
Immersive reading	Immersive reading could also be called *linear reading*: the text is read in a concentrated way from the beginning to the end and each subsequent section, page or chapter builds on what went before. Typical examples of this are novels, essays and lengthy magazine articles.	To be able to be immersed in a text, its design should not be distracting. A reader-friendly typeface that does not draw attention to itself is a prerequisite. Line length and line distance (leading) are just as crucial. For instance, if the reader's eye has trouble finding the beginning of the next line, this is a design flaw.
Informative reading **Selective reading**	When reading informatively and selectively, one usually does not start at the beginning, but first skims the text to pick out the interesting snippets. Newspapers and magazines are good examples, but many illustrated books and text books are also designed for navigating from one useful bit to another. The reader's goal is to quickly and efficiently record information.	Informative reading requires a clear division of the text and a clear hierarchy – a design that distinguishes the various levels in the text. *Navigation* is a common term to designate the typographic elements (choice of type, lines, colours, icons, subheads, boxes) that help do this. In design for informative reading, the rhythm of texts and images can build an interesting *visual dramaturgy*.
Consultative reading	Dictionaries are a typical example of consultative or referential reading. It is a very specific way of reading: a quest for that one item that you want to know more about. In timetables , cultural listings and various other reference books something similar happens. Of course, the classic use of reference books is now gradually being replaced by online search functions.	Again, lucid navigation is crucial. In dictionaries, timetables and similar things, convention plays a crucial role, and breaking expectations makes little sense here. For example, clear contrasts between keywords and explanatory text, and a considered compromise between space saving (economy) and readability are part of the challenges the designer has to get to grips with.

	What, where?	**How?**
Activating typography	A strategy for drawing the readers' attention and stimulating them to read. The first aim of activating typography is looking; the reading happens a in the second instance. Magazines – especially their headlines, subheads, intros and pull quotes – are typical cases of activating typography. Advertising, book covers and packaging could also count as typography that incites to action.	Readability is not of primary concern here, rather the viewer needs to be seduced with all visual means available. There are hardly any rules or recipes, and designers may be able to claim much freedom. Therefore, more ingenuity is expected from them. Activating typography is often done in teams in which designers collaborate with writers, editors and/or marketing specialists.
Staged typography	As pointed out before, any work of typography exists to give a text the stage from which to address its audience. But we reserve the term 'staged typography' for those cases in which typography attains its goals with theatrical means, visual tricks and special effects. It is outside the world of books that the most impressive stagings take place: in advertising, movie title sequences, lettering in public spaces, etc.	Staged typography hardly knows any rules or restrictions. The sky is the limit. This does not necessarily imply that this kind of typographic design is always outrageous or highly decorative – see Gerard Unger's work below. It also does not mean that functionality is not relevant. Striking and distinctive typography is sometimes better placed to perform certain functions than more predictable and cautious solutions.
Informative typography	There are situations in which a poorly designed warning or indication can be fatal, or can be the cause of a missed connection or administrative problems. In a complex society full of risks and regulations, providing good information design should be a matter of common decency for governments and service companies.	More than any other branch of typographic design, information design is the task of a specialist. Given the number of incomprehensible and confusing forms, signage, orientation systems, timetables and medicine leaflets, designers who are interested in specializing in it will have years of work ahead of them

qualities regarded as making him superior to other 1
5 (*pl*) the gallery of a theatre [OE *god*]
God (gɒd) *n* **1** the sole Supreme Being, eternal, spirit and transcendent, who is the Creator and ruler of al and is infinite in all attributes; the object of worshi monotheistic religions ▷ *interj* **2** an oath or exclama used to indicate surprise, annoyance, etc (and in su expressions as **My God!** or **God Almighty!**)
Godard (*French* gɔdar) *n* **Jean-Luc** (ʒɑ̃lyk) born 1930, French film director and writer associated with the Wave of the 1960s. His works include *À bout de souffle* (1960), *Weekend* (1967), *Sauve qui peut* (1980), *Nouvelle V* (1990), and *Éloge de l'amour* (2002)
Godavari (gəʊ'dɑːvərɪ) *n* a river in central India, risi in the Western Ghats and flowing southeast to the of Bengal: extensive delta, linked by canal with the Krishna delta; a sacred river to Hindus. Length: abo

↑ Typography for consultative reading: Mark Thomson's design for Collins' Dictionaries. Maximum clarity with sparse (but not all-too-minimalist) means.

← Staged typography: type designer Gerard Unger created an alphabet called Delftse Poort (Delft Gate) for the Rotterdam building of the same name, in collaboration with the architect Abe Bonnema. The lettering combines a certain theatricality with seriousness and matter-of-factness, which is appropriate for a prestigious office building.

← **The designer's role 16**
→ **Typographic modes 22–39**
→ **Organising & planning 40**

Stream of ideas: immersed in a text

The basic design of the book has remained unchanged for centuries. The average novel or collection of essays looks almost identical to the books printed in late 15th century Venice or early 16th century Paris.

The literary book has little use for a surprising form. In a novel or essay – not counting the odd illustrated novel – language needs to do all the work. The text is a stream of ideas with a linear structure, read from beginning to end. With mere letters, words and sentences, a completely different world is conjured up. The reader is invited to dive deep into the text – that is why this kind of reading is called *immersive*. It usually works best when the type and layout do not call attention to themselves and approach the ideal of 'invisible' typography.

The literary book is only one of many media in which typography plays a central part. As it has such a rich tradition and high prestige, it has long determined the discussion about typography and the design of texts. The criteria for shaping a linear, literary text, however, do not necessarily apply to other ways of reading.

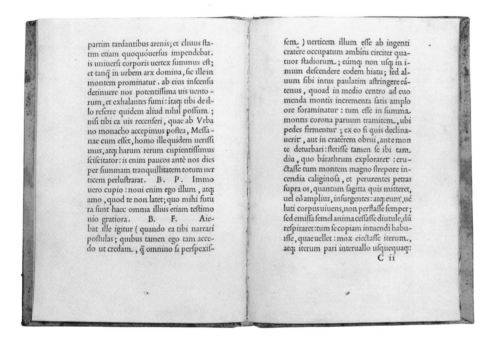

The book as a stream of ideas found its form in late fifteenth-century Italy. A book like *De Aetna* by Cardinal Pietro Bembo, printed at Aldus Manutius' shop in 1495–96, is not significantly different from the literary paperback as it is produced today. Even the 500-year-old font is still relevant: the type, cut for Aldus by Francesco Griffo, was the model for the 1929 Bembo typeface, which is still used in today's digital typography. (→ p. 79)

Wanted: 'invisible' typography. The heritage of Beatrice Warde

The Crystal Goblet, or Printing Should Be Invisible was the title of a lecture held by the American typography historian Beatrice Warde at the British Typographers Guild in 1930. She argued that typography was at its best when it was subservient to the content, the text. Her metaphor is that of a crystal wine glass. The real wine connoisseur, Warde said, has no interest in a decorated chalice: good wine needs no ornament but comes into its own in a delicate, colourless glass. Just like a good wine glass, good typography is neutral and transparent, while obtrusive design gets in the way of reading and understanding.

To many book designers Warde's ideal of 'invisible' design is still a guiding principle. But her argument only applies to immersive reading. In many other reading modes diversity in typography can actually help in reading. Moreover, the concept of 'neutrality' can be interpreted in very different ways. While a typeface like Bembo was neutral to Warde, the modernists preferred the 'objectivity' of industrial sans-serifs. Even neutrality is a matter of taste.

Showing the story

BASTARD BATTLE

gens, peu amoulés, peu versés en art guerrier pour peu dire, nous devions les armer et instruire.
Les tisserands furent dévolus aux long bow et arbalètes, eu égard à leur qualité de vision, item Humblot l'armurier ; samouraï Billy.
Les tonneliers et paysans, pour leur force et puissance, aux fourches, masses et toute arme de jet comme estoc volant, pierre et chauldron ; samouraï Tartas.
Samouraï Vipère-d'une-toise prit sous son aile les femmes, sans distinction, bagasses ou commerçantes, et tous jouvenceaux frêles ou légers.
Oudinet ne voulait entendre que le sabre, aussi le febvre et les fruictiers, aussi la Florinière, iceulx pour AKIRA, samouraï.
À ma façon drunken master, j'enrôlais les tonneliers, tous gens de vigne et bons boyteurs ; samouraï SPENCER FIVE.
Dimanche-le-loup leva une formation d'espions et éclaireurs, samouraï Pipeur.
Et tous ceux qui savoient monter plus ou moins, laboureurs, palefreniers, et pouvaient soutenir le poids d'une lance allèrent au chevalier ; samouraï Enguerrand.
Ainsi partagés et mis en divers corps d'armée, commencèrent en droite heure les manœuvres et répétitions. Les espions du pipeur, Dimanche-le-loup en teste, se séparant au bas du faubourg des tanneurs, s'envoyèrent au travers la contrée prendre le vent.
Nous aultres, Enguerrand, Billy et moy, fîmes le tour des murs et remparts, parchemin de ville en mains, examinant la plaine, les bois, la Suize et les fossés.

66

BASTARD BATTLE

Simon Gurgey, maçon, fut mis à remparer un bout de muraille rue des Poutils. On dressa des bois taillés en pointe, enterrés droits et guingois, devant le mur de la rue d'avant le Four, qui estoit faible, une bonne blinde par devers. Les fossés le long de la rue Chaude sondaient profonds, on n'y fit rien, mais placer à chasque meurtrière une arbalète armée. Il fut dit que de nuit, la Suize qui coulait au faubourg des tanneries serait hérissée de caques-tripes par son fond sur tout le gué et ses costés. Ce qui fut effectué. Icelieu, par en plus des pièges, Vipère-d'une-toise enseigna sa troupe à se camoufler dans les bois et s'embusquer dans les herbes pour crocher les pattes des chevaux et leur attraper les jarrets. Ce pour quoi elle avoit trois méthodes d'attaques secrètes au sol, suivant en cela les traités de stratégie de Sun-Zi et Wu-Zi sur l'avantage des combats en forêts et plaines marécageuses.
Enguerrand assura pouvoir tenir le pas porte de l'Eau à lui seul contre cent cavaliers. On lui porta icy vingt armes d'hast très lourdes et grandes, environ seize empans.
Billy garderait la porte Arse et son magasin atout ses archers et arbalétiers. Il fit bouyllir par Jeannette une pleine marmitée d'herbes estranges, puantes, un jour de long, dans laquelle on tremperait la pointe des flèches avant de bersalder. Fit aussi couler du plomb, par petites boules.
On porta moult pierres au chemin de ronde, et bastons fourches pour balancer les eschielles. Tartas taillait des masses en nombre, pointées de penthères fichantes.
Pour Akira et pour moy, aussi pour nos gens, l'enchas

67

Narrative typography

This booklet designed by French typographer Fanette Mellier treats the body text in a very special way. The text seems to be overcome with fits of madness. Hysterical typefaces and colors reflect the mood and emotions of the story. For this purpose the full text was converted into a bitmap image and processed in Photoshop. Mellier's version of Celine Minard's *Bastard Battle* was part of a series of 'bizarre books' she has made as part of the city of Chaumont's ongoing series of graphic projects.

→ Formulas of book design 48
→ Renaissance oldstyle 84
→ Typographic technology 164

Navigation: guiding the reader

We've seen how book typography attempts to make itself invisible in order to help the reader to sink into the text. For selective reading, the opposite is true: typography makes itself useful by standing out and by helping the reader to skim the text. As the term indicates, selective readers do not read everything. A reader who sets out to make a quick selection from the abundance of information in a textbook, magazine or website will profit from clear navigation. A wealth of resources are available to the designer and the editor to facilitate this. Besides language and type, these include images, lines, colour in different shapes, pictograms – and let's not forget the 'white of the page'. A judicious use of empty space is a first step towards clarity.

Contrast and rhythm

Text that was designed for selective reading has a special texture. *Contrast, rhythm* and *hierarchy* are key words. To begin with the latter: a lucid hierarchy tells the reader, even before the actual reading begins, where the most important information is located. It should make clear, at first glance, which means are used for navigating the layout. Without having to search, the reader must be able to find his/her way to titles and headlines, summaries, intros and captions.

Contrast is an important tool for making this possible – contrast between different typefaces, between bold and lighter text, large and small, calm and busy, empty and full. Colours (including white, black and shades of grey) are means of establishing contrast. By thoughtfully applying principles of contrast and hierarchy a designer can build a page that offers a balanced and natural-looking visual rhythm: a smooth alternation between fragments that call attention to themselves and those that do so less – a unity in diversity.

Wanted: distinctive typography. There are many recipes for creating contrast and articulation by means of typeface selection — light and bold, serif and sans-serif, large and small. Diversity is good, but some restraint is advisable in order to avoid the page becoming a hotchpotch (unless a hotchpotch is what is wanted). The same bold sans that is used for headlines, for instance, can become a secondary font for boxes and introductions in a smaller size. If all this sounds too predictable, then imagination has to kick in.

→ Typejockeys from Vienna are a three-person collective that do both graphic design and type design. To show off their imaginative style – definitely more playful than much of the stern minimalism favoured by many design companies in the German-speaking world – as well as their type designing capabilities, navigation on their website uses a collection of different fonts.

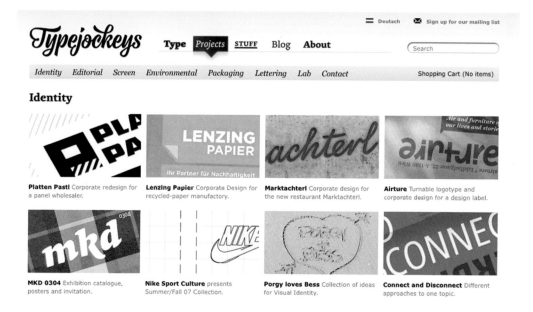

Typejockeys

Type Projects STUFF Blog About   ≡ Deutsch   ✉ Sign up for our mailing list

Search

Identity   Editorial   Screen   Environmental   Packaging   Lettering   Lab   Contact   Shopping Cart (No items)

Identity

Platten Pastl Corporate redesign for a panel wholesaler.

Lenzing Papier Corporate Design for recycled-paper manufactory.

Marktachterl Corporate design for the new restaurant Marktachterl.

Airture Turnable logotype and corporate design for a design label.

MKD 0304 Exhibition catalogue, posters and invitation.

Nike Sport Culture presents Summer/Fall 07 Collection.

Porgy loves Bess Collection of ideas for Visual Identity.

Connect and Disconnect Different approaches to one topic.

Organising information

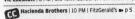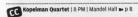

Chicago Reader: at a glance

The Chicago Reader, a popular alternative weekly for the *windy city*, had a somewhat incongruous layout before the revamp by Jardí+Utensil (a collaboration between the American designer Marcus Villaça and Enric Jardí from Barcelona). Their redesign made the magazine more lucid and less cluttered. The main interventions: a clearer hierarchy and improved navigation thanks to a simple grid and clear typographic contrast.

← The designer's role 16
→ Text & display 62
→ Fine-tuning headlines 127

Staging the reader's experience

Browsing and reading an illustrated book, magazine or brochure (or a website that mimics these media) is an activity that makes the mind work at different levels. The text has varying density. Sometimes it encourages the reader to dive in for several pages of immersive reading; elsewhere it requires the reader to make choices about what to examine first. In some places it may interact with the photography or illustrations, and in other places it claims attention for the writing itself. Sometimes the images tell their own story, independently from the text. Whether or not the text can successfully compete for attention with the easily accessible imagery is a question of design. More specifically: of a good *scenario*. On the double page spreads of a publication a story is told, a small drama is unfolding. As a film or theatre director uses the script or play to create a multi-sensory experience involving images, human emotion and movement, the graphic designer uses visual means to keep the reader involved and entertained while interacting with

Wanted: a typographic scenario. The designer, perhaps in collaboration with an author or editor (if they're not assuming that role as well), establishes which means should be employed when. Where should the layout rock, where whisper? When will language do the work and where will images, shape and colour prevail? Will the typography – large or small, loud or quiet – tell part of the story?

 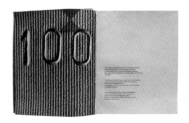  

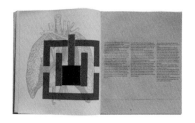  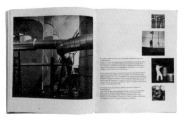

the publication. And although a book, magazine or brochure is a static thing – as still many websites are – the experience itself is dynamic and time-based. The graphic designer is not creating single spreads or pages, he/she is making content work across an entire publication or even a series of publications and, quite probably, a series of interactions.

So when the content is more than just plain text, when it mixes different typographic levels and expressions with different types of images, the designer's task is to create an interesting experience in time; and the way to do that is by introducing tension and surprise. This is done by means that are not dissimilar to the things that make a good film or theatre production or even a piece of music work. Creating contrast. Changing speed. Varying density. Establishing a rhythm which is maintained throughout a publication, or unexpectedly interrupted. A good designer needs to have a sense of drama.

The 1985 Grasso book

During the decades after World War II, the upswing of the European economy was recorded and illustrated by a new kind of publication: the company photo book. In the Netherlands and elsewhere, this genre became a laboratory for top-level designers and photographers, who were allowed ample budgets to give the best of themselves. Although well-written, the texts were usually where the management took control – the least interesting parts of the book. The designers were thus provided with a sound alibi to treat the imagery on an equal level, and create veritable visual scenarios. The 1958 book for Grasso machine works, *100 jaar Grasso*, was a case in point. Conceived by designer Benno Wissing, the book uses a flexible grid as the basis of a dynamic and ever-changing layout.

Wissing went on to co-found Total Design with Wim Crouwel and others, becoming the agency's most ardent champion of systematic grids.

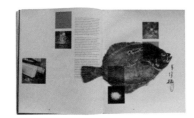

Seducing with type: packaging

We live in a mercantile society and therefore typography is often used to sell things – a form of 'activating' typography. That in itself is good news for designers: when clients know that well-made design sells, they are more likely to find a budget for it. It is not necessarily bad news for consumers either. Admittedly, a deluge of logos, advertising and packaging has been washing over us ever since the invention of the branded product (which is less than a century and a half ago), but even if there were purely commercial reasons behind this, much of it is now considered valuable heritage – and has a beauty if its own.

Unfortunately, on the trajectory from product development to the store there are several places where things can go wrong. One of those places is the marketing department. Among marketing's tasks is to reduce arbitrariness and chance when launching products by attuning these products to what consumers want, or seem to want. But marketing, like design, has a degree of gut feeling (aka intuition), which adds an irrational element to the mix. Trained to rule out such random thinking, marketers often tend to translate their need for security into a predilection for formulaic solutions, copying what has been successful in the past – which can result in numbing uniformity. In packaging this has led to endless shelves of bags and packs showing product photos, lettered with similar-looking 'warm' and 'human' script fonts. Nothing wrong with that, but time and again it is confirmed that things that look special attract more attention and communicate more efficiently. In other words, seducing with type is similar to seducing with words and gestures: it can pay to have the courage to be different.

Wanted: seductive typography. There is no recipe for seduction. Everything is permitted to attract attention and win the favour of the passer-by or customer. The human factor is important, and script fonts are seen to be talking to the customer's heart. If anything, throw the formula overboard and break through the cliché. The personal approach is often preferable to standard solutions.

↙ Informal script fonts are highly appreciated by packaging designers because of their 'friendly' and hand-made character. Two designs made with fonts from Sudtipos in Buenos Aires, who specialise in scripts for packaging.

→ In their design for Rezept-Destillate Thomas Lehner and Christine Gertsch went for an unconventional approach: chemistry-style packaging for a small liqueur brand, designed with a custom-made font. Foto: Studio Koritschan

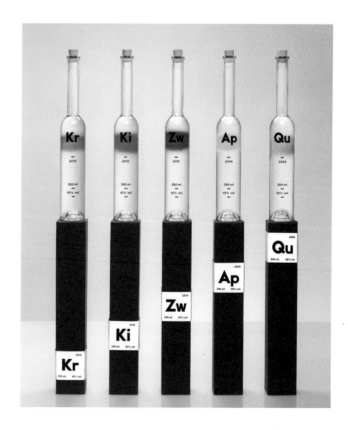

Extreme chocolate branding

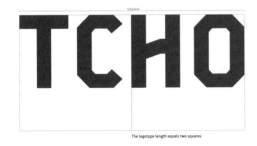

The logotype length equals two squares

TCHO is a new chocolate brand from San Francisco, for which the Berlin office of Edenspiekermann developed the visual identity and packaging. The graphic design is part of a sophisticated branding concept. Its strategy is typical of the *narrative branding* approach that has become popular with marketeers lately – creating a strong brand by intertwining it with a good story.

In TCHO's case the story is about the product itself – a product that is special enough to play the central role in the image-building strategy. TCHO makes its own chocolate from raw organic cocoa, and is one of the few manufacturers in the United States to do more that melt pre-produced chocolate. TCHO's policy – from their contacts with the cocoa farmers to the human resources policy – is socially committed and directed towards sustainability. Yet their methods are pragmatic and hi-tech – one of the founders is a former aerospace engineer and worked on the Space Shuttle project.

The corporate identity encompasses all printed products – from press kits to flyers – as well as advertisements, posters, conference presentations and the TCHO. COM website with its integrated online shop. Every aspect has a uniform design approach, from on- and offline design to logo, colour scheme and typography right through to packaging. The packaging positions the product as a delicacy for modern stylish consumers without being nostalgic. The actual launch was preceded by a beta phase which was presented as such, with hand-stamped brown paper packaging to test the market.

The TCHO logo was hand-drawn on the basis of existing industrial letterforms; as corporate font the designers chose Erik Spiekermann's FF Unit. In 2009 the TCHO packaging design won both the Academy of Chocolate Gold Award and a Gold European Design Award.

← **Visual rhetoric 18**
→ **Fonts or lettering? 104**
→ **Logo strategies 150**

Seducing with type: book covers

Book covers, too, are a form of packaging. Both in high street bookshops and on the web, we shop with less patience and make more impulsive decisions. A striking or recognisable cover is an important weapon in the struggle for attention.

In several European countries, during the past decade a kind of consensus developed about how a literary book should look. An amazing proportion of novels and short story collections came with a cover showing a photo in earth colours, with title and author's name superimposed in a white or creamy, tasteful classic font and usually centred: soporific sameness.

Whilst influences from, mainly, Britain and the USA have begun to change this, in hard economic times publishers remain inclined to make choices they perceive as 'safe' – although there are many signs that in commissioning book covers taking a risk may be a really good investment.

The Anglo-Saxon publishing world has been hit by crisis just as badly as elsewhere and here, too, complaints can be heard about increased tendencies to avoid risk. Yet the situation is radically different from that found in most European countries. In American and British book cover design there seems to be more room for individualist solutions – for showmanship, pastiche, irony and play.

And the choice of type? It is subservient to the overall effect or concept – functional thinking, in a way. In North-America or the UK the struggle for shelf space is even more acute than in Europe. Attracting attention and seducing are a design's chief duty. The lettering may be a font or something improvised, hand-written or meticulously drawn; what counts is the unity and overall impact of the design. To quote a Woody Allen movie title: *Whatever works.*

Wanted: adventurous typography. If books were all written the same way, most readers would soon lose interest. Literature is about variety and discovery. Browsing books in a bookshop, be it on the high street or over the web, should be full of surprises – not the tedious repetition of 'same old' that it often is. Book covers that dared to be different have often been very effective.

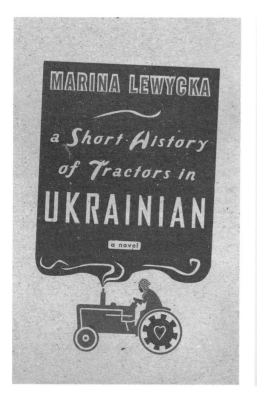 

← Two popular book covers by British designer Jonathan Gray (Gray 318). Both designs became internationally successful: publishers across the world adapted or imitated them for their translations of these books.

Success by design

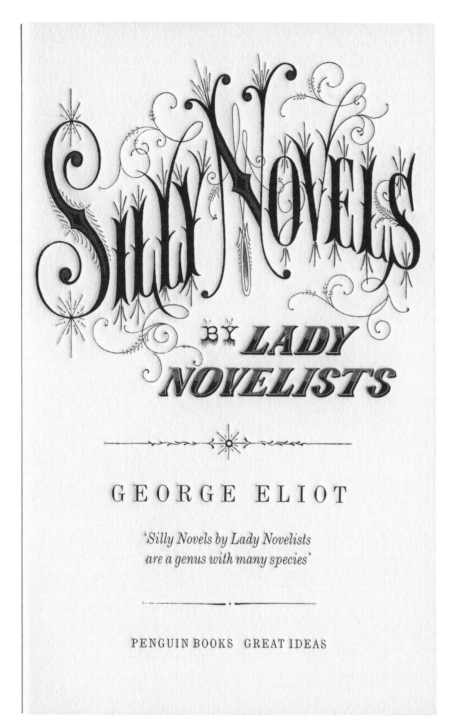

↑→ Once the basic concept of the Great Ideas series was in place, Pearson invited a group of colleagues to design individual covers. The Eliot cover is by Catherine Dixon; the Orwell cover is by Pearson. Among the other participating designers were Phil Baines and Alistair Hall.

Great Ideas

In 2004 Penguin Books launched the Great Ideas series, a collection of classic texts of philosophy and *belle lettres* packaged as pocket-sized paperbacks. Apart from the affordable price (originally £3.99 in the UK) the most striking aspect of the series was its design.

Conceived by David Pearson, a recent graduate of Central Saint Martin's in London, working with Penguin's in-house art director Jim Stoddart, the series' design was hailed as 'dazzling' and 'gorgeous'. The series came in five batches, each printed in black and a single spot colour, with blind debossing to suggest a letterpress process. The lettering and ornamentation reflected the era and spirit of each text.

The Great Ideas series won many design awards, and sales were in the millions. Of its commercial appeal, Pearson says: 'I was once told that a member of the sales team pretended that his laptop was broken so he could get the proofs into the hands of booksellers (instead of via the usual on-screen presentation) and he maintains that the effect was very powerful. Also, because the titles had been previously available in other incarnations we could very easily chart any new sparks in sales. In the case of George Orwell's *Why I Write*, sales jumped from a couple of thousand copies to 200,000.'

Corporate identity, corporate design

↑ The 1990s identity for the Dutch police (Studio Dumbar) did include a logo, but its most conspicuous and talked-about element consisted in red and blue stripes on vehicles. This simple device had the effect of increasing the visibility of police officers in the streets; people had the impression police presence had increased (which was considered a good thing) although this was not the case.

Virtually every organisation has a logo today: the local government, the hairdresser, the doctor's practice. The popularity of logos has led to the assumption that a logo and a corporate identity are more or less the same thing. In the era of web 2.0 this can lead to disturbing situations. Organisations, from small to surprisingly large, think they can acquire a new visual identity by simply renewing their logos; and there's an increasing tendency to do so via crowdsourcing, using dedicated websites or self-organised competitions. Five hundred ideas for free, rewarding the winner with a few hundred (fill in currency) – what more could you possibly want?

Well, one thing that might come in handy is a logo that will work under all circumstances. One that is not only pretty as a GIF on the website, but will also look good in colour and monochrome offset printing, and when used very large or very small; one that can be plotted on a huge banner or milled into a steel fence. Under certain circumstances, the logo will have to be placed on a dark or busy background. Then a white version will be needed, or a logo on a shield. Perhaps this is a job for professionals after all.

Operation CI

But even a logo that works properly does not a corporate identity make. To establish a visual identity that is both visible and recognisable, in order to make an organisation stand out against its environment, a designer will add many more elements to the mix: a colour palette; a set of customised shapes (the red and blue stripes of the Dutch police are a prime example); a consistent way of combining text and image; perhaps a custom typeface (→ p. 152).

Once a corporate identity has been designed, it must also be implemented: embedded in all aspects of the organisation's day-to-day reality. In large companies, this can be a gargantuan task. In many countries, dedicated companies – *identity implementation consultancies* – specialise in this aspect of the project delivery. So corporate identity operations clearly can be a costly business. But if they are well thought-out, they do various things: not only do they help the organisation break through the clutter of today's overload of visual information, they can also provide a more efficient use of resources, and thus save money.

Designing procedures

A corporate identity used to be a static thing. Each detail was pre-designed, after which a thick binder – the branding book – was printed. Any designer that was later commissioned to produce a product as part of the corporate design (a brochure, a pen, a truck tarpaulin) was to comply with this book of rules.

Today much of an organisation's communication is produced in-house. Managers and secretaries become occasional designers who lay out and laser-print reports, newsletters and even stationery. The final product may also be an intranet page or a PowerPoint presentation. With so much non-professional creativity going on, designers have a particular task. Often they don't design a finished product, but a set of rules. And because these rules are applied by people without much design know-how, they should be presented in a clever form. Digital templates need to offer a fool-proof route to a correct design. In the words of the Dutch designer and computer scientist Petr van Blokland, who specialises in such projects, 'we have to make it hard for people to do it wrong.'

Wanted: much more than typography. When developing a corporate identity, typographic decisions often take a back seat to other decisions that take place on many different levels. Precisely because the typography will be embedded in a larger whole and will be a constituent of the organisation's image, it needs extra care. Are the fonts technically flexible and equipped for international use? Has the cost of a group licence for all the organisation's computers been taken into account? When the client is huge, the design agency may propose to have a custom font family designed to save costs on licensing.

Identity for a digital lifestyle

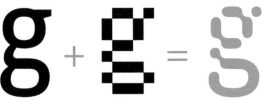
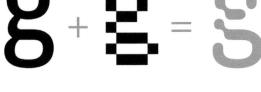

With over twenty-five stores, Gravis is Germany's biggest Apple retailer, and in addition sells many digital products by other manufacturers. This is both a blessing and a curse. Apple guarantees publicity and a growing number of loyal buyers, but how can Gravis maintain itself as an independent retail brand in its own right?

Directed by Susanna Dulkinys, the design team at United Designers (now the Berlin office of Edenspiekermann) developed an identity based on the theme of 'Digital Lifestyle'. The communication concept and design is flexible and simple. It appeals to customers wherever they happen to be standing or sitting, mostly at the point of sale and online. The 'brand experience' is based on a new logo, a colour scheme, a typography and layout concept – and an exclusive typeface for pictograms and accentuated text. Dulkinys designed a custom typeface based on her logo – an ingenious hybrid between a readable text face and a pixel font.

→ Information design   34
→ Logo strategies   150
→ Corporate typefaces   152

Information design, at your service

Long before language-based writing systems were developed, people shared knowledge and intelligence through graphics – early forms of information design. Coded tokens in envelopes of baked clay were used as waybills in ancient Sumer. Cave paintings may have been visualisations of information. Maps were exchanged regardless of a shared language.

Things are different now. Even the prophets of the 'information age' could hardly imagine today's overload of content, refreshed by the minute. We are more savvy than we used to be in interpreting and processing information but there is simply too much of it, in the street and in buildings and on screens, so we have little patience and diminishing attention spans. We need help to cut through the clutter and filter out the information that is important to us. Smart visualisation – be it through well-designed text or maps or images – can be part of the solution.

Software manufacturers like to convince us that they can help us, as producers and transmitters of information, to visualise our content efficiently. Microsoft programs such as PowerPoint, Word and Visio come with functions for making graphs, charts and diagrams, giving people the illusion of having a professional information design toolkit at their disposal. Often the result is the opposite of what this discipline is supposed to do: people change a simple idea or straightforward data into a graph that is anything but efficient, becoming superfluous and confusing.

Sub-disciplines

Information design is a specialised discipline that offers little room for an intuitive approach. It can be defined as *the art of visualising information so that it becomes more accessible and more easily understandable to more people*. It differs from other areas of graphic design in that it requires those who do it to be much more than designers (although some may claim that all good designers *are* by nature information designers). In the words of Terry Irwin, Head of the Carnegie Mellon School of Design: 'Information designers are very special people who must master all the skills and talents of a designer; combine them with the rigor and problem-solving ability of a scientist or mathematician; and bring the curiosity, research skills and doggedness of a scholar to their work.'

Typography and information

Information designers, it has been said, should be capable of 'understanding what it is like not to understand.' Good information typography is always one step ahead of the user. People must sometimes be lured into reading in places where they didn't intend to read at all. Therefore visually powerful solutions are certainly not forbidden.

Most pieces of information design mix different means of visualisation, and language frequently seems secondary to pictograms or maps. Nevertheless, the shaping of text is a crucial factor. In order to work well with other levels of visualisation, without dominating it nor being overwhelmed by it, the typography must be very well thought-out, and possibly tested on a representative group of future users.

There are instances – from road signage to medical information leaflets – where good typography can literally be a matter of life and death. Such instructions don't necessarily need to look special. They should first and foremost be intelligent, and anticipate human imperfections.

Wanted: Typography with empathy

Information design is not one single undivided territory: it has many subdisciplines that require specific skills. These are some of its main areas (which can overlap in one piece of work):

- Mapping
- Calendars, timelines, timetables
- Visualised statistics: charts and graphs
- Wayfinding and signage systems
- Interface design
- Technical illustrations and diagrams
- Tutorials and instructions
- Forms and informative mailings

A place for applied sciences

**Signage system
for Osnabrück University
of Applied Sciences**

Design agency Büro Uebele in Stuttgart, Germany, developed a spectacular yet functional wayfinding system on an astronomic theme for the University of Applied Sciences in Osnabrück. From the company's press release: 'A sky of black letters and numbers, interspersed with red clouds. Words like stars show the way, guiding the traveller. The ceiling is the firmament, scattered with words, the concrete walls are bare. As people look ahead of them, they naturally locate the repeated information that guides them through the building – the text is big enough to grasp instantly, so there's no danger of anyone losing their footing. The space adapts to the user. The pure austerity of the floor and walls reaches a brilliant culmination in this starry sky, with its pattern of images the eye can read: Cassiopeia, Ursa Minor, Pollux, Andromeda.' The project has won numerous awards, including a Red Dot 'Best of the Best' Award, an award of the Tokio Type Directors Club and a gold medal in the Joseph Binder Awards. Photos © Andreas Körner.

← Directing attention 17
→ Typographic placemaking 153
→ Spatial illusions 156

Designing for the web

In its introductory phase, every new medium mimics an older one, only finding its own expression after some time. Just like the earliest newspapers resembled books, most websites in the 1990s were digital versions of brochures. The term 'Web 2.0' is often used to denote a new phase in web design in which the fundamental innovations of the internet over print are reflected: interactivity, immediacy, collaboration and database-driven content.

Web dynamics

When making choices in web design, the functionality of the website – what is under the bonnet – plays a decisive role. Certain visual solutions that seem obvious to designers with a background in print design simply cannot be achieved on a site that makes full use of all the interactive and dynamic features of modern web technology.

For instance, many websites have a flexible width to allow the page to be scaled to the size of the screen. In the vertical direction, the 'depth' or length of the page is virtually infinite, especially when there is a comments function in place. As Typekit's creative director Jason Santa Maria has pointed out, a designer who wants to take these dynamics into account won't be helped much by traditional rules for a balanced design such as the Golden Ratio and the Rule of Thirds (both

are discussed briefly in the next chapter). It is impossible to predict the exact ratio of the page the user will perceive, and therefore there is no visually ideal or perfect way to fill that page.

In other respects, too, form and content of a website are often subject to change. Commercial web pages especially are increasingly being compiled on-the-fly, driven by databases and in interaction with the user's behaviour, which is recorded using cookies at each visit. The selection and order of the articles may change, localised ads may be added, and so on. So the web designer often does not create ready-made pages, but a set of possibilities.

New and old guidelines

So should a designer who designs for the web forget everything he or she learned about print design? Yes and no. Much works differently on the web, yet the basic principles of classic and modern (typo-)graphic design have not become worthless. Proven guidelines for good layout and typography are still relevant, but they must be applied intelligently and adapted to the new environment. The typographic grid as it was developed in the 1950s, for example, is a good starting point for creating order on a website; but because contents are dynamic and windows must be scalable, the grid must be re-thought from the inside out – more about this on → p. 56.

↓ Web pages don't have to scroll vertically; that is just the established convention. This online magazine from Singapore (designer: Max Hancock) scrolls in the horizontal direction instead, which feels more true to the notion of a double page spread – not to mention being a more appropriate aspect ratio for most users' widescreen monitors.

Wanted: a fusion of aesthetics and usability. Designing for the web must find a middle ground between control over the look of the page and web-specific functionality.

Static and dynamic text

Understandably, many designers hope to exert control over web typography just as precisely as they would in print. Surprisingly often they still choose the shortest route, converting text – even body text – into image files (GIF or JPEG), or for enhanced excitement embedded into a Flash movie. Seemingly this offers a great deal of control, but it has several drawbacks. Search engines such as Google scan and catalogue language. In order to achieve good search results, the right words and names must be prominently mentioned on a site – as text, not image.

There are other factors as well. Users may want to copy text fragments. Text must be scalable (in Flash it's often not), otherwise it defies legibility when read on a high-resolution display like that of a smartphone. Moreover, static, inflexible, rasterized text allows for no input of new data. At every change, the web designer must come into action to convert the new text into new GIFs or JPEGs. Finally, converting text into images makes it impossible for the visually impaired to have it read aloud via special software add-ons.

In short, all the signs indicate that the future of web typography does not lie with Flash movies or 'pretty' pictures of text, but with genuine typography using real fonts. Sophisticated web typography has come into reach of those designers willing to explore the possibilities of *cascading style sheets* (CSS) and well-hinted webfonts. While this requires the web designer or developer to leave the WYSIWYG editor and get stuck into code, the rewards are worth the trip – web type is getting better and more versatile every week. See the pages on screen typography and webfonts (→ p. 112–115).

→ The website of web design agency Kitchen Sink Studios, based in Phoenix, Arizona, abounds with a rich variety of typographic flavours – all rendered in real, indexible, screen-reader-friendly text, and created using HTML5 and CSS3 with multiple viewing devices and browsers in mind. Shown are the top and borrom sections of the long scroll.

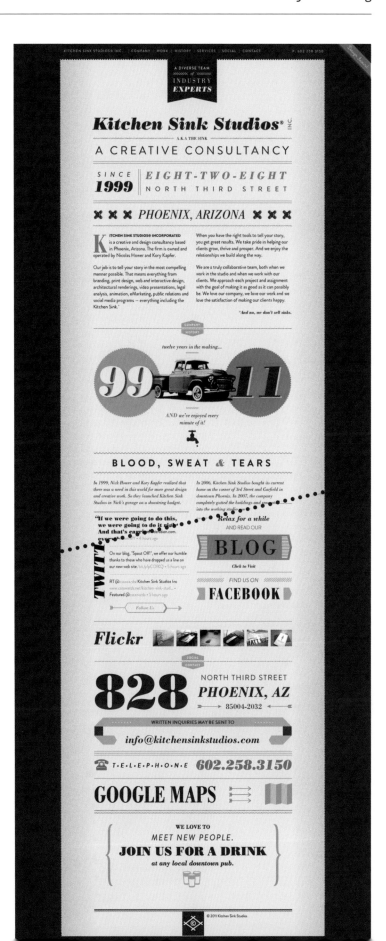

Type for type's sake: products for typophiles

What did graphic design buffs hang on their walls in the old days? Perhaps they got their hands on a vintage poster or two from the 1930s or 1960s; they might show work done by a friend. Almost invariably this was work originally made for a client, now leading a second life as a pseudo piece of art. Designers of a certain stature seldom decorated their walls with graphic design: they preferred paintings and art prints.

The past few years have seen the advent of a whole new kind of product that has found ready buyers thanks to the internet. Designers produce self-initiated graphic work – from posters and calendars to t-shirts and assorted objects – with the sole purpose of marketing them as typo-

graphic merchandise. Posters for rock concerts are made not as an assignment from the promotor but to be sold online and in galleries. Much of this printed matter is (to some extent) hand-crafted using techniques such as screenprinting and letterpress (→ p. 161).

There seems to be a fast-growing public for typographic merchandise. Type fans are alerted to new products through their social networks. It has become easier for designers to find their niche – provided that their product is special. As all of these exchanges take place in the equally excitable and critical world of designers and type geeks, conceptual and technical excellence are absolute conditions for success.

Wanted: unique voices, grand gestures, technical ingenuity. Anyone into breaking with convention, taking risks and being a little entrepreneurial, can create a new market for typographically flavoured gewgaws. It's a big challenge to find specialised manufacturers; technical ability and a willingness to improvise are essential.

House Industries in Delaware has been a trendsetter in the field of typographic objects. Their merchandise – production usually coincides with the release of a new digital type family – includes furniture, games, sculptures and these cast metal bookends.

These bicycle helmets sporting House Industries' patterns of letters ('H' from the Photolettering font Banjo, and curly brackets/braces) were produced for Giro's new Reverb line, 2011.

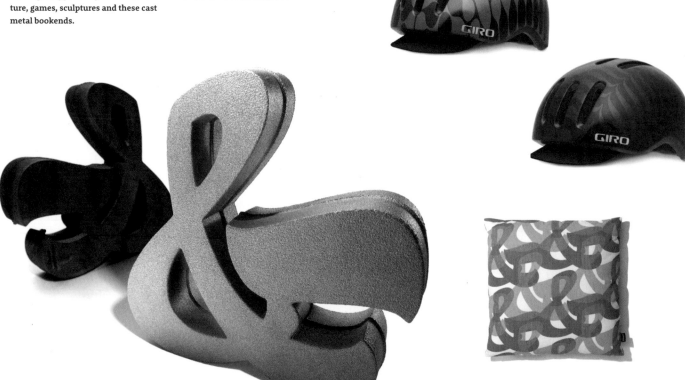

Object of desire

Seb Lester was for many years on the payroll of the British division of Monotype, where he made his name with the fonts Soho and Neo, both very clean, corporate typefaces. His personal work, on the other hand, revealed a dramatically different character. These exuberantly silkscreened posters recalling seventeenth century calligraphy were published as limited edition prints and enthusiastically snapped up by glamour-hungry graphic designers, allowing Lester to venture out on his own in 2010 as a highly proficient, high-profile custom lettering designer.

→ Fonts or lettering? 104
→ Style and statement 146
→ Material technologies 160

When Ben Faydherbe of Faydherbe/de Vringer was asked to design a series of posters for the art foundation Stichting Ruimtevaart in The Hague, it was clear that he needed to think of a system that allowed him to take on this sizeable low-budget project, and not have to start from scratch with every poster design. He constructed a template on the basis of a simple grid. The approach was time-saving and yet allowed enough room for variations.

Organising
and planning

Controlling the canvas

What we see when we look at graphic work is usually a flat surface. In a book or magazine this surface is a double-page spread. In other cases it is a poster, a sign, a frame in a movie title sequence, a screen of a computer or mobile device. This 'unity of graphic design' can be called a *canvas* – the area on which a designer arranges graphic elements the way a painter fills his or her painting.

Even when a design is purely typographical and contains no photography or illustration, in order to make it interesting as well as usable it is helpful to look at its composition as if you were looking at a picture. The division of the surface into dark and light parts (the *white* and the *black* in typographic terms), balancing the elements or creating a deliberate unbalance, while maintaining legibility, is as much an act of conscious form-giving as making a painting is. If the work is designed for print, it makes a lot of sense to hang it on the wall and take a few steps back. Judging digital designs on the computer screen alone can be limiting.

Creating a sequence

The canvas is often part of a larger whole. In a book, magazine or website, the pages or spreads form a sequential unit in which rhythm, relationships and contrasts are established throughout the publication. Something similar is happening with series. A string of posters or adverts for a concert venue, or a weekly or monthly newspaper can increase their recognizability when visual connections between the individual issues are established. A predetermined basic layout, and more particularly a template or grid, can help. It ensures that pages with diverse contents still have common elements. Not only does this create a sense of unity, it also helps readers to feel at home in a publication or on a website and to find their way without unnecessary searching or guessing.

(Mind you, the opposite can also be true. If a theatre or club distributes program leaflets that are unpredictable and different each month, and made without any apparent visual pre-planning, that, too, can result in a striking identity.)

Organising and planning

It is not the grid's only task to structure the user's and reader's experience. Designing on a grid is also a method to rationalise and systematise the design itself. It provides a framework, a kind of pre-design that limits the number of decisions that need to be taken for each page. It can be a means to streamline the production (the 'workflow') of a project and to make sure that, when several designers are working on a project, the outcome is consistent.

Graphic designers always need to take their context into account. Therefore design – especially within an agency structure – is generally a much less spontaneous activity than painting or music (not counting music for films or commercials). Most jobs are assignments: there is a client, there is a brief and a strict timing. We need to work within technical and budgetary constraints. In a studio structure there's often a specific distribution of tasks and workflow: if one designer gets too busy, another must be able to take over the work.

Many designers and studios produce work in roughly three stages: first the basic design; then a layout for each page; and finally the master document – the digital 'working drawings' from which the printed work, website or display panel is directly produced. Even when the workflow is not as systematic as that, it is a rule in many studios that if one designer is not available, another must be able to take over. Such practical circumstances imply that many graphic designers benefit from a systematic and rationalised approach ensuring that, when several designers work on a project, the outcome remains consistent.

So at the start of any project, the actual design work is preceded by another step. Planning, or designing, the process in many cases involves planning the design itself – preparing the canvas.

One step beyond: automated layout

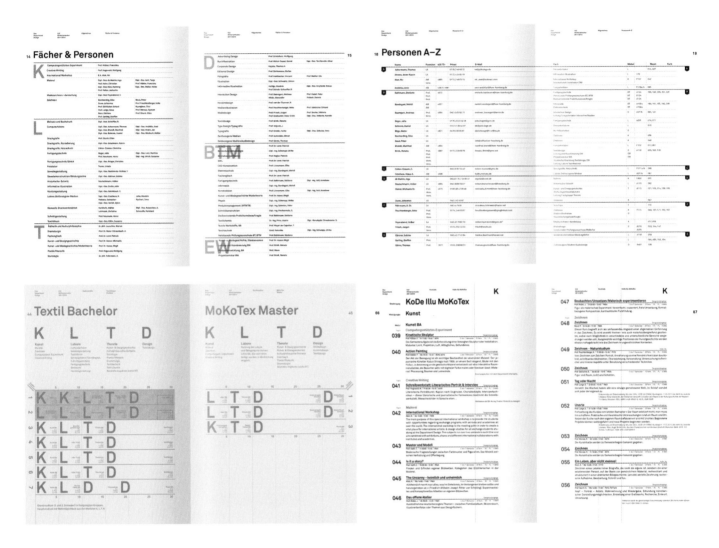

University Calendar, Hamburg University of Applied Sciences

Grids and templates were originally developed as guidelines for designers and their assistants – in other words: as instructions to be executed by human beings. The next step, inevitably, is the partial elimination of human intervention, letting the computer carry out the most time-consuming part of the work – the layout of individual pages. In fact, without automated page layout many printed publications containing large amounts of data would be impossible to produce within the given timing. Travel brochures, mailorder catalogues, timetables, cultural listings and the like have become too complex to design page by page. Using data input from one or more databases, the final layout is therefore often generated by a computer using carefully prepared basic designs.

At the Design Department of the Hochschule für Angewandte Wissenschaften (HAW) in Hamburg, Germany, students learn the ins and outs of automated page layout by producing a very real piece of work: the department's calendar booklet. It is designed by a different work group of students each semester, developing the basic design from scratch each time. The calendar of the 2011–2012 winter semester was conceived and designed by students Larissa Völker, Sören Dammann, Aljoscha Siefke and Dodo Voelkel under the supervision of Prof. Heike Grebin.

← Dramaturgy 26
→ Grid systems 50
→ Concepts 144

Modularity and efficiency

Modularity is a basic principle of many artefacts as well as forms in nature. Building an endless variety of things by combining and repeating simple components – modules – is crucial to most areas of human construction: architecture, machine building, music, typography.

Typography, in its original meaning of composing and printing with movable type, was probably the first human activity in which a modular approach enabled production on an industrial scale.

The stages of book production combined various levels of modules of increasing complexity: metal letters were collected into lines; lines built columns; columns and margins were combined into pages; printed sheets, consisting of 4, 8 or more pages, were folded into signatures; these were bound to make a book. In each phase, the components or units had to have a certain uniformity. Letters had equal height, lines were of equal length, and pages were usually laid out in a repeating pattern of symmetrical double page spreads. It would have been irrational and inefficient to break that regularity. The modular approach was inherent to the mechanic nature of typesetting and printing.

Around 1900 avant-garde poets and artists began breaking the moulds of traditional composition in page layout. They wanted to 'free' the text from the constraints of static, symmetrically organised rectangles; replace the classic decorative mode of centred titles by dynamic arrangements, introducing asymmetry, diagonals or pure chaos. Sometimes these experiments went hand in hand with ambitious claims for straightforwardness and functionality. In truth, building a diagonal page layout or random setting in letterpress required hours of trial and error and from a printer's practical point of view was the opposite of efficient – utter madness.

Experimentation soon made way for pragmatism; the Bauhaus was one of the places where Modernist principles of simplicity were advocated as a way to streamline mass production. It was only a matter of time before Modernist typographers returned to modules, having absorbed the lessons of the New Typography of the 1920s and '30s. During and after World War II, Swiss typographers fine-tuned the concept of the grid into an all-encompassing system of regular units, which became both a practical and a theoretical tool.

↑↑ Page from the Gutenberg 42-line bible with the underlying basic grid structure superimposed.

↑ 1659 Elsevier edition. For centuries, the technicalities of book printing dictated the basic grid of a page: a frame of margins surrounding rectangular blocks of justified text, with centred titles reflecting architectural tradition.

↑ Leaflet for Bauhaus books, designed by László Moholy-Nagy in 1925, mixing traditional justified text with a dynamic, asymmetric grid .

← The Italian Futurists were among the artists that upset the typographic applecart in the early decades of the twentieth century. This 1919 page by Ardengo Soffici is an example of what they called *Parolibere* ('words in freedom').

← At the height of his Modernist period, Jan Tschichold wrote *The New Typography*, in which he proclaimed that the days of centred typography were over: the new age needed a dynamic, asymmetric layout based on a flexible grid. This famous example from Tschichold's book (redrawn) focuses on magazine spreads. Tschichold would later return to a more traditional approach, for instance in his centred cover designs for Penguin books.

The total grid

Over the course of six decades, the grid was systemised, dogmatised and mythologised. Several designers of the 'Swiss school' published books describing and prescribing grids. This fragment from Josef Müller-Brockmann's book *Grid systems in graphic design* (still in print after thirty years) gives an idea of the universal ambitions of the grid's advocates as well as their fascination with exact science: 'The use of the grid as an ordering system … shows that the designer conceives his work in terms that are constructive and oriented to the future. This is the expression of a professional ethos: the designer's work should have the clearly intelligible, objective, functional and aesthetic quality of mathematical thinking. His work should thus be a contribution to general culture and itself form a part of it. … Design which is objective, committed to the common good, well composed and refined, constitutes the basis of democratic behaviour.'

This identification of a formal method with a morally just attitude has been questioned many times since. From a practical standpoint, the grid is certainly not a must any more. While desktop layout software is full of rulers and guides, these are not indispensable: computers also facilitate the creation and multiplication of the 'words in freedom' which fascinated the Italian Futurists. But as a practical means of structuring both the production process and the design itself, grids are still the most influential device carried over from Modernist functionalism into today's practice. To many typographic designers, the modular grid is the essential starting point of a design.

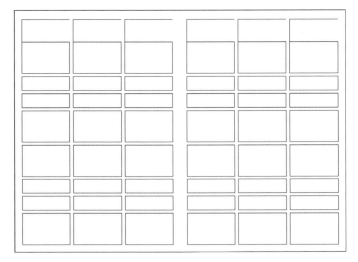

↖ Modular grid by Massimo Vignelli for Knoll brochures (redrawn, used by permission).

↑ In the decades following the introduction of the Swiss-style grid, millions of books, magazines and brochures were given modular structures based on text blocks and photos of equal size or related sizes. *Linoleum* magazine, Netherlands, 1966. Design Nan Platvoet.

→ Grid systems 50
→ Grids on the web 56
→ Manual typesetting 166

Divine proportions

Design is an attempt to banish coincidence and randomness. Consequently, a rational or systematic approach usually inspires more confidence than a design that is based solely on personal preferences and intuitive choices. A modular structure as discussed on the previous pages is a powerful basic principle, but it leaves many variables unsolved. The central decision to be made, one that has always intrigued city planners, architects and print designers, is about size: how big should the modules be, how big the complete thing? Or, on a more abstract level: what proportions make a thing look 'right'?

Devising (or 'discovering') so-called ideal proportions has traditionally been an important tool for designers to be able to present at least part of their decisions as inevitable and logical. From time immemorial the makers of signs and artefacts have tended to derive the proportions and characteristics of their designs from shapes found in nature or in naturally-derived geometry.

Trade secrets and the Da Vinci Code

In the same way that Vitruvius and Leonardo da Vinci rationalised human proportions by placing a human body within a circle and a square, letter-forms and books have often been constructed and analysed by means of geometric shapes and formulas. Sophisticated constructions were devised to determine the correct or ideal proportions of the page and the layout. Many of these were 'trade secrets' that were never documented at the time and were reconstructed centuries later. For instance, it wasn't until the early nineteenth century that art historians discovered the importance of the *Golden Section* or *Divine Proportion* (a well-known mathematical formula which you may remember from *The Da Vinci Code*) as a guiding principle in classic and renaissance architecture, painting and book design.

Whether or not such proportions actually make for better design is to be seen; we often like what we are used to. But both the Golden Ratio and simpler, but related principles like the *rule of thirds* can give designers a head start in creating a considerably more dynamic composition than that which is suggested by, say, a centred PowerPoint template.

↑ The human body, like the bodies of most other animals, is more or less symmetrical. This may have influenced our predilection for symmetrical objects and signs.

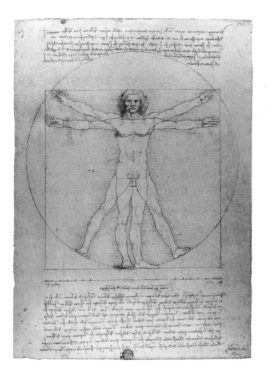

← In his famous drawing based on the theories of the architect Vitruvius, Leonardo da Vinci related the human proportions to the basic geometric shapes of the circle and the square.

→ Rationalisation was one of the great obsessions of the Renaissance. Many artists and architects tried 'explaining' the beauty of the roman alphabet by deriving each letter from a grid and its details from circles, squares and simplified geometric proportions. Albrecht Dürer, who also wrote *Four books on human proportion*, tried to provide the perfect recipe for the construction of letters in the treatise 'On the just shaping of letters' published in his geometric handbook *Course in the Art of Measurement with Compas and Ruler* (1525) from which these two examples are taken.

Fibonacci and the Golden Ratio

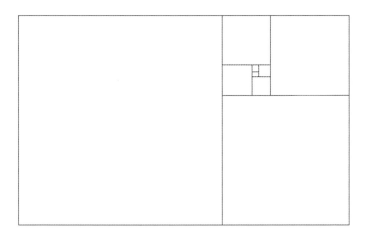

$\varphi \approx 1{,}6180339\ldots$

$$\frac{a}{b} = \frac{a+b}{a}$$

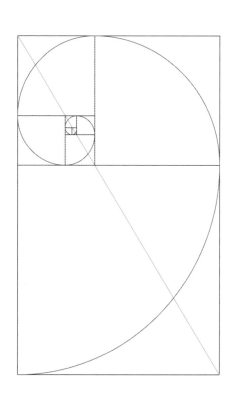

0
1
1
2
3
5
8
13
21
34
55
89
144
233
377
610
987
1597
2584
4181
6765
10946
17711
28657

The Golden Ratio or Golden Section divides a line into two parts relating to each other at about 1:1.618, an 'irrational' number represented by the Greek letter *phi*. The Golden Ratio plays a significant role in geometry, especially in the construction of pentagons and pentagrams. Ever since the pyramids were built, the Golden Ratio appears to have been used in architecture, art and crafts to establish harmoniously and rationally proportioned shapes. The Golden Ratio can be constructed with the help of a ruler and compass. (If you're interested, a quick web search will tell you how.)

↑ When subtracting a square from a 'golden' rectangle, the result is again a rectangle with golden proportions.

↗ A line divided in two according to the Golden Ratio, and the formula describing how the two parts of the line relate.

→ The Golden Ratio is interconnected with the Fibonacci sequence, a series of numbers in which each number is the sum of the two preceding ones. In nature, spiralling shapes often follow patterns similar to the one shown here, built with squares that increase in size according to the Fibonacci sequence. Fibonacci-related formulas are used in many fields, including computer science and the financial markets. In graphic design, the sequence as been used to create unorthodox grids.

Rule of thirds. Creating visual tension

Among the many prescriptions for visual composition, the rule of thirds is probably the most famous. First described by John Thomas Smith in his book *Remarks on Rural Scenery* (1797) the rule states that visual tension can be obtained by dividing the canvas into horizontal and vertical thirds. Placing key elements along the four dividing lines, and near the 'power points' where these lines cross, should result in a more interesting composition. The rule of thirds is now a staple of many a photography course, especially in North America, but can of course be useful in graphic composition as well.

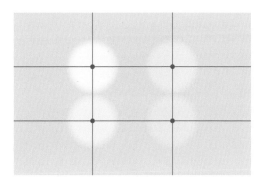

← Modularity & efficiency 44
→ Grid systems 50

Secret formulas of book design

The designer-writer Jan Tschichold found that most books produced between 1550 and 1770 were made according to some kind of 'divine' or rational proportion: a specific canon of page sizes from which the proportions of the type area and its position on the page was derived through sophisticated, 'secret' constructions. He was convinced that readers intuitively recognise such relationships as more pleasant and harmonious. Small books, Tschichold also decreed, must be tall (you should be able to hold them with one hand) and for square books, he wrote in 1962, there certainly is no need whatsoever.

Today square books are produced in relatively large numbers – it is an economic way of making books using a limited quantity of paper. For square formats, it makes little sense to construct page layouts according to renaissance diagrams. Designers must rely on their intuition and eye.

In general, subjectivity and practical considerations are the main guidelines in establishing the proportions of type on a page today. Contemporary designers are often rather fond of extremely narrow margins. These are achievable because printing and binding techniques are so much more precise than in 1600.

Yet there still is interest in the formulas that Tschichold (re-)discovered. His books are still reprinted and translated. In the influential book *The Elements of Typographic Style* by Canadian Robert Bringhurst, several pages are devoted to the construction of double-page spreads using the Golden Section and related formulas.

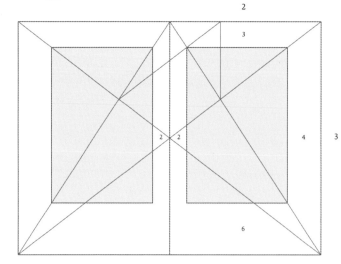

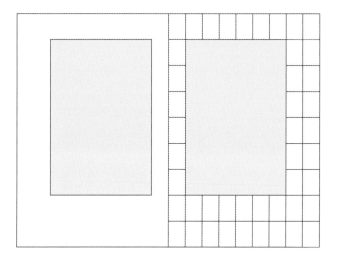

↑ 'Ideal' proportions as reconstructed by Jan Tschichold were devised long before the invention of printing. Based on a manuscript by Villard de Honnecourt (c. 1280), this page scheme is characterised by Robert Bringhurst as 'a sound, elegant, and basic mediaeval structure.' Shown are both the construction and the resulting 9 × 9 'grid'. Using these formulas and the resulting wide margins today will result in a design that looks deliberately classical and precious, rather than 'natural'.

← Rosbeek Printers' goodwill publications were square books of c. 198 mm. Unsuitable for traditional structures, square formats often prompt the designer to use unconventional layouts. Piet Gerards's design of the complete catalogue of the Rosbeek series is a case in point. The book was published in 2010 by Gerards's own publishing firm, Huis Clos, which has also published writings by Tschichold.

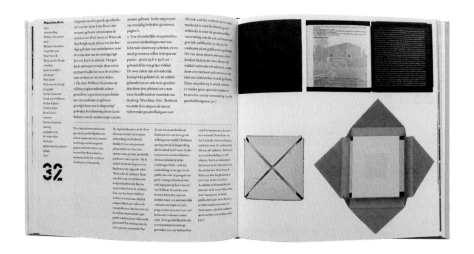

Rationalisation: the DIN standards

Even if we rarely come across books made according to mediaeval formulas, in many parts of the world we are in contact on a daily basis with a system similar to the Golden Ratio: that of the paper formats of the German DIN institute. Created in 1917, DIN (*Deutsches Institut für Normung* or German Standardisation Institute) has established standards in many fields, including health and the environment, but the 1922 standard paper sizes are among their best known and internationally most influential.

The Berlin engineer Walter Porstmann based his design on a forgotten formula from the late eighteenth century, in which all sizes have an equal proportion of $1:\sqrt{2}$ ($\approx 1:1.414$). The advantage is that the range of sizes is perfectly consistent and easy to scale: to get to the next, smaller size in the range you simply fold the sheet of paper in half. When employed throughout the production and distribution process of, say, a publicity campaign with handouts, posters and brochures, the DIN system will lead to minimal loss of paper; it will also save space when storing or transporting the printed matter.

There are four series of standard DIN sizes, A to D, of which the first three have become worldwide ISO standards. The A series is by far the most used: in many countries, a sheet of office paper is referred to as 'an A4'. The B series provides a range of in-between sizes, while the C series is used solely for envelopes, compatible with A-size sheets: an A4 sheet will fit into a C4 envelope; folded once, into a C5 envelope.

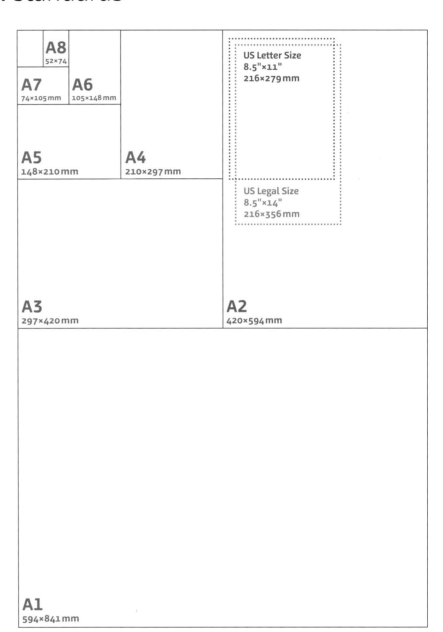

A8 52×74
A7 74×105mm
A6 105×148mm
A5 148×210mm
A4 210×297mm
A3 297×420mm
A2 420×594mm
A1 594×841mm
A0 841×1189mm≈1m²

US Letter Size 8.5"×11" 216×279mm
US Legal Size 8.5"×14" 216×356mm

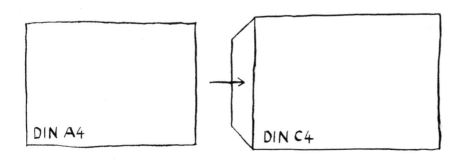

DIN A4   →   DIN C4

← Stream of ideas 22
← Modularity 44
→ That Swiss feeling 92

Looking into grid systems

↑ The modular construction of a grid is similar to the design principle of a half-timbered house. The woodwork is a grid, and the rectangles it defines may be filled at will – with masonry, windows or doors, just like the grid of a page is filled with text, images and other elements.

There are many ways to create coherence within a design and provide it with an inner logic, but as we have seen, the modernist grid has obtained a special position. This is not only the case for graphic design: cities, buildings or interiors can also be grid-based. Simply put, a grid is a division of the canvas through lines. Most grids use rectangles, but there are also grids in which circles, triangles and diagonals play a role.

In a modular grid, each box can be filled with varying contents – text, image, colour planes, and the elements necessary for articulation and navigation. Often a grid contains rules defining which elements may be placed where, what the distances between them can be, what typefaces and body sizes are used, what the colour palette is, and so on. A grid full of such rules and regulations is a template.

Self-imposed constraints

Most designers like constraints: a client brief, a budget, a maximum size. Constraints give direction to their thinking and provide the motivation to think in terms of function and structure, not shape and skin. Thanks to constraints, designers can think of themselves as problem solvers.

In finding a form, grid systems provide a more or less artificial constraint, and that too can help to guide the mind. But the use of a grid or template should not lead to self-delusion or to a situation where designers thoughtlessly fill in the blanks. As it is a self-imposed restriction, it can be overridden or ignored.

An all-too strict or simplified grid may limit the designer's freedom of movement, which can be frustrating and inefficient. A finely-woven, flexible grid is one possible way to prevent the grid from becoming a straitjacket. The other solution, however, is more common: some basic guidelines are given to establish column widths and a simple vertical division; the designers are given (or take) the liberty to break the grid as soon as they have painted themselves into a corner.

A final warning: in spite of the attraction of grid-based order, grids are optional. They are just one way of looking at page-making. Like talented painters and draughtsmen, a brilliant designer may not need a pre-designed framework for designing a well-made page. Sometimes the grid is in the head; and sometimes a certain amount of disorder can be a good thing.

→ In his book *Grid systems*, Josef Müller-Brockmann, one of the masters of the Swiss functionalist school, presented this example of a three-dimensional grid for a trade fair stand. Josef Müller-Brockmann, *Rastersysteme für die visuelle Gestaltung. Ein Handbuch für Grafiker, Typografen und Ausstellungsgestalter. Grid systems in graphic design. A visual communication manual for graphic designers, typographers and three dimensional designers.* 7th printing, Niggli Verlag, Sulgen/Zürich 2010 (orig. 1981).

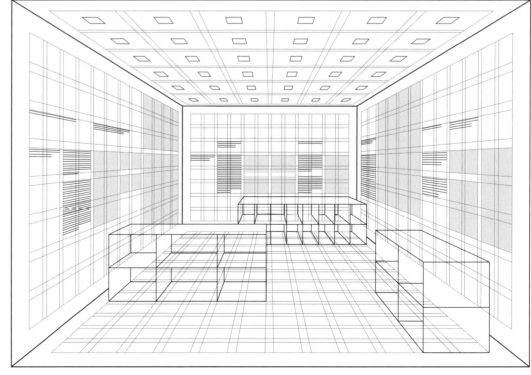

A flexible grid

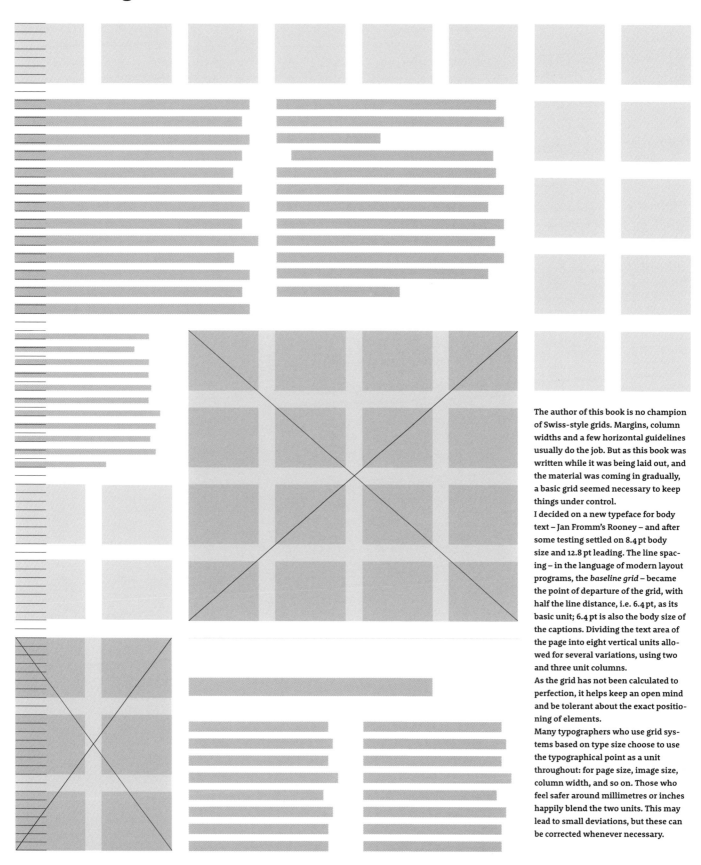

The author of this book is no champion of Swiss-style grids. Margins, column widths and a few horizontal guidelines usually do the job. But as this book was written while it was being laid out, and the material was coming in gradually, a basic grid seemed necessary to keep things under control.

I decided on a new typeface for body text – Jan Fromm's Rooney – and after some testing settled on 8.4 pt body size and 12.8 pt leading. The line spacing – in the language of modern layout programs, the *baseline grid* – became the point of departure of the grid, with half the line distance, i.e. 6.4 pt, as its basic unit; 6.4 pt is also the body size of the captions. Dividing the text area of the page into eight vertical units allowed for several variations, using two and three unit columns.

As the grid has not been calculated to perfection, it helps keep an open mind and be tolerant about the exact positioning of elements.

Many typographers who use grid systems based on type size choose to use the typographical point as a unit throughout: for page size, image size, column width, and so on. Those who feel safer around millimetres or inches happily blend the two units. This may lead to small deviations, but these can be corrected whenever necessary.

Types of grid

Grids are not just a way of organising what you want to put on the page. More importantly, perhaps, they are a way of controlling the space that is left empty: the *white* of the page. White space in graphic design is not a recent invention, the huge margins of mediaeval books had a similar function – creating a frame around the painting, silence around the music. But in modern design, the white is not a frame, it is a dynamic thing that moves around the canvas and helps focus the attention first here, then there. When used well, a grid prevents a complex composition from looking random. To use a musical analogy: a grid provides the time signature – the beat against which the melody of the text, image and white space can be played.

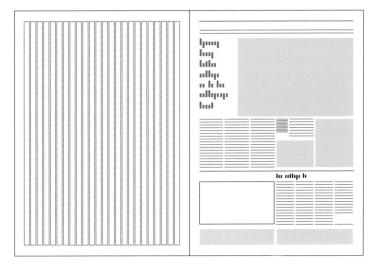

↑ Newspaper grids are almost invariably column grids, with no fixed division in horizontal rows. This design, based on the eight-column layout of many broadsheet newspapers, has a 24-column master grid, making possible a high degree of variety of smaller and larger columns and photos.

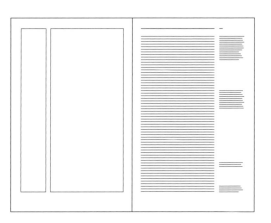

↑ A classic and widely used grid for books with footnotes and/or illustrations. The main text is in a wide column, in its outer margins is a secondary column for accommodating notes and captions. Besides the axial (symmetric) layout, an asymmetric variant is also possible, for instance one in which the margin column is always left of the main text, on both odd and even pages.

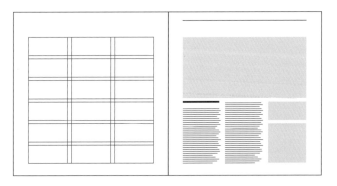

↑ Simple grid for an illustrated book or brochure.

↑ When designing a poster, advertisement or magazine spread, a grid of squares – which, in this case, was tilted a few degrees – can help to keep things under control.

A Baroque framework

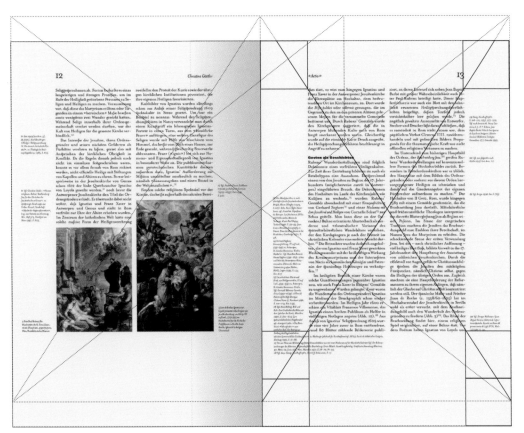

Barocke Inszenierung (Baroque staging) is a book containing the proceedings of a conference of the same title held at Berlin's Technical University. designed by Andreas Trogisch of Berlin's Blotto studio, the book is a fascinating collision of ancient constructions and contemporary thinking. Trogisch used a mediaeval formula such as the one shown on page ← 48, shifting the grid so that its highest point is about an inch over the top of the page, resulting in exact squares and double squares defining the margins. This strict scheme formed the basis of an ever-changing page layout that breaks the mould of the grid wherever necessary and uses the marginal footnotes of mediaeval manuscripts, enclosing the text like a frame of reassuring scholarship.

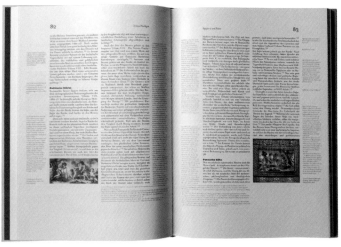

← **Dramaturgy** 26
← **Controlling the canvas** 42
→ **Grids on the web** 56

The grid exposed

Some designers swear by designing on a grid, others don't think it is very useful and prefer a more spontaneous approach to layout. But as the grid has been such an elementary aspect of graphic design over the past six decades, it is hard to ignore even for experimental or postmodernist designers. Confreres from both camps – strict functionalists as well as postmodern eclectics – have commented on the grid as a visual and ideological device by making it visible in their designs. The effect can be ironic or tongue-in-cheek; it can also be way of visualising the point of view that (typo-)graphic design is practically unthinkable without the underlying logic of the grid, as in Wim Crouwel's classic poster and catalogue for the 1968 *Vormgevers* ('Designers') exhibition at the Amsterdam Stedelijk Musuem, shown below.

British functionalist designer Anthony Froshaug was of that opinion as well. In his essay *Typography is a grid* he wrote: 'To mention both typographic and, in the breath/sentence, grids, is strictly tautologous.' Typography, he pointed out, per definition means arranging standard modules in a regular pattern.

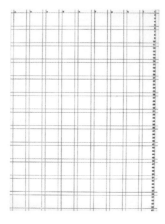

↑ For the exhibition 'Vormgevers' (designers) at the Stedelijk Museum in Amsterdam, Wim Crouwel made a self-referential poster. As a basis for the layout, as well as the custom-made alphabets, Crouwel used the grid he had introduced a few years earlier for the Stedelijk catalogue designs. On the back of the 'Designers' exhibition catalogue the same grid was reproduced at true scale. With thanks to Ben Bos and Tony Brook.

A wink to the grid

Anette Lenz's design for the 2001–2002 programme of the Angoulème city theatre in France explicitly used the grid as a design element. The grid is presented on the cover, then provides a strict ordering of the season's programme on page 3 and on the editorial pages marks the rhythm for a variegated play of text blocks, colour planes and photos. The rectangular order is broken by impulsive circles and diagonal bars that mostly stay on the lower level but sometimes find their way to the top.

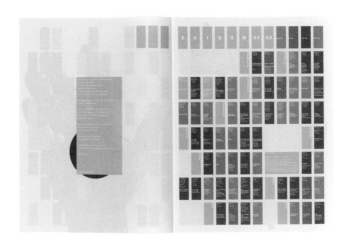

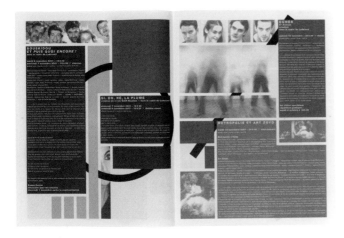

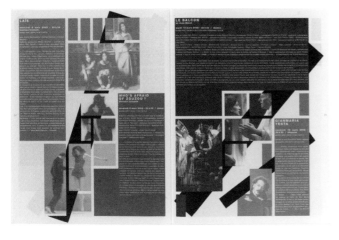

← Dramaturgy 26
→ Modular type 92
→ Concepts 144

Grids on the web

In print design, the use of grids has gradually become an optional thing. Many designers are interested in concepts and structure rather than perfectly lined-up elements, and use grids loosely, if at all. In web design the opposite has happened. During the past few years it has become a hot topic, and the subject of dedicated websites, blogs and books. It is presented as a cure to all the things that are frustrating or annoying about web design: scalable windows, ever-changing content, inconsistent fonts, and more. The grid for the web, however, is something radically different from grids in print.

While grids for print can take the page size and proportions as reference and create margins, text areas, or patterns of regular modules from there, a grid for the web can rarely do that. As we saw (←p. 36) the vertical size of many web pages is unknown and so the division of the canvas is often purely vertical – a column grid. Columns are often calculated pixel-perfect – which is great for controlled website design, see below. But pixel sizes do not make as much sense when the page is viewed on the tiny, high-resolution screen of a mobile device. Multi-column layouts become ridiculous on a smartphone, while images with a fixed pixel width become too small.

So mobile browsing calls for yet another paradigm shift in web page design. A possible solution is to create sliding scale of virtual designs for different *viewports*: big monitor – smaller monitor – tablet – smartphone. What can be an aesthetically pleasing, multi-column magazine-like design on a computer screen may become a purely pragmatic one-column layout on a mobile device. Grids will help to guide the scaling of designs from one device to the next.

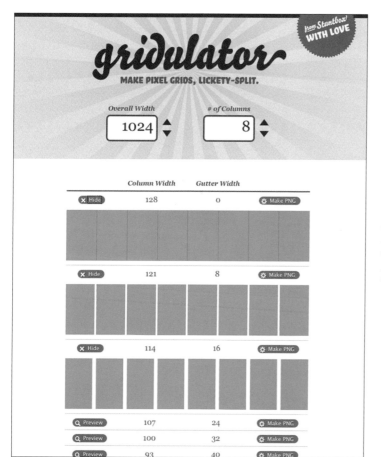

Gridulator

David Sleight, the owner of New York web design agency Stuntbox, built a simple online application for calculating column grids on the web. Originally designed for in-house use, Gridulator was later made available as a free download from gridulator.com. As Sleight explains, he built Gridulator because 'most of the existing desktop grid calculators are geared heavily towards print (widths like 58.766666666 aren't exactly helpful to a web designer).' Gridulator was designed to be 'something that would make the act of creating a grid so easy as to make the output nearly disposable. No more cringing at the thought of rearranging umpteen gazillion guides in Photoshop. And no more fretting that the numbers wouldn't add up in PixelLand.'

Lively, lucid, manageable

Creative Capital

Creative Capital is one of the largest funders of the arts in the USA. The organisation has many programs, including their artist grant program that showcases some of the finest artists in the world.

Area 17, a web design agency with offices in Paris and New York, developed a website for Creative Capital that is almost as ambitious as their programs. The goal of the website was 'to clearly communicate the many offerings of the organisation while creating opportunities to showcase the artists themselves and the role of Creative Capital in their professional growth.' The use of a strict yet flexible grid helps in keeping the website lucid and easy to update.

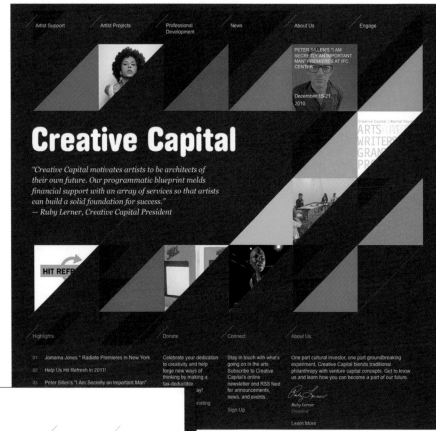

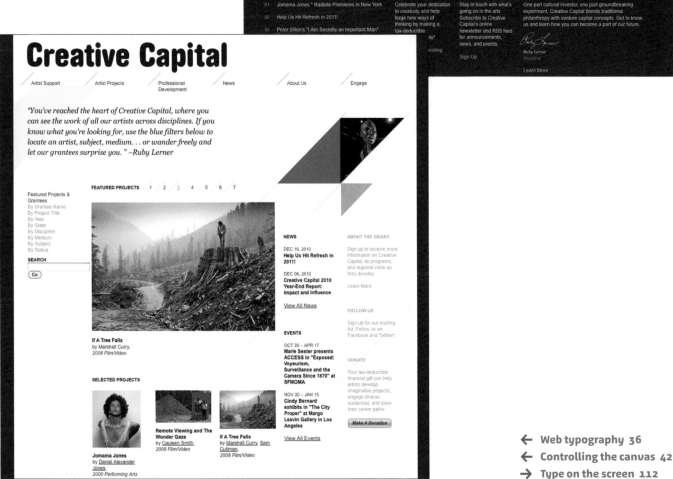

← Web typography 36
← Controlling the canvas 42
→ Type on the screen 112

Niemands Land, a war poem by Flemish
author Tom Lanoye, was designed in an
expressionist style by Gert Dooreman.
While he used dozens of typefaces,
Dooreman chose to limit himself to
fonts produced by Czech type designer
František Štorm (plus Rhode and
Barcode from Font Bureau). 'Every kind
of expression I wanted to achieve was
represented by those typefaces,'
Dooreman commented. Prometheus
Publishers, 2002.

40

INSLAG & KABAAL

luider & luider steeds lui—
der nog luider & luider

EEN STORTVLOED VAN LOOD

raast over
ons heen

« HET KOMT VAN LINKS !!! »

[ons gebeurt niets] .... *[wij zijn goed beschut]*

BOEM ·
Weerkaatsing
BOEM · patáát!

bijtende rook ZWELT ....moffenlinie GEVELD ....*verdwijnt in verwarring*
....*in rook*
....*in smook*

kreten en *g...e...k...e...r...m*

onze troepen roepen *« GIJ VARKEN GIJ*
GAAT ER GODVER AAN GIJ !! »

Crash! Reverberation! Crash!
Acrid smoke billowing. Flash upon flash.
Black smoke drifting. The German line
Vanishes in confusion, smoke. Cries, and cry
Of our men, 'Gah, yer swine!
Ye're for it,' die
In a hurricane of shell.
One cry:

Knowing and
selecting type

vergaan in een orkaan **VAN GRANATENDICTATEN**

1 KREET *['WE KOMEN ERAAN KIJK UIT']*
DAAR IS DE HEL AL OPENGEGOOID
DAAR
DAAR, JA!
stukken
brokken
brokstukken
vanvanvan
mensen
&messen
&pensen
&pezen
&ezels
&schedels

vliegen
vlammen
vallen
allen *DE LUCHT IN* begot

SMAK!
SMOOR!...[oh!]
OPSTOOT!...KRAK!

MACHINEGEWERENGEBABBEL
BOMBARDEMENTENGESCHETTER
BLOTEWAPENGEKLETTER

'We're comin' soon! look out!'
There is opened hell
Over there; fragments fly,
Rifles and bits of men whirled at the sky:
Dust, smoke, thunder! A sudden bout
Of machine guns chattering ...
And redoubled battering,
As if in fury at their daring! ...

Thinking about type selection

The selection of a typeface can be crucial to the attractiveness and functionality of a piece of graphic design. But it shouldn't be forgotten that type is only one element of many. Choosing proven, famous typefaces does not guarantee good graphic design. The opposite is also true. It is entirely possible to make a convincing piece of design with a mediocre typeface. The communicative power of a graphic product depends on many other factors besides type.

This doesn't alter the fact that anyone who is professionally engaged in shaping text should be well-informed about the properties of letters. By this I don't just mean the aesthetics of letterforms – do they look good? – but also about what happens under the bonnet. Often the technical characteristics of a typeface, its specifications, are crucial to the decision to use or not use a typeface or type family for a specific project. Does it have a sufficient range of weights, such as Light or Black for striking headlines? Numerals of equal width for setting tables, small caps for acronyms such as UNESCO and ASCII? Are they OpenType fonts that are compatible with Windows as well as Mac computers? Is the regular weight of the typeface sturdy enough for small sizes, or is it perhaps too contrasted, with skinny hairlines that risk becoming invisible in small sizes or when reversed out of a dark background? Does the font come with specially designed ligatures and alternate letter combinations to help designers create spectacular headlines?

While the supply of well-equipped (text) fonts was still very limited as little as fifteen years ago, there are now hundreds of well-designed and affordable type families offering impressive possibilities for high-end typography.

'Uninteresting type, please'

In short, today's demanding typographic designers have a huge array of usable fonts at their disposal. Besides sophisticated text typefaces there are tens of thousands of charming, dramatic or powerful display fonts to make a design stand out; new fonts are released on a daily basis.

But not everyone *wants* beautiful letters. In contemporary graphic design there is also an opposite tendency that has a strong predilection for 'faceless' type. Many designers who are conceptually inclined think that ideas are a thousand times more important than typographical detail; they feel that all that attention to perfect typesetting and traditional finesse is exaggerated – a kind of fetishism. They prefer typefaces that have little to say, fonts that are so familiar that we almost perceive them as being 'non-designed'. Helvetica, Times New Roman and DIN are such typefaces. In the Netherlands, well-known designers such as Mieke Gerritzen or International Jetset have relied almost exclusively on Helvetica and similar typefaces for a large part of their careers. Catalogues and cultural papers set in Times are now hip (a trend that started more than ten years ago), while that choice was considered to be a rather lazy, safe solution in the early days of digital type.

This is a remarkable paradox in the Dutch – and also British – graphic design world. Our young type designers enjoy worldwide admiration for their technical skills, sophisticated tastes and innovative ideas, but trendy graphic designers of their own generation have other priorities and tend to use anonymous typefaces designed in the mid-twentieth century or fonts that come at no extra cost with operating systems.

↓ Some designers like using unusual, exclusive typefaces as a distinguishing element. Weiss-Heiten Design Berlin (Birgit Hoelzer, Tobias Kohlhaas) developed this identity for Fuchsauge, an office for art history and editing. The typeface is Andrea Tinnes's Switch, which can only be purchased directly from the type designer and is not distributed by other companies.

THERE IS NO INTERNET REVOLUTION. TECHNOLOGY IS IMPROVING AT A SNAIL'S PACE AND IT CERTAINLY WON'T KEEP UP WITH THE SHORT-CIRCUIT VISIONS OF THE IT MARK-

ETERS. DO NOT BECOME DISAPPOINTED WITH THE CRUEL LIMITATIONS YOU ARE CONFRONTED WITH. EMBRACE THEM. BE NICE TO THEM AND THEY'LL WORK HARD FOR YOU.

← ... while other designers, such as Dutchwoman Mieke Gerritzen (who is also director of MOTI Museum Of The Image in Breda, formerly the Graphic Design Museum) prefer typographic simplicity. Most of her work was designed using bold Helvetica, Franklin Gothic and other industrial, 'no-nonsense' typefaces. In her approach to type, Gerritzen is a heir of Piet Zwart; a fragment of Zwart's 1930 plea for 'uninteresting type' is reproduced below.

Both approaches are firmly rooted in their respective international traditions. In the 1920s and 1930s designers such as Jan van Krimpen in the Netherlands and Eric Gill in Great Britain created sophisticated typefaces that were internationally innovative within the idiom of classical book faces. The development of this 'modern traditionalism' coincided with the advent of a much more radical typography influenced by Modernist movements such as De Stijl and Constructivism. One of this tendency's most prominent representatives in the Netherlands was Piet Zwart, who was proclaimed Dutch 'designer of the century' in 2000. Zwart believed in a sparse typographic style that did not allow for any kind of frippery. In 1930 he wrote (making demonstrative use of all-lowercase): 'ornate and antiquarian mediaeval types have lost their right to exist. we require more businesslike letters. ... the less interesting, the more typographically usable. a typeface is less interesting when it has fewer historical relics, and is more related to the precise, tense spirit of the 20th century.' As the ideal modern typeface had not yet been invented, Zwart preferred no-frills sans-serifs from the late nineteenth century: grotesques, still called 'antique' or *antieke* in Dutch at the time.

It wasn't until after 1945 that type designers in Switzerland and France created the types Zwart had dreamed of, types based on nineteenth-century grotesques, but colder, more rational, more precise. Helvetica was the most successful of these 'exact' faces. It was immediately embraced by the postwar heirs of Piet Zwart and company – by 'functionalists' such as Wim Crouwel in Amsterdam and Massimo Vignelli in Milan and New York. The young generation to which the likes of International Jetset belong are their spiritual children.

Know first, reject later

If you are a budding designer looking for clues in type selection it is probably a good idea to look beyond current trends. If not, you risk making imitations of an imitation without realising it. There's little merit in blindly using 'undesigned' typefaces in the idea that your work will at least look contemporary. Perhaps the nuance of a newly designed book or display typeface better matches what you want to express. It therefore makes sense to get an idea of these nuances, however cursorily. That is what this chapter is for.

←   Navigation 24
→   Choosing typefaces 102
→   Buying fonts 110

Text and display: bread and butter

Different ways of reading require different kinds of typefaces. The main distinction is so obvious that it is easily overlooked: the question of whether we are dealing with plain text (*body text*) or headlines, slogans, etc. For the former we need a text face, for the latter a display face. A good text font will often work well as a display typeface. The reverse is usually not such a good idea.

Workhorses and jobbing faces

For centuries, the range of special typefaces available for setting titles and headlines was very limited. Almost invariably, the types used for title pages, bills and pamphlets were large roman capitals. This changed in the early nineteenth century when the Industrial Revolution brought new production methods and consumption patterns, as well as large-scale entertainments such as circuses, resulting in a need for mass publicity. This triggered a demand for loud, attention-grabbing letters, leading to the creation of a whole new breed of letterforms: extra bold letters (*blackface*), letters with no serifs or with very fat or unusual serifs, shadowed letters or three-dimensional letters (→ p. 88).

These special headline and advertising type-faces came to be called 'jobbing type' in English: they were the types used for the odd jobs outside the realm of book or newspaper printing. The Dutch name, 'smoutletter', referred to *smout*, 'lard'. It made sense, because in German as well as Dutch, body type was and still is called 'bread type' (*Brotschrift, broodletter*). In a society where lard was just about the only type of sandwich filling available to the common man, the name had impeccable logic to printers and typesetters: try selling your clients some tasty display type – 'the icing on the cake' – and you might be able to feed your family more than just dry bread.

Case study: Quadraat text and display

The FF Quadraat type family by Fred Smeijers was a small series of contemporary oldstyle faces when it first came out. Later Smeijers added a sans-serif version and a narrower (Condensed) variant. Although the Quadraat family was introduced as a family of text faces, both the serif and the sans worked well for display purposes – see the example on this page. Nevertheless Smeijers felt there was room for a series of display variants designed for effect. He therefore introduced FF Quadraat Display and FF Quadraat Headliner. Both these sub-families have a huge x-height and are narrow in width, which makes them economic in use – that is to say, they allow a line of text to be set larger and thus have more impact in the same amount of space than a line set in the more modest Quadraat variety. The use of Quadraat Display and Headliner for longer texts in small body sizes is to be discouraged.

↓ **Poster for a Dutch-German arts festival designed by Wim Westerveld. Tasteful use of the sans-serif (text) face Quadraat Sans in a display setting.**

Niederländische Kultur in Jena 1997 · Eröffnung 20. Juni, Theaterhaus Jena
Literatur · Ausstellungen · Musik · Theater · Kleinkunst · Film · Architektur ·
Wissenschaft · Technik · Schülerprojekte · Vorträge · Workshops

Nederland in Jena

Quadraat Regular, *Italic*
Quadraat Bold, *Italic*
Quadraat Sans, *Italic*
Quadraat Sans Bold, *Italic*

Quadraat Display Italic, **Bold**
Quadraat Sans Display, Black
Quadraat Headliner Light
Quadraat Headliner Bold

Contemporary jobbing faces

Display or headline fonts are fashion items. The preferences of art directors and graphic designers change every five to ten years, and the crowds quickly get used to the new trend. This was as true in the nineteenth century as it is today. Type foundries and type designers benefit by creating new fashions to keep their businesses going.

A number of trends from recent years are shown below. Several of these are retro styles. There is almost no style in the history of typography that is not represented in type design today. Script fonts are not listed below: they are dealt with elsewhere.

My receding hairline

Taz H09 (LucasFonts)

Bold, black beauties

Taz UltraBlack (LucasFonts)

Typewriter references

Typestar (FSI)

Into the matrix

BPdotsPlus (Backpacker)

'The modern face'

Poster Bodoni (Bitstream)

19th-century wood

Maple (Process Type)

The Roaring 20s & 30s

Sympathique (Canada Type)

POST-WAR STYLE

Miedinger (Canada Type)

Disco|Techno|Geo

Dublon (Paratype)

Extremities

Ever more text families are coming with extreme weights to set spectacular headlines, from ultra thin (hairline) to extra black.

Technical

Graphic designers like using typefaces with a technical look and feel when trying to resist the polished aesthetics of 'sensible' typography. Often these fonts refer to visually simplified letterforms designed for typewriters, dot matrix printers, displays in trains and buses and on airports, or automatic character recognition (OCR). → p. 92

Nineteenth-century echoes

Most text faces in the 19th century were based on the Bodoni/Didot model with its pronounced contrasts. For large format posters, extreme forms of this genre were developed, as well as typefaces with exaggerated serifs, and the first sans serifs. Today there are myriad interpretations of these dramatic genres. → p. 88

Twentieth-century echoes

In the first half of the twentieth century changes in typographic fashion happened in rapid succession. The botanical ornaments of Art Nouveau were supplanted by Art Deco's rigid ornamentation and the geometric simplicity of Contructivism; after 1955 several waves of geometric type design followed, with 1990s and techno style as the latest major current. → p. 90

Typeface, font, family, character set, font format

When typefaces consisted of cases full of heavy metal type, they were sold by the pound. If you wanted to set a thick book without redistributing the type for re-use, you would need large quantities of the stuff: a huge investment of money and muscle. Today, a digital font allows you to set as many books as you like. Buying a new typeface is not as weighty a decision as it used to be. But good fonts come at a price and deciding what to buy hasn't become easier. The structure and characteristics of fonts can vary greatly, depending (among other things) on the *font format*: TrueType, PostScript Type 1 or OpenType. Here's a concise introduction to fontology.

↓ In the age of metal type, letters were sold by the pound, priced separately for each point size. Foundries established the smallest quantity of type that could be acquired. Below is such a 'fount' of type.

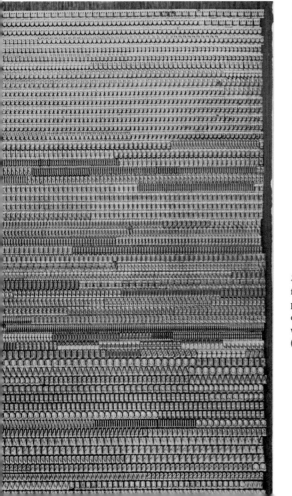

What is a typeface – and what is a font?

Agile *Italic*

↗ Edgar Walthert's Agile is the headline typeface of this book. Agile consists of ten weights, from Hairline (very thin) to Ultra (extremely bold) with italics and small caps for each weight. When we mention Agile in general (as an idea, a concept, a group of related fonts) then we can speak of the *typeface* Agile.

Typeface is the word used to describe the design: a typeface is not so much a certain quantity of characters but rather the basic drawing, a set of underlying principles. Sometimes the word is used for a specific *style* or *weight*: 'As headline typeface we chose Agile Bold' – but more often than not it stands for all the variants together: 'The Agile typeface was released in 2010.'

Garamond Regular, SMALL CAPS, *Italic*
Garamond Semibold, SMALL CAPS, *Semibold Italic*
Garamond Bold, *Bold Italic*

↗ As harddisk space was a big issue in the early days of digital typography, even all-purpose text families such as this Garamond were of modest size. Small caps were not deemed necessary for the Italic styles and Bold weight. Today many of the new all-purpose font families are very extensive: they consist of five or more weights and are often available in various widths.

Type family A collection of related fonts based on the same basic design. These fonts can vary in thickness (weight), style (normal, italic, small caps) and width. The digital design process facilitates the design of very large families, which are often referred to as *suites* or *superfamilies*. Such a family consists of a number of related sub-families; Luc(as) de Groot's Thesis, for instance, consists of a sans-serif, serif and semi-serif series as well as monospaced and 'Typewriter' varieties.

Agile **BLACK**

↗ One weight of Agile. This OpenType font has the small caps built in (see next page). As usual, the italic is accommodated in a separate font. So Agile's Black weight consists of two fonts : normal (or roman) and italic (Agile Black Italic).

Weight and style Originally 'weight' referred to stroke thickness: the Bold version of a typeface is a weight. In the 1990s font suppliers began using the word as a synonym for *font*: 'weight' was used to denote a specific *style* (e.g. Italic) within a weight: TheSans Bold Italic was called a weight. This complicates matters; it is better to speak of a style there. So let us agree that 'weight' denotes the stroke thickness within a typeface (Light, Semibold, Black, etc.) within a type family, and that a weight can contain the italic, small caps and other style variations.

Font and character set

↓ Part of the character set of one font of TheSans, the sans-serif component of Luc(as) de Groot's Thesis superfamily. This diagram shows the state of things a few years back, with c. 1,500 glyphs per font. A full font would come with diacritic signs (accents) for virtually all languages that use the Latin alphabet; with Cyrillic and Greek, and small capitals for each of these scripts, plus special punctuation for small caps (like smaller '?' and '$'); nine different ampersands (&-signs) and four kinds of @-signs, lining and hanging (oldstyle) numerals, numerals for fractions and tables, mathematic signs, arrows and 'dingbats'. Many glyphs have been added since – among others, a huge set of phonetic signs as well as pictograms for signage and siacritics for Vietnamese. Besides, there is also TheSans Arabic. TheSans now consists of c. 6,000 glyphs.

Font, or 'fount' in the old British spelling (from *to found*, meaning 'to cast'). In its American spelling the term font is now generally accepted as 'basic unity' of the type trade. In brief: *A font is the smallest salable part of a typeface family*. Even shorter: fonts are digital typeface files.

This may sound somewhat vague, but there is a reason for that. An 'obsolete' digital font format such as PostScript Type 1 could accommodate 221 or 214 *glyphs* (characters) respectively on a Mac or a Windows machine, allowing for one style only to fit in a font. Special numerals, small caps, diacritics (accented letters) for less common languages such as Czech or Icelandic, non-Latin scripts like Greek or Cyrillic – each of these required separate fonts to be produced.

OpenType fonts (the new standard) are much more extensive: one font can hold a character set of c. 65,000 glyphs. This allows the manufacturer to accommodate several scripts in one font – like Arabic, Cyrillic and even Chinese – but also small caps and a choice of numerals, ligatures, and so on. However, as the character set cannot be subdivided, it is still one font.

Under PS Type 1 and TrueType it was also common to produce separate fonts for typographic embellishments and extras, e.g. a font of 'swashes' (letters with decorative curls), a font of arrows and/or ornaments, etc. You'll probably still encounter such 'specialist' fonts for several years to come. In OpenType such extras have become part of the standard font.

This doesn't imply that *every* OpenType font is equipped with all those goodies. Also, not all computer programs support extensive character sets; Microsoft Office suite (Word, PowerPoint, etc.) has been the most notable spoilsport in this respect. But conformity across platforms and software is growing each year.

Family members

In a family all members have their respective tasks, and it is no different with type. Here is a brief overview of the members of an extensive type family: TheSans by Luc(as) de Groot.

TheSans
TheMix
TheSerif

Superfamily

TheSans is part of a so-called superfamily: an extremely extensive system of fonts built around the same basic design. TheSans is the sans-serif variant, TheSerif is the version with (slab) serifs and TheMix has serifs in selected places only, making it a 'semi serif'.

ABCDEFGHJKabcdefghjk

Upper- and lowercase

Each variant of a family usually consists of two basic alphabets: uppercase (capitals, majuscules) and lowercase (minuscules).

TheSans
AaBbCcDdFfGgSsTtWwYyZzÁáÊêÑñÖöŠš@!

TheSans Italic
AaBbCcEeFfGgSsTtWwYyZzÁáÊêÑñÖöŠš@!

THESANS SMALL CAPS (SC) + *SC ITALIC*
AABBCCDDFFGGSSTTWWYYZZÁÁÊÊÑÑÖÖŠŠ@!
AABBCCDDFFGGSSTTWWYYZZÁÁÊÊÑÑÖÖŠŠ@!

Roman, italic, small caps

Most text type families come in a number of weights (stroke thicknesses). Each weight of a well-equipped family such as TheSans contains a roman, an italic and small caps for both. When the Thesis superfamily first came out in 1994, italic small caps were exceptional. They have become much more common since.

TheSans Black **Theodore gives up**

TheSans ExtraLight Jackie tries again

TheSans ExtraLight • TheSans Light
TheSans SemiLight • TheSans Regular • TheSans SemiBold
TheSans Bold • **TheSans ExtraBold** • **TheSans Black**

Hairline H13
Hairline H31

Weights

TheSans originally consisted of eight weights, from ExtraLight to Black. It was later expanded with a broad range of 'Hairlines', ultra-thin variants for large-size yet subtle headlines. The heaviest and lightest weights of any family (and certainly its hairlines) are usually not well suited for body copy. At text sizes (from c. 7pt to 12pt) the medium weights of ThaSans, SemiLight to ExtraBold, are the most usable. These weights also work well in large sizes.

SemiCondensed · Condensed
XCondensed · XXCondensed · XXXCondensed

ABCDEFGHIJKLMNOPQRSTUVWXYZ
abcdefghijklmnopqrstuvwxyz
1234567980&()[]$£€#§@&+=!?

Condensed versions

Many families (including popular typefaces such as Helvetica) come with narrow and extra narrow variants. These have names such as Condensed, UltraCondensed, Compressed, etc. TheSans has a particularly broad range of narrow fonts, with 'x-rated' names as with sizes in fashion.

Mono-spaced

In a typeface's monospaced version each letter takes up exactly the same width, just like the letters on an old typewriter. They can be used to make nice, rad-looking headlines but are mainly meant for typesetting computer code.

← At its initial release in 1994, Luc(as) de Groot's Thesis was the largest type family ever designed by one person. Besides three variants (sans-serif, serif and semi-serif) in eight weights, the family also offered a large number of extras, such as small caps, multiple numeral styles, arrows, pictograms and a collection of ampersands (&-signs). Back then, the PostScript Type 1 font format with its limited character set required several fonts per weight to accommodate all these goodies. This resulted in a staggering 144 fonts on Thesis' first release. In the OpenType-system all the extras of each weight fit into a single font. Therefore the font list shown is now a historical document.

FFThesis™ © Luc(as) de Groot 1994

→ Combining typefaces 104
→ OpenType features 130
→ Numerals 138

Italics true and false

aefgiv

aefgiv

aefgiv

Italics usually play a secondary role in typography. When an *italicised* word turns up in a text set in roman, something special is probably going on. The word may be the title of a book or magazine – publishers' style sheets often specify that such titles should be italicised. Italics can also express emotion or emphasis, 'I am *important* so I want to get my way *now*!' Many authors italicise foreign words, which can be useful and/or amusing: 'Snobbish, *moi*!?' or 'The French take a lot of fresh *pain* with their meals.'

This distinguishing use of italics is surprisingly old: as early as the sixteenth century, italics became used for emphasis alongside romans. Yet the italic originally started out as a solo artist. The Italian punchcutter Francesco Griffo cut the first italic printing faces for the printer Aldus Manutius, who applied them as stand-alone text faces in small-size editions of the classics – the earliest printed paperbacks.

Handwriting

Griffo's italic was a faithful copy of Italian humanist handwriting. This explains the etymology of the term *italic*. Another common word for calligraphic italics is *cursive* (from the Latin

currere: 'to run'), referring to the uninterrupted flow of the writing: most of the letters are written without lifting the pen from the paper.

For centuries Griffo's type was the basic model for all italics, and even today most italics have calligraphic characteristics that derive from that early example. The cursive forms of the 'a', 'e', 'f' and 'g' differ significantly from those in the roman, but other letters also show marked differences. In addition, a typeface's italics are often lighter and narrower than the roman.

Real italic and slanted roman

In short, in many cases an italic is characterised by a unique structure – not just by the fact that it is not upright. Yet a number of typefaces released during the twentieth century did not have calligraphic traits but were slanted (*oblique*) versions of the roman. Type designers and foundries had several reasons to do so, and often their chief motivation was a financial one. New photographic design and production processes made it possible to tilt a roman type at a 10 to 14 degree angle at the push of a button, and pass it off as an italic. Typesetting italic texts or even producing complete fonts in this way obviously meant

Upright italics: the Joos typeface

As italics are characterised by a particular shape, the angle at which they are tilted is of secondary importance. It is therefore quite possible to design an upright italic, or one that is leaning to the right at a virtually imperceptible angle of, say, 1 or 2 degrees.

One of the earliest typefaces that can be described as an upright italic was cut by Joos Lambrecht, an opinionated printer in sixteenth-century Ghent (Flanders). In 2008 the young French type designer Laurent Bourcellier produced a digital version of Lambrecht's typeface, called Joos.

FF Seria by Martin Majoor and Auto 3 by Underware are among some of the recent, newly designed digital typefaces featuring upright italics.

Italique

considerable savings in design costs. Moreover, there were historical precedents. Many early sans-serifs, such as Akzidenz Grotesk, also had no 'real' italics, a trend that was continued in modern grotesques like Helvetica and Univers. Type designer Adrian Frutiger was convinced that an italic with calligraphic traits was not fit for a modern sans-serif such as his Frutiger typeface and produced an oblique roman instead.

In practice such an *oblique* or *slanted roman* is not always ideal: it may lack impact as it is simply not different enough from the roman. In the design of sans-serifs, the 'real' italic has made a comeback since the early 90s. This prompted Linotype to equip Frutiger Next, the 2000 version of the Frutiger family, with a true italic; yet a more recent version, Neue Frutiger (produced in close collaboration with Frutiger himself), saw a return to the slanted roman.

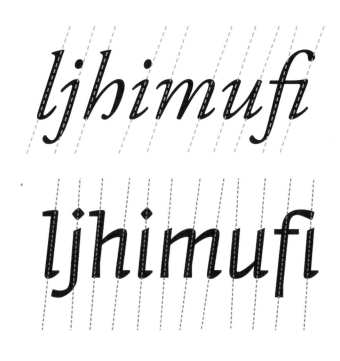

Hamburge — Frutiger Italic 1976

Hamburge — Frutiger Next Italic 2000

Hamburge — Neue Frutiger Italic 2009

↑ Classic italics such as Garamond's (top) do not have a consistent slope: the slight variations of the angle lend liveliness and spontaneity to the text. This principle was taken up in contemporary typefaces such as Fedra Serif by Peter Biľak (bottom).

Quickly jumping zebra

Quickly jumping zebra

← Bree, an upright sans-serif by TypeTogether's Veronika Burian and José Scaglione, comes with a number of letterforms borrowed from italics, such as 'a', 'g', 'k', and 'z' (top). The more conventional roman forms (bottom) are offered as alternates.

Auto 1 *Quel fez sghembo ha*

Auto 2 *Quel fez sghembo ha*

Auto 3 *Quel fez sghembo ha*

← Auto by the design group Underware is a lucid, contemporary sans-serif with a unique feature: its roman can be combined with three different italics. Auto 1's italic is restrained and simple, while Auto 2 has a subtly swinging italic, and Auto 3 an upright italic with unusual details.

Typeface anatomy: serifs and dry sticks

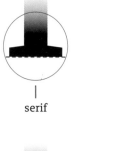

serif

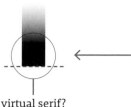

virtual serif?

Many parts of letters have names that refer to parts of the human and animal body: arm, leg, eye, waist, tail. Metaphors from other areas also found their way into typospeak – flag, stem, bowl – as well as descriptive workshop terms: ascender, crossbar, diagonal.

In the dictionary of type jargon, *serif* is probably the only word never spotted outside the typographic realm. The Dutch word is *schreef*. As type designer Gerrit Noordzij has pointed out *schreef* is simply the past tense of *schrijven*, to write; in his view it denotes the scratch or line with which a punchcutter might mark the end of a stroke on an unfinished punch; the schreef was simply the end of a stem or leg.

In all probability the etymology of the English word *serif* goes back to that ambiguous Dutch term – remember that until well into the seventeenth century English printers imported type and typographic knowledge from the Netherlands.

Thus, the English *sans-serif*, also written as *sanserif*, can be unmasked as a somewhat silly fantasy word based on the assumption that 'se-*reef*' must be French. It's not. Sans-serif in French is *sans empattements*. The most colourful term is the one used in the Hispanic world: they call a sans-serif a 'dry stick': *palo seco*.

Measuring type

↑ Line thickness is measured in points as well in modern layout software. The lines are, respectively, 0.3 – 0.5 – 1 – 2 – 4 and 6pt; on the far right, a line with the width of the old cicero.

	MM	DIDOT POINT	PICA POINT	DTP POINT
1 MM =	1.00000	2.65911	2.84527	2.83463
1 DIDOT POINT =	0.37607	1.00000	1.07001	1.06601
1 PICA POINT =	0.35146	0.93457	1.00000	0.99626
1 DTP POINT =	0.35278	0.93808	1.00375	1.00000

In the graphic world, the size of letters – the body size – is traditionally measured in points: Didot points in Europe, pica-points in America. The typographic point was invented in France around 1700 as a replacement for the attractive but imprecise size names that had previously been used. And as this was France, its size was derived from the king's shoe size. In the system established almost a century later by the influential printer François-Ambroise Didot, there were 864 points to the *Pied du Roi* (king's foot) which amounts to c. 0.376 mm for a Didot point – just over three points in a millimetre.

In the United States the point system was adapted to the standard American foot, resulting in the Pica system. A pica point is equivalent to about 0.3515 mm, with 12 points to the pica.

Both traditional points systems were superseded after the advent of digital typography by the fractional or DTP pica. Measuring 1/72 of the standard Anglo-Saxon foot (1/6 of an inch) it is equivalent to 4.233 mm; the point is 1/12 of a DTP pica, or c. 0.353 mm. When Adobe's PostScript adopted the system, it soon became a standard in digital graphic communications.

In the early days of digital typography, the graphic industry on the European continent lobbied hard for a decimal system to replace the old points. It would have been efficient, as document and image sizes were usually measured in millimetres. But tradition proved powerful, and the points system prevailed. Many traditionally trained typographers – even younger ones – still use points to define the size of their documents and the units of their grids.

English-language typographers abbreviate 10 points as '10pt'. In the pica system 'p' stands for pica; so for instance, when choosing Picas as the ruler unit in InDesign, 10 points is notated as 0p10 (zero pica, ten points).

European users may still come across other typographic units used by a minority of typographers. The most widespread is the *cicero*, equivalent to 12 Didot-points or 1/6 of the historical French inch (*pouce*) and similar to an English pica. The cicero was named after a great Roman, Marcus Tullius Cicero: the printers Pannartz and Sweynheim used a 12pt typeface (1 cicero) for their 1468 edition of Cicero's *Ad Familiares*.

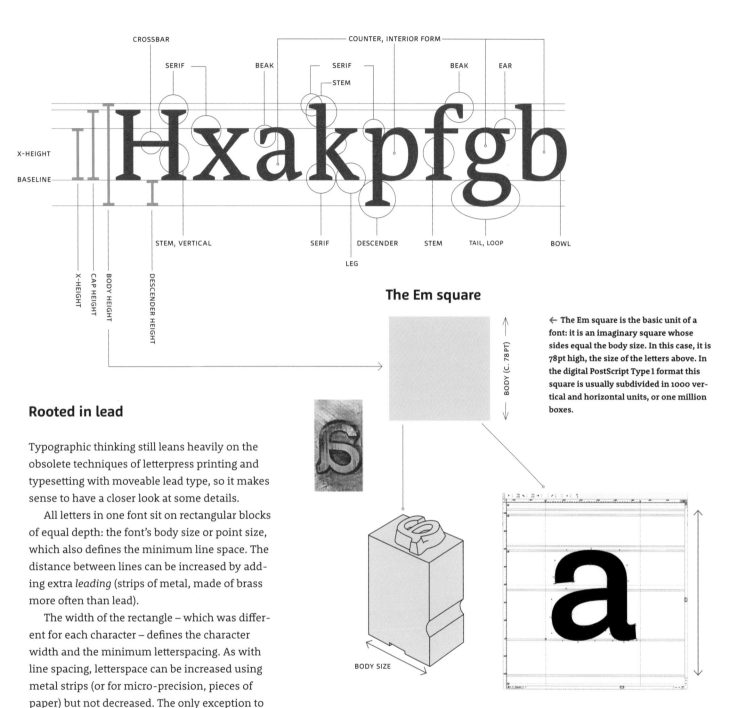

CROSSBAR

SERIF

BEAK

COUNTER, INTERIOR FORM

SERIF

STEM

BEAK

EAR

Hxakpfgb

X-HEIGHT

BASELINE

X-HEIGHT

CAP HEIGHT

BODY HEIGHT

DESCENDER HEIGHT

STEM, VERTICAL

SERIF

DESCENDER

STEM

TAIL, LOOP

BOWL

LEG

The Em square

BODY (C. 78PT)

← The Em square is the basic unit of a font: it is an imaginary square whose sides equal the body size. In this case, it is 78pt high, the size of the letters above. In the digital PostScript Type 1 format this square is usually subdivided in 1000 vertical and horizontal units, or one million boxes.

BODY SIZE

Rooted in lead

Typographic thinking still leans heavily on the obsolete techniques of letterpress printing and typesetting with moveable lead type, so it makes sense to have a closer look at some details.

All letters in one font sit on rectangular blocks of equal depth: the font's body size or point size, which also defines the minimum line space. The distance between lines can be increased by adding extra *leading* (strips of metal, made of brass more often than lead).

The width of the rectangle – which was different for each character – defines the character width and the minimum letterspacing. As with line spacing, letterspace can be increased using metal strips (or for micro-precision, pieces of paper) but not decreased. The only exception to this is that type manufacturers may choose to avoid generously overhanging shapes, like the arc of the lowercase 'f', which would cause a gap with the next letter, by *kerning* that letter: the overhang protrudes from the body and rests on the next letter. This is the original meaning of the word kerning, which is used in digital typography for all corrections to the standard letterspacing between two or more characters (→ p. 128).

→ **Comparing fonts 72**
→ **Ligatures 134**
→ **Typesetting 166**

Comparing fonts

When choosing a headline typeface for a poster or book cover, the designer has much freedom. When choosing a typeface for body text the range of possibilities is narrower, especially in cases where factors such as accessibility and efficiency (economy) play a role. While all 'book faces' were designed for longer texts, their characteristics may differ a great deal. Besides, some fonts that are advertised (or tagged on font websites) as being suitable as text or book faces are in fact far from ideal. For example, some work well only in point sizes of 12pt and up because they are simply too thin for an enjoyable read at smaller sizes. Or they may have been designed for display use but have come into fashion as text faces thanks to graphic designers who find a hip look more important than ease of reading.

In short, the only way to come to decisive conclusions when choosing a text face that should look good and perform optimally is by testing it. You can do it on your own, or involve acquaintances and relatives (preferably of different generations). In case different fonts must be compared, it is not a good idea to blindly select the same point size for all possible options: just zoom in on the screen to ensure that the x-heights of the letters are the same.

Point size and x-height

What do we talk about when we talk about a 12-point character? As seen on the previous page, the point or body size traditionally referred to the lead block on which the typeface was cast. So the length of ascenders and descenders was part of the body size. This has remained unchanged. At one and the same size, letters with long ascenders and descenders (and therefore a relatively small x-height) look smaller than letters with short extenders and a large x-height.

In addition, digital design technology allows for more flexibility of sizing the character within the virtual body height, making it appear smaller or larger. By way of example, here are two Dutch contemporary typefaces – FF Seria, a font family with generous ascenders and descenders, and PMN Caecilia, a familly with a relatively large x-height and 'face'.

PMN Caecilia 48 pt   FF Seria 48 pt

→ What is more economical, a large or a small x-height? The answer is not as obvious as it seems. In practice, the body of a text face is chosen in relation to the optical properties, including the x-height. The economy of a letter (i.e., the amount of text of a certain level of legibility that fits in a given area) depends more on other factors – such as how well the characters are drawn, and whether their shapes are wider, more open, etc.

Murciélago

PMN Caecilia 18 pt

Murciélago

PMN Caecilia 16 pt

Ex et, officip suntotatur susapictota dolum laut plibus idel ium a quam, sita volut officat empeles porestrum et laborum harum quam rem in coriberat fuga. Xim quiatate venimus dendist, non pe molorae stiorerro blaborio.

PMN Caecilia 55 (Regular) 8 pt

Murciélago

FF Seria 18 pt

Murciélago

FF Seria 22.8 pt

Ex et, officip suntotatur susapictota dolum laut plibus idel ium a quam, sita volut officat empeles porestrum et laborum harum quam rem in coriberat fuga. Xim quiatate venimus dendist, non pe molorae stiorerro blaborio.

FF Seria Regular 11 pt

8pt!

11pt!

Reading test

Six typefaces in two broad categories – serif text type with oldstyle proportions, and sans-serif – in a rather compact, flush-left setting. The body size was adapted for each typeface so that the text occupies the same number of lines, and x-heights are similar. Which typefaces are the most readable? Which ones are disappointing? Bottom row: three justified text blocks, identical except for the leading.

The *clear* and *readable* effect of the old-style roman text letter is produced not so much by its angular peculiarity, or any other mannerism of form, as by its relative monotony of color, its thicker and shortened hair-line, and its comparatively *narrow and protracted body mark*.

An over-wide fat-face type that *emphasizes* the distinction between an over-thick stem and an over-thin hairline, necessarily destroys the most characteristic feature of the oldstyle letter. It then becomes necessary to *exaggerate* the angular mannerisms of the style.

Digital revival of a sixteenth-century classic:
Adobe Garamond Pro 9/11

The *clear* and *readable* effect of the old-style roman text letter is produced not so much by its angular peculiarity, or any other mannerism of form, as by its relative monotony of color, its thicker and shortened hair-line, and its comparatively *narrow and protracted body mark*.

An over-wide fat-face type that *emphasizes* the distinction between an over-thick stem and an over-thin hairline, necessarily destroys the most characteristic feature of the oldstyle letter. It then becomes necessary to *exaggerate* the angular mannerisms of the style.

Contemporary text face design:
Vesper Pro 8/11

The *clear* and *readable* effect of the old-style roman text letter is produced not so much by its angular peculiarity, or any other mannerism of form, as by its relative monotony of color, its thicker and shortened hair-line, and its comparatively *narrow and protracted body mark*.

An over-wide fat-face type that *emphasizes* the distinction between an over-thick stem and an over-thin hairline, necessarily destroys the most characteristic feature of the oldstyle letter. It then becomes necessary to *exaggerate* the angular mannerisms of the style.

Digital version of a twentieth-century revival:
Bauer Bodoni 9/11

The *clear* and *readable* effect of the old-style roman text letter is produced not so much by its angular peculiarity, or any other mannerism of form, as by its relative monotony of color, its thicker and shortened hair-line, and its comparatively *narrow and protracted body mark*.

An over-wide fat-face type that *emphasizes* the distinction between an over-thick stem and an over-thin hairline, necessarily destroys the most characteristic feature of the oldstyle letter. It then becomes necessary to *exaggerate* the angular mannerisms of the style.

Industrial sans-serif from around 1890:
Akzidenz Grotesk 8,5/11

The *clear* and *readable* effect of the old-style roman text letter is produced not so much by its angular peculiarity, or any other mannerism of form, as by its relative *monotony* of color, its thicker and shortened *hair-line*, and its comparatively *narrow and protracted body mark*.

An over-wide fat-face type that *emphasizes* the distinction between an over-thick stem and an over-thin hairline, necessarily destroys the most characteristic feature of the oldstyle letter. It then becomes necessary to *exaggerate* the angular mannerisms of the style.

Contemporary humanist sans-serif:
LF TheSans 8/11

The clear and readable effect of the old-style roman text letter is produced not so much by its angular peculiarity, or any other mannerism of form, as by its relative *monotony* of color, its thicker and shortened *hair-line*, and its comparatively *narrow and protracted body mark*.

An over-wide fat-face type that *emphasizes* the distinction between an over-thick stem and an over-thin hairline, necessarily destroys the most characteristic feature of the oldstyle letter. It then becomes necessary to *exaggerate* the angular mannerisms of the style.

Geometric sans serif based on 1960s lettering:
AvantGarde Gothic 7,5/11

The *clear* and *readable* effect of the old-style roman text letter is produced not so much by its angular peculiarity, or any other mannerism of form, as by its relative *monotony* of color, its thicker and shortened *hair-line*, and its comparatively *narrow and protracted body mark*.

An over-wide fat-face type that *emphasizes* the distinction between an over-thick stem and an over-thin hairline, necessarily destroys the most characteristic feature of the oldstyle letter. It then becomes necessary to *exaggerate* the angular mannerisms of the style.

Chaparral Pro 8,5/13

The *clear* and *readable* effect of the old-style roman text letter is produced not so much by its angular peculiarity, or any other mannerism of form, as by its relative *monotony* of color, its thicker and shortened *hair-line*, and its comparatively *narrow and protracted body mark*.

An over-wide fat-face type that *emphasizes* the distinction between an over-thick stem and an over-thin hairline, necessarily destroys the most characteristic feature of the oldstyle letter. It then becomes necessary to *exaggerate* the angular mannerisms of the style.

Chaparral Pro 8,5/11,5

The *clear* and *readable* effect of the old-style roman text letter is produced not so much by its angular peculiarity, or any other mannerism of form, as by its relative *monotony* of color, its thicker and shortened *hair-line*, and its comparatively *narrow and protracted body mark*.

An over-wide fat-face type that *emphasizes* the distinction between an over-thick stem and an over-thin hairline, necessarily destroys the most characteristic feature of the oldstyle letter. It then becomes necessary to *exaggerate* the angular mannerisms of the style.

Chaparral Pro 8,5/10,2 ('auto' leading in InDesign)

→ Choosing type 102
→ Line length and leading 174

Type classification

Like animals and plants, typefaces are divided into classes and species in order to facilitate recognising them and talking about them. Some designers find classification a useful expedient in combining various typefaces within one piece of graphic design.

In generally accepted classifications such as the one invented by Maximilien Vox (c. 1954, below) text typefaces or 'workhorse' faces are the main point of focus. Classic serifed book faces receive special attention, with Vox devoting no less than four separate categories or classes to this genre. No attempt is made to subdivide most other kinds of type, such as scripts or unconventional display types, into sub-categories. This is,

of course, related to the fact that typographers of Vox's generation often were inclined to value serious book typography over other forms of graphic communication.

It still makes sense to have a generally accepted terminology when choosing and evaluating type. The most common practice today is to use a mixture of categories from conventional classifications and all kinds of ad hoc terms. These pages offer an introduction to the rich but complex lingo of type descriptions and to the historic background of the various kinds of typefaces.

manuaires
Humanes
Garaldes
Réales
Didones
Mécanes
Linéales
Incises
Scriptes

↑ Title page of the original brochure with which the Vox classification was announced. Published by the friends of the Rencontres de Lure, a yearly conference organised by Vox in the town of Lurs in Provence, 1954

Still relevant: the ATypI/Vox classification

The French typographer and type historian Maximilien Vox (pseudonym of Samuel Monod) invented a new way of classifying typefaces around 1955. Vox' proposal responded to a need for clarity, especially in France, where the typographic terminology was unstructured and obscure. Names like *labeurs* (similar to the English 'workhorse'), *elsevirs* and *antiques* were used interchangeably without much sense of history. To replace the hodgepodge of names used in France and internationally, Vox had coined a series of fanciful new names referring to the historical background of the different type styles. Thus 'Humane' became a name for typefaces with roots in Italian humanism, 'Garalde' is a contraction of the famous names Garamond and Aldus, and 'Reale' connotes the regime of Louis XIV, who had

ordered the Romain du Roi to be designed for his *Imprimerie Royale*.

The Vox system was a success: the world-wide typographers' association ATypI adopted it with some minor changes. The system has survived to the present day and is still recommended in many typographic handbooks, although in view of the current situation it shows considerable gaps (more about that later). In mid-2011 a group of young ATypI members began investigating the possibilities of updating the classification using modern tagging techniques.

For the overview on the opposite page we used the common English translation of the Vox categories.

Type categories and history

Typographers and graphic designers often mix different terminologies when describing fonts. Below is an explanation of the Vox classification in relation to other, equivalent terms. From page 80 we look at modern versions of these genres.

Vox/ATypl

Humanes are based on the earliest romans, derived from the humanistic handwriting, which were introduced around 1470 in Venice. A typical feature: the 'e' with an oblique crossbar. **Garaldes** follow the model of the romans used by Claude *Gar*amond (Paris) and *Ald*us Manutius (Venice) and their 16th and 17the-century heirs.

Reales are the types that were developed from Renaissance and Baroque models in the 18th century. They are more regular and have rather pronounced vertical stress.

The name **Didone** refers to the *Didot* family of Parisian printers and to Giambattista Bo*doni* from Parma. Their types from around 1800 are characterized by clear lines, thin, straight serifs and strong vertical modulation.

Lineales is the Voxian name for all sans-serifs, regardless of their construction. It is one of the categories where Vox's classification is hopelessly inadequate.

Mecanes show low contrast between thick and thin parts and sturdy, straight serifs. In Vox' time these faces usually had a geometric, mechanical structure – hence the name.

Glyphic typefaces are those that are reminiscent of stone-carved letters. Typically, the stems are slightly tapered (narrower in the middle).

Manuares is an umbrella term for a variety of typefaces derived from handwriting, such as uncials and Gothic (broken, blackletter) types. Scripts are all the typefaces that look like hand-drawn or-painted lettering.

Common names

The difference between Humanes and Garaldes is subtle and of little use to today's reality. They are often jointly referred to as *oldstyle, Renaissance oldstyle* or, in sources influenced by German usage, *Renaissance-Antiqua*. Some authors use *Mediaeval* for Humanes – typefaces based chiefly on Jenson's types. → p. 84

As a prelude to the rationalist Didone style, this genre is often referred to as *transitional*. Which is somewhat unfair, as it is an accomplished style with no 'in-between' feel. → p. 86

The most common name in English is the nineteenth-century moniker *modern face*. The historically correct *classicistic* is used as well. Advocates of Gerrit Noordzij's theory (→ p. 76) speak of 'pointed-pen-typefaces'. → p. 86

The 19th-century names *grotesque* and *Gothic* denote different variants in English. It is also useful to distinguish between genres such as *humanist* and *geometric* sans-serifs. → p. 97

The nineteenth-century name *egyptian* is still common today. The most used term is *slab-serif*. As with sans-serifs, it makes sense to distinguish *humanist* and *geometric* slab-serifs. → pp. 88–89

There are several other terms: *incised, glyphic, flare serif*. The French-derived term *lapidary* is sometimes encountered.

It is preferable keep blackletter and uncials in separate categories. For scripts, the English usage discerns a mass of subgenres: brush script, copperplate script, formal script, and so on. → pp. 80, 104

Vox has no separate genres for fonts that fall outside the traditional categories: they all end up in a big bag with the label 'Other' or 'Exceptional'. Yet it is entirely possible to be more specific about those genres, so that we all know what we are talking about. → p. 77 and 90–93

Edgefirst — Humane: Jenson

Edgefirst — Garalde: Garamond

Edgefirst — Reale: Baskerville

Edgefirst — Reale: Arnhem

Edgefirst — Didone: Bodoni

Edgefirst — Geometric sans: Futura

Edgefirst — Humanist sans: TheSans

Edgefirst — Geometric slab-serif: Rockwell

Edgefirst — Humanist slab-serif: PMN Caecilia

Edgefirst — Glyphic: Optima

edgefirst — Uncial: Libra

Edgefirst — Brush Script: Bello

Edgefirst — English Roundhand: Bickham Script

Classifying by stroke modulation

The earliest printing typefaces were imitations of hand-written letters, and in letterforms of a later date many of the characteristics of handwriting have been preserved. The Dutch typographer and teacher Gerrit Noordzij has even postulated that there is no essential difference between writing by hand and 'writing' with fonts. He therefore defines typography as 'writing with prefabricated letters'. Noordzij has devised a simple type classification that subdivides letterforms according to the tool from which they derive, directly or indirectly.

Contrast

A crucial element of his theory is the *contrast* between the thick and thin strokes of the letter (also called *stress* or *modulation*). In traditional text characters this contrast can be *diagonal* or *vertical*. Typefaces with a predominantly diagonal contrast have their roots in writing with a broad-nibbed pen, while those that show vertical stress link back to writing with a pointed nib. Noordzij calls these two distinct types of contrast *translation* and *expansion*. These terms are explained in more detail in the adjoining diagrams.

Besides this subdivision based on contrast there is another grouping based on internal structure: *interrupted* versus *cursive* writing. With the first manner of writing, the pen is briefly lifted off the paper after each stroke; in cursive writing, the letter is written in one continuous movement. Traces of these writing styles can still be found in many typefaces designed for printing. Plotting each of these two variables on an axis results in a very simple classification system with four main classes, as shown in the diagram on the right.

Translation

When writing with a broad-nibbed pen, the nib slides across the paper at a constant angle. Strokes drawn from the bottom left to top right are thinnest (the thickness of the pen); strokes from top left to bottom right are thickest (the pen's width). In drawing straight lines and curves on the paper we move the front of the pen along the path that our hand travels, resulting in a stroke that naturally widens and narrows. You could say that the line formed by the front of the pen is *projected* on the irregular shape of the letter. This is called translation in mathematics. (Brush-rendered letters by Gerrit Noordzij.)

Expansion

When writing with a pointed pen something totally different happens. The thick-thin contrast is not caused by a moving line, but by the pressure exercised on the pen. The tip of the pointed pen is split and when the two halves come apart under pressure, the stroke widens. Expert calligraphers bend their strokes in virtuoso ways. As they do not hold their pen at a constant angle, the direction of the contrast may change. But it feels natural when writing to put more pressure on the pen when drawing from top to bottom, with a predominantly vertical contrast as a result. (Lettering by Gerrit Noordzij.)

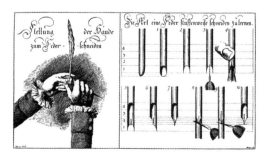

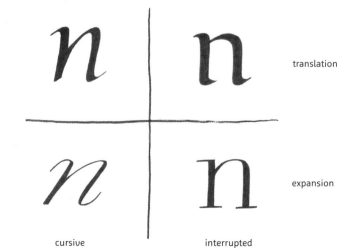

translation

expansion

cursive   interrupted

New type, new genres

FontFont classes

Classifications like the one proposed by Vox have little to offer when it comes to categorising non-traditional letterforms. In its early years, FontShop's FontFont library was especially known for its experimental fonts. In order to bring some method to the madness, Jürgen Siebert and Erik Spiekermann thought up a classification that was as unusual as the typefaces themselves. All serious text faces, with and without serifs and from classical to modern, were placed in a single group labelled *typographic*. The many unusual (typically display) typefaces in the FontFont library, on the other hand, were subdivided into categories that had as much to do with concepts or motivations as with formal design principles: *ironic, historic, intelligent, destructive*, and so on. This playful classification was later simplified, but it still remains a relevant attempt to make some sense of the multitude of type design strategies of the early nineties.

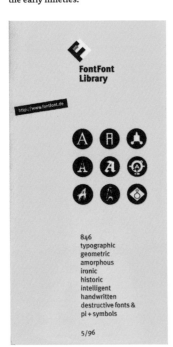

846
typographic
geometric
amorphous
ironic
historic
intelligent
handwritten
destructive fonts &
pi + symbols

5/96

FontFont classification, 1996

FF Balance Celeste **Dax** Meta Quadraat Scala Scala Sans

Typographic

Everything that can pass for a serious text and titling face, serifed and sans-serif, from oldstyle to contemporary.

FF Amoeba Blur Harlem Moonbasealpha Penquin Rekord

Amorphous

'Amorphous' means formless; these are typefaces exploring the cutting edge of type design. Often rebellious or anarchic, some would be at home in the 'Destructive' category as well.

FF BerlinSans Liant **Brokenscript** Humanist DISTURBANCE LUKREZIA

Historic

FontFont, too, has its revivals: from the Art Deco BerlinSans to digitalisations of 15th century printed and hand-written alphabets. Jeremy Tankard's Disturbance, a mix of upper- and lowercase shapes, is perhaps ironic rather than historic.

FF Atlanta DirtyThree **DirtySevenOne** Fudoni **Schmelvetica**

Destructive

Other terms used for 'destructive' fonts are 'deconstructive' and 'grunge' – the former a reference from twentieth-century French philosophy, the latter from rock music. Many of these fonts are remixes of existing fonts: they were achieved through a distortion filter, or are a 'mashup' of two contrasting fonts (Fudoni = Futura + Bodoni).

ff Dome DotMatrix **Gothic** Isonorm3098 **minimum** Scratch tokyo

Geometric

Experimental fonts constructed using ruler and compass, from the likes of Neville Brody, Max Kisman and Pierre di Sciullo.

FF Cavolfiore KARTON Dolores DYNAMOE Knobcheese Trixie

Ironic

These are tongue-in-cheek typefaces: illustrative, deliberately sloppy or based on trivial alphabets from daily life, such as those from stamp kits, typewiters or dymo devices.

FF Advert Rough Baukasten **Kipp** Kosmik Primary Beowolf

Intelligent

The very first FontFont was Beowolf, a font that executed a 'random' script on its way to the printer so that each letter was distorted in a somewhat different way. Kosmik also had a built-in random function. Other 'smart fonts' allowed for layering in multicoloured stacks.

FF CHELSEA DuChirico DuGauguin ErikRightHand JustLeftHand **Instanter**

Handwritten

Like Beowolf, Kosmik and Trixie, FF Hands was an invention by a twosome called LettError (Dutchmen Erik van Blokland and Just van Rossum): a digitalisation of their own handwriting. The 'handwritten' category also contained advertising scripts and handwriting-inspired display fonts.

Old letterforms, new fonts

Ovink: reinterpretation

The Ovink typeface is a contemporary reinterpretation of an alphabet by architect Knud V. Engelhardt, one of the fathers of the Danish tradition in type design. Designer Sofie Beier examined Engelhardt's 1926–1927 alphabet for the street signs of Gentofte, a suburb of Copenhagen. She freely interpreted Engelhardt's drawings, expanding the typeface into a large and usable text family that manages to maintain the spirit of that bold 1920s design throughout its nine weights. The font's name has little to do with Denmark: it pays homage to Willem Ovink, a Dutch scholar who conducted remarkable research into functionality and legibility. Beier's work as a type designer, too, has been informed by academic research on legibility.

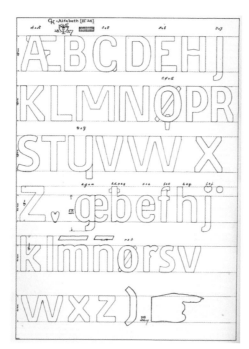

↑ Original, 1927
← Interpretation, 2011

Ever since the invention of printing, every era in Western culture has had its favourite typeface genres. Types that went out of fashion were melted down mercilessly into fluid lead from which new typefaces could be cast (or bullets in times of war). This has not been necessary for the last sixty years or so, but in the fast succession of technologies during the past century, a great many typefaces have threatened to vanish, as well as the knowledge of them.

The last couple of decades have brought a change as ever more people realise that type design is a significant aspect of our culture. The internet has contributed to the proliferation of 'typemania': thousands of type geeks around the world use social networks to exchange information and keep each informed on their most recent (re-)discoveries. Many are type designers who, with or without thorough historical research, make digital versions of typefaces and lettering styles from the past.

Total recall

This has brought us to a unique situation: for the first time in the history of typography we have a virtually complete overview of the printing types that have been made over the course of the centuries. Typefaces from each period are now actively used. Moreover, it is characteristic of our postmodern culture that there are relatively few prejudices about which styles are 'right' and 'wrong': in principle every operating procedure is allowed and every historic style is a legitimate source of inspiration. There is not a dominant ideology of form any more; there are only personal preferences.

Of course, only a portion of new digital typefaces are based on designs from the past. Type designers invent their own original letterforms on a daily basis. They often quote elements from different periods and traditions, blending them with contemporary techniques and attitudes. In some cases they are inspired by a single attribute of an existing typeface to create a ground-breaking contemporary form.

First, the legibility

of isolated

CHARACTERS HAS BEEN NEGLECTED HITHERTO,

WHILE IT IS

at the same time highly important

for the science

AND ART

OF PRINTING AND ADVERTISING,

and experimentally more accessible

than the legibility

of continuous reading-matter.

Revival and digitisation

[Image: Detail from an original copy of De Aetna, showing text in original type]

montem magno strepore
caliginosa, et perurentes
supra os, quantum sagitta quis
vel eo amplius, insurgentes:
corpus vivens, non perflasse

← Detail from an original copy of *De Aetna* by Pietro Bembo, published in 1495 by the Venetian printer Aldus Manutius in a typeface cut by Francesco Griffo. On the right are some words reset in digital Bembo, with 'v' substituted for 'u' where appropriate, and the mediaeval long 's' replaced by the normal 's'. Designed on the basis of this original, the hot-metal Monotype Bembo (1929) was a successful book typeface for many decades. But the digital version that was published in the 1980s turned out much lighter. Not only was it less handsome, it was also problematic – too skinny – when set in small sizes. Apparently, the digital design had been based on large-scale working drawings that were too delicate for a text font to be used at small sizes. Nowadays, revivals are often newly drawn on the basis of vintage printed samples of the originals, with sturdier fonts as a result.

A revival is a new edition of a typeface that has become unavailable, either because the original manufacturer has disappeared or because the technology it was produced for has fallen into disuse. A revival is not necessarily a copy of one specific old printing type. Punchcutters such as Claude Garamond (sixteenth century) or Giambattista Bodoni (eighteenth century) never made a typeface called 'Garamond' or 'Bodoni'. Font names were generic and technical, denoting a size (e.g. *Paragon*, around 18pt) or a style (e.g. *Inglese*, English script).

The earliest Bodoni and Garamond revivals, designed in the early twentieth century, were not based on one single model but on an entire body of work, from which an 'ideal' revival was distilled. In the case of Garamond there was even a serious misunderstanding: Beatrice Warde discovered that the types on which the most successful Garamond revivals were based had actually been the work of Jean Jannon, who lived about fifty years later.

Changing technologies

Revivals travelled from one technology to the next: from metal to photocomposition, from early digital machines to desktop typography. Some typefaces suffered from those adaptations. Early digitalisations of classic Monotype revivals such as Bembo and Van Dijck, for instance, were too thin; the specific qualities of the new technology – the precision of digital typesetting, the sharpness of modern offset printing – had not been sufficiently taken into account.

What makes digital revivals of pre-twentieth-century typefaces especially tricky is the fact that digital type is scalable; one font can be used in any size, from tiny to huge. In the old days, fonts were hand-cut at true size. Big fonts had more detail, small fonts had less contrast and were more robust. Scalable fonts based on an ancient model inevitably have an element of compromise – unless they are designed at specific *optical sizes* (→ p. 100).

Baskerville *& Italic*   BERTHOLD

J Baskerville *& Italic*   FRANTIŠEK ŠTORM

J Baskerville Text *& Italic*   FRANTIŠEK ŠTORM

Baskerville No2 *& Italic*   BITSTREAM

Mrs Eaves *& Mrs Eaves Italic*   EMIGRE

Mrs Eaves XL *& Mrs Eaves XL Italic*   EMIGRE

← Although all these digital typefaces are based on John Baskerville's types from the eighteenth century, no two are identical, and some are very different indeed. Each designer approached the source material in a different way. The Bitstream typeface was based on Baskerville's large sizes and is meant for headlines (titling). The Berthold is a compromise, designed for text as well as display. Both František Štorm and Emigre's Zuzana Licko designed versions that are more robust and well suited for text sizes. Both based their revivals on a fresh examination of printed samples of the original Baskerville types.

→ Text typefaces 98
→ Optical size 100
→ Type technology 162

'Type' before Gutenberg

The prehistory of our Latin alphabet is fascinating. It harks back to the pictograms of the Sumerians, from which abstract symbols were developed around the third millennium BC. That history has been told and re-told compellingly in numerous books and on websites. I will limit myself here to the writing system that has made our civilization what it is: the Latin alphabet. Of the many types of scripture, designed for writing on parchment or paper, for scratching and cutting into stone, many are still relevant today. This double-page spread presents a very concise anthology of writing genres in the first millennium-and-a-half of our era.

↓ Besides famous monuments such as Trajan's column, there are hundreds if not thousands of examples of beautifully preserved Roman stonecarving. Here is an example of a modest memorial with an inscription in *capitalis*.

↗ A fictitious movie title set in Trajan.

QUATASTROPHY II

DISASTER MOVIE

Capitalis monumentalis, Hollywood's darling

At the beginning of our Latin writing tradition are the capital letters that the Romans developed from the Greek alphabet. Cut in marble, the *capitalis monumentalis* was the Empire's corporate typeface – an impressive sign of power reaching the farthest corners of the empire as it was carved into landmarks and milestones.

With the capitalis begins the history of the serif. The priest and scholar Edward Catich argued that serifs were a by-product of the preparations for stone carving: letter painters drew the letterforms on the marble with a flat brush, each stroke ending in a pointed dash: the serif.

Hollywood loves the capitalis – or at least, it did throughout the past decade. The most used font by far for setting film titles is Trajan, which Carol Twombly designed for Adobe Systems. The typeface was derived from the lettering on the Trajan column in Rome, the most famous example of the capitalis.

Twombly's version respects proportions of the the the monumental alphabet – the solemn rhythm of broad and narrow letters (roughly based on a square and half square respectively) although Trajan's serifs are longer and its 'N' narrower. The slightly larger 'initial capitals' must have been an invention of the designer or of Adobe's type director. They are very un-Roman, but look really pretty on posters.

Roman handwriting: capitalis rustica, uncial and half-uncial

For writing on papyrus and parchment and for *graffiti* (literally: scratching) on walls, the Romans developed informal versions of the monumental alphabet, such as the elongated *capitalis rustica*, which was written with a broad reed pen. Gradually the letterforms became rounder, and around the fourth century emerged a style in which something of our minuscule (lowercase) can be discerned: the uncial. A later variant, the half-uncial with its long ascenders and descenders is a more obvious precursor to our minuscules.
From these types developed Anglo-Saxon scripts. The Irish uncial was frequently used for printing texts in Gaelic and can be found on road signs everywhere in Ireland.

TIONE·UBIErt·morrY·acULeUrtUUrUbIertn
CONTENTIOtUAl·INrubIecTIONem·Itaque
corum·morYuINcITUr·etmorteTedeUIc
INmortalY·tUtIruItUruccedIt·quaeu
rubIecTIONIrbenrectUlltUbortHdeIn

ZAUBERFLÖtE mEDIOR

↑ ↑ The half-uncial remained in general use until well into the ninth century.

↑ Some contemporary type designers have revisited uncial forms, such as Andreas Stötzner with Lapidaria.

Carolingian minuscule: an alphabet for my kingdom

The roman uncial and half-uncial were adopted and developed in several European countries. From there, around 800AD, arose the system that probably had the strongest impact of all mediaeval scripts: the Carolingian minuscule. Emperor Charlemagne, after whom the script is called, wanted to further the cultural unity of his vast empire by introducing a uniform, legible handwriting style that could be used and understood in all regions. A driving force behind the reform was the British scholar Alcuin of York, whom Charles had appointed to run the palace school and *scriptorium* (writing workshop).

The Carolingian minuscule was the first fully developed script which used a double alphabet of capitals and 'lowercase' letters: all subsequent lowercase alphabets can be traced back to it. The script is round, open and clear. It is still popular with calligraphers.

Not only were the letterforms themselves innovative, so was the way the Carolingian writing workshops structured the text. For the first time on the European mainland (the Irish had done it before), word spacing was introduced on a wide scale. Uptothatpointthewordshadbeenthreadedonastringwithoutanyspacingwhatsoever.

Humanist handwriting: a happy accident

From the thirteenth century the Carolingian minuscule was displaced by a new, square modular script: *Gothic* or *broken script* (aka *blackletter*). More about this on the following pages. While Gothic types, written with a broad pen cut from a goose feather – a *quill* – conquered Europe, there was resistance in Italy. Its scholars and poets (whom later historians would call 'humanists') studied the literature and philosophy of classical antiquity. They knew those works from manuscripts written in a clear hand with an openness that seemed to fit the lucidity of the of the authors so well. In reality they were reading texts that had been copied between the ninth and the twelfth century in different variants of the Carolingian minuscule. Yet the Italian humanists believed this was the handwriting of the ancient Roman writers.

So the humanist script developed in Italy from Petrarch's time onwards was not a rebirth of classical handwriting, like the humanists believed, but a 'revival' of Charlemagne's minuscule. Thanks to that misunderstanding, Italy created a new, lucid style of writing that, over a century later, would serve as an example to printers in Venice and Rome who were in search of alternatives to the rigid Gothic letters from Germany.

→ Sample of humanist handwriting in an early fifteenth-century manuscript. From around 1470 onwards this style became the model for the revolutionary roman printing types cut in Venice.

Broken script (blackletter)

↑ In 1984, American director Rob Reiner made the satirical 'rockument-ary' *This Is Spinal Tap* about the rise and fall of a fictitious heavy metal band. Even back then, Gothic scripts (used here in an airbrush-treated variant) were a highly recognisable cliché in the hard-rock scene. They must owe their popularity to a combination of factors, from the mediaeval-mystical undertones to the sharply cut shapes. Possibly the Gothic script's dubious reputation as a 'Nazi typeface' (see below) plays a role as well: a special recommendation for metalheads, gangsters and hip-hoppers in search of a controversial image.

There are many names for this typeface: broken script, Gothic, fraktur, German type. In English, blackletter is most common. 'Old English' is the variety often used for pubs and for the name-plates of many British and American newspapers. The script was developed in the second half of the twelfth century in the *scriptoria* (writing workshops) of Northern Europe as a simple and space-saving text script written with a new kind of tool, the broad-nibbed quill pen. The name 'broken script' is based on the movement of the hand when writing: at the end of each stroke the pen is briefly lifted, so that the stroke is interrupted. *Fraktur*, the German name for the most popular variant of the script, also means 'broken' – think of 'fracture'.

The types used in the earliest printed books, such as those from the workshops of Gutenberg and his successors, were imitations of the handwritten broken scripts. In England and the Netherlands the genre remained in use for considerable time alongside roman types (Renaissance oldstyles). In Germany, fraktur remained the default text face until the Second World War.

Gothic script has many variations. The most uncompromising version is *textura*, developed in the fourteenth century, which was the letter that Gutenberg took as the model for his metal types a century later. It is a script that consists entirely of straight lines: all curves are broken. A later variant is Bastarda, which is called that because it is a 'hybrid' of different styles – the broken nature of textura combined with round strokes. Fraktur, too, is a combination of curved and straight sections. It became so common in Germany that the term 'fraktur' came to denote all broken scripts.

Vanitas

Textura by an unknown Dutch punch-cutter, late fifteenth century

Muttersprache

Kleist-Fraktur, 20th-century German printing typeface based on manuscripts from the 16th and 17th centuries

Dedicatio

Bastarda-K, digital typeface by Manfred Klein based on German Bastarda handwriting

Shadows of the past. Fraktur, a doomed typeface?

Ich war in meiner Jugend Arbeiter so wie Ihr!
Adolf Hitler.

'In my youth I was a worker just like you!': election bill with an advertising-like blackletter.

In the course of the twentieth century the reputation of blackletter underwent a remarkable evolution. In Germany, early attempts to replace blackletter by roman types, especially in advertising and on book covers, were made around 1900; however, blackletter types remained popular. After Hitler and his henchmen seized power in 1933, fraktur went through a renaissance as a display type. Its distinctive shapes became part of the visual Nazi rhetoric. Fat blackletter variants were used to create powerful, Germanic-looking slogans. It made a lasting impression and to this day blackletter is associated with Nazism.

Yet the Nazis themselves had already banned fraktur. In 1941 the party's head office published a circular denouncing Gothic script as a 'Jews' letter'. According to this statement, Jewish printers had maliciously distributed 'their' typeface across Germany for centuries; now that its true nature had been revealed, it had to be outlawed. The regime's real motives, however, were more practical. They were about to steamroller the rest of Europe, where texts were printed with roman typefaces. A typographic U-turn was called for to assure smooth communication with the conquered peoples.

As one of their favourite new types the Nazis embraced the modernist Futura. Such irony! Its designer, Paul Renner, had been persecuted for years by the Nazi regime. He had always advocated the abolition of the German fraktur as a standard text face.

Fraktur, mon amour

→ When did broken scripts become cool? When Gerard Huerta designed his logos for hard rock bands Blue Öyster Cult and AC/DC around 1975? When California gangsters began using it in their tattoos, inspired by the traditional black-letter tattoos of their fellow Mexican prisoners? The fact is: no other genre has the kind of street credibility blackletter has. Young German designer-writer Judith Schalansky recognised the phenomenon and made the book *Fraktur mon Amour* (2006), a visual declaration of love to blackletter.

← Fakir, a contemporary fraktur by the design group Underware.

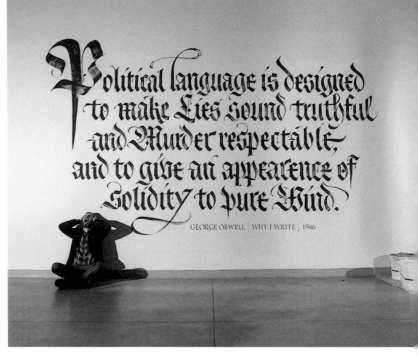

Today's designers use the ambiguity (Is it evil? Is it cool?) of Gothic scripts to add a suggestive layer to their message.

← David Pearson's cover for the Penguin Great Ideas series highlights the vicious nature of Machiavelli's political pragmatism.

↑ Luca Barcellona's hand-painted blackletter adds ambivalence to George Orwell's clear statement.

The renaissance oldstyle: indestructible model

Johannes Gutenberg, c. 1445

Pannartz/Sweinheim, 1464

Letterforms developed very quickly once printing types began to be produced *en masse*. In 1455 Gutenberg printed his Bible in Mainz in a type that was a successful imitation of the handwritten *textura* of the era – a narrow, square Gothic script. In 1464 Sweinheim and Pannartz took the art of printing from Germany to Italy. To meet the local demand for 'roman' letters, they cut a new font that bent the rigid Gothic shapes into something that began to resemble the handwriting of the humanists.

Around the same time the Frenchman Nicolas Jenson, who had learned the art of printing in Mainz, arrived in Venice. He printed his first work in 1470 using a newly designed face – a sophisticated leaden variation on humanist handwriting. With his typeface, the model for the next few centuries was established. Every later text typeface of 'roman' inspiration was derived from Jenson's alphabets or followed the same logic.

This is not to say that development was at a standstill. Francesco Griffo, also in Venice, cut his typefaces slightly sharper and somewhat lighter in colour. Moreover, Griffo made the first Italic printing face, a novelty that was here to stay. The French punchcutters from the sixteenth century, with Claude Garamond as undisputed master, brought more elegance into the lettershapes. The Flemish and the Dutch, from Van den Keere to Van Dijck, reduced the ascenders and descenders, increasing the relative x-height so that smaller body sizes could be used with equal legibility – an exercise in economy.

Jenson's model remained the guideline for more than three centuries. The basic construction, with its subtle diagonal contrast derived from handwriting with the broad-nibbed pen, remained unchanged. From the mid-eighteenth century onwards, new Neoclassical styles came into fashion with a tighter construction and more static look, but after 1890 typefaces by Jenson, Griffo and Garamond were rediscovered and became the starting point for a new generation of text faces which we encounter, with slight changes, on our Macs or PCs even today. What many people agree on as being the ideal book typeface is essentially still that design from 1470.

Nicolas Jenson, around 1475

Claude Garamond, around 1545

Hendrik Van den Keere, around 1576

Christoffel Van Dijck, around 1660

Typefix
Typefix

Typefix
Typefix

Typefix
Typefix

Typefix
Typefix

Adobe Jenson
Robert Slimbach, 1996
(Italic based on
cursive types by Arrighi)

Adobe Garamond
Robert Slimbach, 1989

DTL Vandenkeere
DTL studio,
Frank E. Blokland, 1995

Monotype Van Dijck
Monotype studio, 1935
(advisor Jan van Krimpen)

Twentieth-century classics

Three successful examples of modern text faces made along classical lines. These are not revivals of existing types, but innovative designs that continue a tradition of centuries.

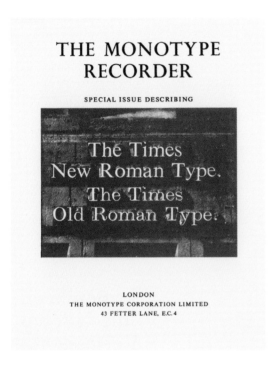

Times New Roman, 1932

In 1929, typographer and type historian Stanley Morison advised the London newspaper *The Times* to rigorously improve its old-fashioned design and have a new typeface designed in the process. The typeface chosen was a proposal by Morison himself: a modernised, crisper version of Monotype Plantin. That earlier typeface was in turn based on a sixteenth-century model: a type from the Frenchman Granjon for the Plantin printing shop in Antwerp. Morison's instructions were executed by Victor Lardent of *The Times*' advertising department. A year after its exclusive debut in the newspaper, Times New Roman hit the market. Its clarity and modernity make it a bestseller to this day.

Trinité, 1982

Trinité is an indirect heir to the seventeenth-century letters of Christoffel van Dijck. The intermediary is Romanée by Jan van Krimpen, which the Enschedé foundry had commissioned in 1932 as the roman companion to an italic by Van Dijck. Romanée is an innovative text typeface of classical proportions. When Enschedé wanted to adapt it for photocomposition in 1978, in-house typographer Bram de Does advised against it. The metal Romanée was a little different in each body size and de Does believed these subtleties would not survive a redesign. To his surprise, the management invited him to design a new typeface himself. The result was Trinité, a groundbreaking contemporary text face. It is a type family in three variants, with different extender lengths – hence the name 'Trinity'. After a short life as part of the Bobst phototypesetting system, Trinité was reborn in 1992 as a digital typeface released by a new company, The Enschedé Font Foundry.

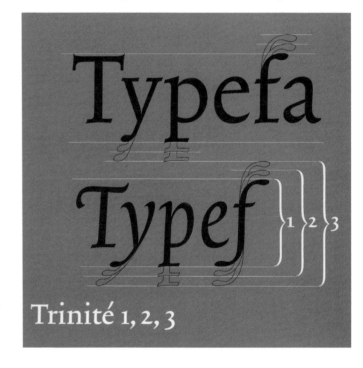

Trinité 1, 2, 3

Scala, 1988–91

When Dutch designer Martin Majoor had to do his civil service in 1988, he landed a job at the in-house design department of the Vredenburg Music Centre in Utrecht. The centre was in need of a bespoke typeface for its internal publications and signage, preferably with the typographic finesse of small caps and mediaeval figures, which were rare at the time. Majoor drew a remarkably original text face with unconventional details. Scala was not based on a specific model but respects the proportions of sixteenth- and seventeenth-century book types. In fact, Majoor refers to himself as a 'modern traditionalist'. In 1991 FF Scala became the first text typeface in FontShop's newly launched FontFont type library.

Passage, a version of Scala adapted for signage, in use at the Vredenburg Centre. With thanks to Peterpaul Kloosterman

Royal contrasts

Oiga

Two digital Didone revivals.
Above, a Didot: Ambroise from
Porchez Typofonderie. Below:
Bauer Bodoni, the digital version of
a twentieth-century metal revival.
Both fonts shown in Bold.

Oiga

There is one category of classic text typefaces that is radically different from the Renaissance and Baroque models: Didone, the classicist roman and italic. The first typeface in this genre, which in English is usually called *modern face*, was cut in 1784 by Firmin Didot. He was twenty at the time and had just been hired as a punch-cutter at his father's printing shop. The face is characterised by straight strokes and geometric curves, a pronounced contrast between the heavy vertical shapes and the thin horizontal hairlines and serifs.

Around the same time in Parma, Italy, the successful printer Giambattista Bodoni experimented with new variations on typefaces by Fournier and Baskerville (see below), both of whom he greatly admired. Bodoni's types, too, were rational faces characterised by extreme vertical contrasts between bold and thin parts.

Both Bodoni and the Didot family enjoyed the support of the royal courts of their time. This may have helped to acquire broad acceptance for their rather radical letterforms. At the beginning of the nineteenth century the Didot-Bodoni-model became the default book typeface in all of Western Europe. Many second-rate imitations with puny hairlines showed an amazing lack of readability: in small sizes the setting had an annoying 'glitter' to it.

Bodoni has remained especially popular: throughout the twentieth century every foundry had its own version. Designers of (American) glossy magazines still like using extremely contrasted Didot variants to set stylish headlines. To this end, many type designers during the past decade or so published refined digital revivals.

'Transitional', type in an interim stage?

The Didone-style faces with their clear and strong vertical contrast did not fall from the sky. During the mid-eighteenth century, typographic pioneers throughout Western Europe made faces that contributed to technological and stylistic innovation. They did not exclusively base their letterforms on the Renaissance model but also looked at contemporary writing and engraving. A new writing tool, the pointed pen with a split nib, enabled a vertical contrast that fitted in well with the somewhat rigid symmetry of the era's neo-classical arts.

In English-language typographic literature this genre of typeface is called *transitional*: in other words, an intermediate step towards *modern face*. The name suggests that the eighteenth-century style was somewhat tentative and immature,

but nothing is further from the truth. The fonts from that era are among the brightest and most self-assured book typefaces ever cut.

The style's most influential representative is John Baskerville, a calligrapher and stonemason in Birmingham who also pioneered inventions in the fields of ink and paper manufacturing. In France, typographical innovation was ushered in by Fournier, and in the Netherlands by Johann Fleischmann (aka Fleischman), a German who cut brilliant typefaces for Enschedé printers in Haarlem.

It took a long time for the eighteenth-century style to be rediscovered (although newspaper faces were often based on it); but during the past decade it inspired many type designers.

John Baskerville, 1757

Johann Fleischman, around 1750

Typefins
Typefins

Mrs Eaves
Zuzana Licko, 1996

Typefins
Typefins

Fenway
Matthew Carter

Typefins
Typefins

J Baskerville
František Štorm, 2000

Typefins
Typefins

Farnham Display
Christian Schwartz, 2004

Bodoni appeal

← A true original: one of the many different sizes and variants of Bodoni's unique style of type design, as presented in the *Manuale Tipografico* published by his widow in 1818, five years after the printer's death.

→ One of the great advocates of Bodoni-style typography is the Italian designer and publisher Franco Maria Ricci, whose art luscious magazine *FMR* enjoyed world-wide fame in the 1980s and whose Biblioteca di Babele was a sophisticated series of literary masterpieces.

↓ A sumptuous Bodoni-style display face seemed perfect for the Spanish-language *Playboy*: Pistilli, a custom typeface by Cyrus Highsmith, the Font Bureau, after a design by John Pistilli and Herb Lubalin.

↑ New York designer Massimo Vignelli famously said that the design world needs only five or six typefaces – Bodoni among them. Emigre invited him to design this poster when they launched Zuzana Licko's Filosofia.

The typeface takes a fresh approach to the Bodoni model, emphasizing the hand-made liveliness of the original faces, which in most revivals is abandoned in favour of rigidity and over-rationalisation.

Typographic noise

ENS ANDERS GOE

CADEMISCH PROEFSCHRIFT

TER VERKRIJGING VAN DEN GRAAD VAN

n het Romeinsch en Hedendaagsch

AAN DE HOOGESCHOOL TE LEIDEN,

OP GEZAG VAN DEN RECTOR MAGNIFICUS

Dr. C. EVERS,

HOOGLEERAAR IN DE FACULTEIT DER GENEESKUNDE,

lag den 8sten Juni 1869, des namiddags te

OR DE FACULTEIT TE VERDEDIGE!

DOOR

LIUS HERMANUS PETRUS KLAVERWIJ

GEBOREN TE LEIDEN.

↑ Detail of the title page of a doctorate thesis, Leiden 1869. For a standard scientific publication like this, the printer dipped generously into his type case, using about ten different fonts.

The nineteenth century used to have a bad reputation in typographic circles. The industrial revolution, made possible by the steam engine and other inventions, had brought about high-speed mass production in many areas. Industrially produced objects were standard products lacking in style, often decorated with randomly selected ornaments from the past. In book printing, much craftsmanship was lost. New text types were rigid imitations of the Bodoni-like faces that were popular around 1800. Books of classical simplicity were rare in the machine age; foundries literally melted their stock of baroque fonts in order to cast type to fit the latest fashion. The stately title pages of yesteryear were replaced by lush compositions of illustration, typography and ornament.

Commercial experiments

Type historians have long regarded the nineteenth century in graphic design with some disdain. But those historians looked mainly at book design, while the real innovations occurred in other areas. The nineteenth century has now been rehabilitated as we realise that the rich typographic palette available today owes a lot to the discoveries, follies and fashions of that era.

One of the big achievements – if that's the right word – of the nineteenth century is advertising. With mechanisation many products fell in price, brands were introduced, competition was on the rise and advertising became a must. New graphic reproduction techniques such as wood type, faster printing presses, stone lithography and more were employed to create and promote brands, and also to lend books and magazines the appearance of a desirable product. In short, the new consumer era was accompanied by a radically new and commercial approach to graphic design.

The radical changes in communication were reflected in the spectacular new typefaces and type genres published from around 1810 onwards, first in Britain and the United States; fonts whose main asset was their novelty value: letterforms with an exaggerated contrast or no contrast at all, with monstrously fat serifs or no serifs whatsoever.

Since the mid-1990s, young graphic designers and type designers have shown a renewed interest in the nineteenth century. They have taken up printing with wood type again or use the era's 'monster fonts' as a source of inspiration for new digital typefaces.

→ 'Brigade de Shoe Black', City Hall Park. From the popular series 'Anthony's Stereoscopic Views', c. 1865. One of the few photographic records of a mid-nineteenth century urban poster wall, showing a large collection of entertainment posters printed largely with wood type, in their original context. This is a monotone photo; the colouring of the posters was probably done by hand.

A fresh look at the nineteenth century

↑ The Adobe Wood Type series is a digital reinterpretation of some of the best known nineteenth-century styles of wood typefaces for posters.

↓ The Shire Types by Jeremy Tankard, a parody of nineteenth-century typographic styles. The characters of the six fonts are mutually combinable; the family was used for the cover and title page of the present book.

↗ Erik van Blokland's FF Zapata tackles one particular style of poster types – wide slab serifs – and takes it to new levels of extremity, with a choice of five weights.

→ The Proteus Project from Hoefler & Frere-Jones, based on four styles of nineteenth-century wood types.

**Ziggurat
Saracen
Leviathan
Acropolis**

abcdefg   CHESHIRE
ABCDEFG   DERBYSHIRE
ABCDEFG   SHROPSHIRE
ABCDEFG   STAFFORDSHIRE
ABCDEFG   WARWICKSHIRE
ABCDEFG   WORCESTERSHIRE

Dominant type: commercial art, Modernism, Art Deco

During the first quarter of the twentieth century, various things happened simultaneously in letterform development. In advertising, the medicine show style of nineteenth-century billboards and ads gave way to a more sophisticated tone of voice. A new profession saw the light of day: commercial artists who developed personal styles of illustration and lettering. The most successful among them were persuaded by type foundries to draw designs for metal typefaces.

In Germany, Lucian Bernhard pioneered a bold, simplified style of advertising and packaging that became known as *Plakatstil*, 'Poster Style'. He soon began designing type in the same vein. In the United States, Oswald 'Oz' Cooper was a successful commercial artist and type designer. Marketed as 'a dominant typeface' when it came out, Cooper Black was an immmediate hit; it travelled through the changing technologies as a permanently popular display face.

Modernist movements

Meanwhile a new artistic movement swept over Europe. It had many manifestations and names, including Constructivism, 'Style' and Elemental (or New) Typography; it is now often collectively referred to as Modernism. For Modernist artists and designers, typographic research became part of a program that banished ornament and figuration, striving for abstraction, rationality and objectivity.

To illustrate their ideals and theories, many artists drew letterforms, almost exclusively for their own use as display alphabets. Although functionalism was a key word in their theorising, the Modernists' idealist thinking seldom led to

↑ A compliment card hand-lettered by Oz Cooper for his own agency, c. 1918; this lettering style formed the basis of what later became Cooper Black.

← Two typical Art Deco faces from the Amsterdam Typefoundry, both based on Morris Fuller Benton's Broadway, 1929.

↓ Several artists connected to *De Stijl* magazine – including founder Theo van Doesburg – drew experimental alphabets using straight lines only. This envelope for a door and furniture factory was designed by the Dutch-based Hungarian graphic artist Vilmos Huszár.

letterforms that were successful as text type, or had readability as their principal aim. Most Modernist alphabets were geometrical ruler-and-compass affairs, concerned as they were with simplicty and rationalism. Some refrained from using curves altogether, like the straight-lined alphabets by Dutch designers Lauweriks, Wijdeveld and Van Doesburg. There was one notable exception: Futura by Paul Renner was a well-wrought compromise between Modernist geometry and the optical concerns of traditional typography. It became immediately influential and spawned myriad imitators (← p. 6).

Art Deco

In the 1920s a less revolutionary breed of lettering artists began drawing decorative letterforms using the compass and ruler. The results were more pleasing and acceptable to the mainstream than Modernist experiments. They were part of a graphic tendency that is often connected to similar trends in architecture, product design and the arts, which we now refer to as Art Deco – a term that was in fact invented in the 1960s. A mixture of simplified Art Nouveau, watered-down modernism and influences from exotic cultures, Art Deco was arguably the dominant style from around 1925 onwards. In graphic design and typography, it resulted in a new approach to display typography, mixing exuberant forms based on handwriting with the geometric structures borrowed from the Bauhaus and the Constructivists.

After Swiss-style functionalism became dominant around 1960, Art Deco got a bad name in design circles, and so did commercial scripts and exuberant display faces. They survived, however, in the colourful hippie styles of the rock posters and underground magazines of the 1960s and 1970s. More recently, type designers and lettering artists have rediscovered Art Deco and mid-century commercial lettering as a source of inspiration and ideas. Hundreds of fonts have been released in which the twisted spirit of Art Deco is celebrated and imitated.

↑ In North America there is a virtually uninterrupted Art Deco lineage, from the 1920s originals via mid-century neon signs and 1970s–1980s LP and book covers to today's manifold quotations. This 2009 poster by Josh Korwin of Three Steps Ahead (Los Angeles) references the shapes and gradients used by A.M. Cassandre, the quintessential Deco designer. It makes use of Mostra Nuova by Mark Simonson, one of today's most popular digital reinterpretations of Art Deco letterforms.

↓ Lettering designed in 2002 by Paul van der Laan for the converted school by Dutch modernist architect Jan Duijker in The Hague-Scheveningen where van der Laan's studio is based. Like the building, completed in 1931, the alphabet has both Art Deco and avant garde-Modernist elements.

Modularity in type and lettering

↑ Josef Albers, Kombinationsschrift, 1931. Setting text with just four elements, instead of the 114 sorts that were standard in the typesetter's upper and lower case.

↑ Wim Crouwel, art catalogue, 1963. Crouwel's hand-drawn letterforms referred to the vertical brush strokes in Edgar Fernhout's paintings.

→ Modular alphabet designed by Crouwel in 1970 for the artist Claes Oldenburg, recalling the latter's giant soft objects. Digitized by The Foundry in 2003 as Foundry Catalogue. Crouwel's display alphabets have become immensely popular lately; many of them have inspired modular fonts designed with FontStruct, see below.

Objectivity, rationality and simplicity were among the main planks in the modernist platform; the Bauhaus was one of the places where these ideas were turned into practical proposals. Geometric construction and modulair structures were seen as valuable means to achieve clarity as well as maximum efficiency in many fields of design, including typography. While constructing letters with compass and ruler was not a feasible principle for text type (← p. 91) it led to some interesting projects in display typography.

Josef Albers's Kombinationsschrift, designed for foundry type, proposed to replace the usual 100+ sorts in the typesetter's case by just four – a square, a circle, a quarter circle, and a square space – with which all letterforms could be built

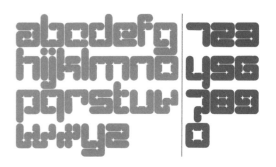

FontStruct, modular type in the digital age

Developed by designer Rob Meek, FontStruct is a free online font-building tool sponsored by FontShop. FontStruct allows users to quickly and easily create fonts constructed out of geometrical shapes, which are arranged in a grid pattern, like tiles or bricks. Once an alphabet (or any collection of signs) is done, FontStruct generates high-

quality TrueType fonts, for use in Mac and Windows applications. There is also a community where 'FontStructions' can be shared, commented and jointly developed.

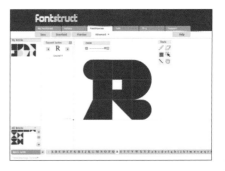

Tyrone: unusual lettershapes made with FontStruct by Belgian designer Peter De Roy, better known among fellow FontStructors as Typerider.

in a number of heights. The project was presented in *Bauhaus* magazine as way to reduce the typesetter's material 'by more than 97%' (that the typesetter's work load would increase accordingly seemed less important).

While these pre-1940s experiments did not catch on in the composing room, modular and geometrially constructed letterforms did become ubiquitous in graphic studios in the 1960s and 1970. They provided a methodical way of drawing personalised alphabets. In today's digital type design, this is equally true: modular letterforms are a safe place to start dabbling in type design.

↓ Poster for the annual 'Young People's Day' of the Evangelische Omroep in the Netherlands, a Christian broadcast organisation. Made with modular letterforms based on squares and quarter circles; coloured in a way that was inconceivable during Bauhaus times. Design by Lava, 2009.

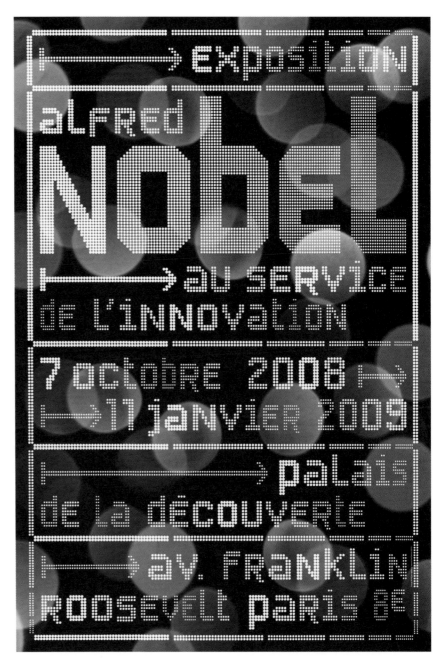

↑ For Parisian designer Philippe Apeloig, developing one-off typefaces for specific projects is a means of personalising his designs. It is also a way of visualizing concepts on what is probably the most abstract level of visual language – type. This poster uses a specially designed monocase alphabet (i.e. with mixed upper- and lowercase forms). Drawn on a simple matrix, the round modules of varying size lend dynamism to the text and suggest scientific exploration. Designed in 2008 for the Palais de la Découverte, Paris, 2010 reprint. Silkscreen, 118×175 cm.

← Modularity and efficiency 44
← The grid exposed 54
→ That Swiss feeling 94

That Swiss feeling

In most European countries World War II put an abrupt end to the development of Modernism, with its functional and objective thinking and rationalist design idiom. It would only continue in neutral Switzerland, where functionalist thinking was developed into a systematic method that, after 1945, became the world's most influential current in graphic design. It is often referred to as Swiss style, although the name 'International Style' is often used in English as well. Among its characteristics are asymmetric layouts, use of grids, text set ragged-right using sans-serifs like Akzidenz Grotesk, and an awareness and aesthetic use of white space on the page. The style is also associated with a preference for photography instead of illustration. Much of the 1950s and '60s work we have come to know as Swiss typography refrained from the use of imagery altogether and relied on type as the principal design element.

→ Photography instead of illustrations, shapes and colours combined with unromantic, sans-serif text, and a grid-based layout: these are some characteristics of what became known as 'Swiss style'. Poster by Nelly Rudin, 1958.

The amazing success story of Helvetica

↑ Neue Haas Grotesk appeared in 1957. Two years later it received its final name: Helvetica. In 2007, fifty years of the font's existence was widely celebrated. There was even a feature-length documentary film about the font, made by director Gary Hustwit, who took the film on a one-year long tour.

Swiss typography conquered Europe in the mid-1950s and was soon adopted in North and South America. Flush-left typesetting and sans-serifs were all over the place. As geometric sans-serifs such as Futura and Kabel evoked the atmosphere of pre-war Modernism somewhat too explicitly, designers preferred advertising typefaces from the late nineteenth century. Berthold's Akzidenz Grotesk was immensely popular, as was Monotype Grotesque or, to a lesser extent, Venus from Bauer.

Yet it was a Swiss company that finally produced the most successful typeface in this genre. Around 1956 the Haas foundry in Münchenstein near Basel commissioned typographer Max Miedinger to draw a new typeface to match Akzidenz Grotesk. Using as his model a grotesque from Schelter & Giesecke (Leipzig, 1880) Miedinger, in close collaboration with Haas' general manager Eduard Hoffmann, designed Neue Haas Grotesk in a few months.

Its success was initially modest, but the tide turned when the Stempel foundry in Frankfurt, Germany, decided to include the typeface in its program. In a letter to the management dated June 6, 1959, sales manager Heinz Eul proposed to re-launch the face under a new name: Helvetia – Switzerland. It was finally released as Helvetica (Swiss) in early 1961.

What followed was a remarkable triumph. Helvetica became a dominant force as the world's corporate typeface. Its overall popularity made it a safe choice, all the more because it soon became available at every printing and typesetting shop. Helvetica's career is convincing proof of the dictum that nothing is as successful as success.

In 1983 Stempel released Neue Helvetica, a subtle reworking of the original, with increased harmony between family members. When Adobe chose (the old) Helvetica as one of the four core fonts of its PostScript software, Helvetica's position as a mainstay of digital typography was assured.

Meanwhile, various manufacturers of printing devices and typesetting systems had concocted their own Helvetica clone – with names like Swiss or Helion or Triumvirate. Finally, Arial came along, the clone that did not want to be a clone. See the opposite page.

Helvetica – the jubilee

Posters to mark Helvetica's fiftieth anniversary.

↖ Experimental Jetset, Amsterdam, Poster to promote the Helvetica movie.

↑ Winning poster in a Linotype competition, made by German designer Nina Hardwig.

So what's up with Arial?

Arial is a system font on most computers. Among ordinary users it is better known than Helvetica. It was designed at Monotype in the late '80s by Robin Nicholas and Patricia Saunders on the basis of a respected older sans-serif, Monotype Grotesque. Yet its proportions and widths are not those of MT Grotesque but correspond exactly to Helvetica's; also, many details are almost identical. The one typeface can be replaced by the other with no noticeable difference. This was not a coincidence: many vendors wanted an alternative system font to replace the popular but expensive Helvetica (sold by Linotype) as system font but preferred not to use a one-to-one clone. So in a way, Arial's design was a foray into the gray zone. One of the companies that opted for Arial was Microsoft. The rest is history.

As a conscientious designer, are you supposed to avoid Arial or not? Well, Helvetica is more authentic and more consistent, so it is not a bad idea to choose the original, or a more exclusive new font in the genre, such as Neutral or Akkurat. But Arial is often considered the inevitable choice as office font in a not-too-ambitious corporate identity program. Why? It's a safe choice and, as it already sits on every computer, it is *free*.

GRaster

↑ In orange: the champion, Helvetica. In blue: Arial – the contender. Many letters are almost identical. That in itself is not necessarily plagiarism, as many typeface inspired by the late nineteenth century have very similar shapes. The most conspicuous differences: Arial's 'G' lacks a spur at bottom right, Arial has a different 'R', no tail on the stem of the 'a', obliquely cut terminals on the curves of letters such as 'c', 'e', 'f', 'g', 'r', 's' and at the top of the 't'.

The emancipation of the sans-serif

Among traditionally trained typographers the view still prevails that nothing is more suited for setting body text than a serifed oldstyle or a contemporary variety of this genre. Virtually all newspapers and novels are printed with this kind of type. Until recently, sans-serifs were seen as a typical secondary typeface, suitable only for headlines, subheads, boxes and captions. There was a brief period in the 1970s when modernist designers began selecting typefaces like Helvetica and Univers for body text under the influence of 'Swiss typography'; but as those types were not designed for comfortable immersive reading, the results seemed to prove the conventional adage: nothing beats a Garamond or a Times for a text face.

But sans-serifs are back to the fore. They are increasingly being used for long text settings. This is not only due to the changing tastes of graphic designers. It is also a result of the type designs themselves: contemporary sans-serifs are becoming more readable and user-friendly. Sans-serif text typefaces have played a central part in typographic experimentation and design of recent years, with type designers proposing more open, less monotonous alphabets. While up until the early 1990s 'sans-serif' implied 'neutral' or 'emotionless' (or simply 'Helvetica') there is now a wide choice of usable typefaces with low stroke contrast and no serifs.

The humanist sans-serif genre, based on the proportions of classic book faces, is especially known for its readability. But in other categories as well, type designers have achieved a degree of reader-friendliness that was previously rare. Sans-serif is now gradually becoming a standard for magazines and brochures, for art catalogues and non-fiction books of all kinds. The supply of usable sans-serifs is growing fast.

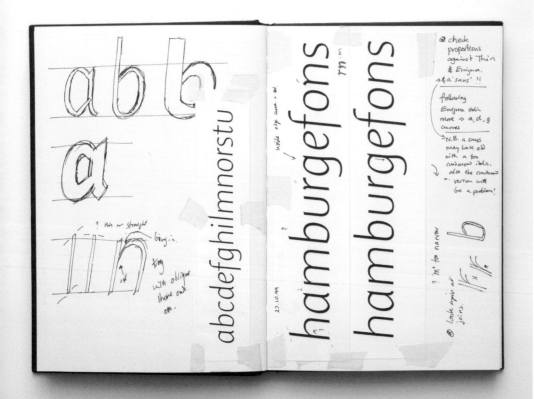

← Sketches for the italics of Shaker, a humanist sans-serif designed by Jeremy Tankard.

→ A concise overview of genres and styles in sans-serif around today. The first four of these genre designations seem to have been generally accepted; 'squarish' and 'technical' are informal but common; the last two are personal attempts at grouping hard-to-define subgenres. The difference between grotesque and gothic is not well defined; it is rather a question of historical and formal affinities. In North-America there has long been a tendency to call all sans-serifs 'Gothic', hence Avant-Garde Gothic and even Copperplate Gothic (which has tiny serifs). This list is certainly not exhaustive. Arguably, there is room for a category of soft and rounded sans-serifs; and the 'Unorthodox' category could be further analysed. Whether that exercise would be very useful remains to be seen. Please note that each of the typefaces shown comes in a wide range of weights and, in some cases, multiples widths.

Sans-serif genres

European Grotesque

Mangfions
Portez ce vieux whisky *au juge blond*
Akzidenz Grotesk (1898 → 1980)

Mangfions
Portez ce vieux whisky *au juge blond*
Univers (1957)

Mangfions
Portez ce vieux whisky au juge blond
Akkurat (2004)

English & American Grotesque, Gothic

Mangfions
Portez ce vieux whisky *au juge blond*
News Gothic (1909)

Mangfions
Portez ce vieux whisky **au juge blond**
Bureau Grot (1989–2006)

Mangfions
Portez ce vieux whisky *au juge blond*
Figgins' Sans-Serif (1836) → Figgins Sans (2009)

Geometric

Mangfions
Portez ce vieux whisky *au juge blond*
Futura (1927)

Mangfions
Portez ce vieux whisky *au juge blond*
AvantGarde Gothic (1970–1977)

Mangfions
Portez ce vieux whisky *au juge blond*
Proxima Nova (2005)

Humanist

Mangfions
Portez ce vieux whisky *au juge blond*
Syntax (1969)

Mangfions
Portez ce vieux whisky *au juge blond*
FF Quadraat Sans (1997)

Mangfions
Portez ce vieux whisky *au juge blond*
Shaker 2 (2000–2009)

Squarish

Mangfions
Portez ce vieux whisky *au juge blond*
Eurostile (1962)

Mangfions
Portez ce vieux whisky *au juge blond*
Klavika (2004)

Mangfions
Portez ce vieux whisky *au juge blond*
Geogrotesque (2008)

Technical

Mangfions
Portez ce vieux whisky *au juge blond*
DIN (1936) → FF DIN (1995)

Mangfions
Portez ce vieux whisky *au juge blond*
Isonorm (1980) → FF Isonorm (1993)

Mangfions
Portez ce vieux whisky *au juge blond*
Interstate (1993–2004)

Office, hybrid, no-nonsense

Mangfions
Portez ce vieux whisky *au juge blond*
FF Meta (1991–2003)

Mangfions
Portez ce vieux whisky *au juge blond*
Corpid (1997–2007)

Mangfions
Portez ce vieux whisky *au juge blond*
Facit (2005)

New directions

Mangfions
Portez ce vieux whisky *au juge blond*
FF Balance (1993)

Mangfions
Portez ce vieux whisky *au juge blond*
Dancer (2007)

Mangfions
Portez ce vieux whisky *au juge blond*
Bree (2008)

Text typefaces: an update

While sans-serifs have come to the fore as viable alternatives to traditional text faces, a quiet revolution has also gone on within the realm of 'oldstyle' faces. Young, often unknown type designers make fonts that are technically more advanced than many of the well-known classics offered by large manufacturers such as Adobe or Monotype. For instance, their character sets are more complete, offering things like multiple styles of numerals, and they often come in an extended, balanced range of weights.

Newly designed text faces have an additional advantage. They are not adaptations of a design made for a past era and an obsolete technology – they are contemporary, both from a technical and an aesthetic point of view. This means, for instance, that they were drawn to look good and work well in small sizes (on screen and/or in razor-sharp offset printing), but also have the detailing needed to make them attractive and communicative as display faces.

There has been an impressive crop of such well-made, well-equipped text faces lately. Part of this is due to the growing quality of specialized education in Type Design, with the Master's programmes from the University of Reading (UK) and the Royal Academy of Arts (KABK) in The Hague (the Netherlands) taking the lead.

Many new text faces combine traditional proportions with sharp, contemporary detailing, finding a reader-friendly balance between familiarity and invention. I hesitate to call these faces 'oldstyle' or 'transitional' or some such historical notion, although that is where they will probably end up when trying to classify them according to common practice. It might be more useful to range them by function: news, literary, heavy-duty, all-purpose … but maybe that would be setting things too firmly in stone.

W.A. Dwiggins and the M-Formula: learning from marionettes

↑ Detail of a woman's head from Dwiggins's marionette theatre.

↓ Reconstruction (by Tim Ahrens) of a letter drawn by Dwiggins using the M-Formula.

William Addison Dwiggins was a brilliant American lettering artist and illustrator who wrote witty and insightful essays on design and type – he is credited with the first use of the term 'graphic designer'. He was also a dedicated puppeteer and maker of marionettes.

Dwiggins was convinced that typefaces had to be contemporary. In a piece about his innovative Electra typeface, he described a meeting with an imaginary Japanese type specialist, who has this to say: 'The trouble with you people is that you are always trying to reproduce Jenson's letters, or John de Spira … You are always going back three or four hundred

years and trying to do over again what they did then. … This is 1935. Why don't you do what they did: take lettershapes and see if you can't work them into something that stands for 1935? … Electricity, sparks, energy.'

In his search for unorthodox yet practical solutions, Dwiggins devised something he called the 'M-Formula', 'M' standing for marionettes. He had noticed, when designing puppets for his own theatre, that in order to be able to recognise the features of, say, a beautiful young woman from the back row, her features had to be exaggerated. The same, Dwiggins argued, goes for

letterforms. To be optimally readable in small sizes, their shapes profit from some extra articulation. When blown up, some of Dwiggins's shapes are very striking. When viewed at text sizes, they are simply crisp. During the past decades, several type designers have adopted Dwiggins's principles in order to create non-traditional, clear-cut letterforms. Prensa by Cyrus Highsmith, Whitman by Kent Lew and several typefaces by Gerard Unger are among those that show Dwigginsian influences.

Text type strategies

Weight-watching
Novel ↔ **Bembo**

aaiimm

Novel Portez ce vieux whisky au juge blond
Bembo Portez ce vieux whisky au juge blond

Nancy suffisant
Nancy suffisant

Compared with the metal type
originals, many digital revivals are too
thin, making for an uncomfortable
read when set small. Newly designed
text faces such as Novel (Christoph
Dunst) address this problem by
compensating for the sharpness of
today's printing – Novel is considerably sturdier than the digital Bembo;
yet its details are interesting enough
for display use.

set in Novel Pro Regular 7/10

Stress factor
Caecilia ↔ **Joanna**

aaiimm

Caecilia Portez ce vieux whisky au juge blond
Joanna Portez ce vieux whisky au juge blond

Royal splendor
Royal splendor

While Eric Gill's Joanna was an excellent text face in the metal version, its
digital offspring is but a spindly shadow
of its former self in text sizes (although
it works beautifully when used large on
book covers). PMN Caecilia by Peter
Matthias Noordzij is a contemporary
alternative: also a typeface with
straight slab-like serifs and humanist
proportions, but with less contrast or
stress and a rounder italic, making it a
good face for on-screen reading.
Consequently, Caecilia was selected as
the default typeface of Amazon's
Kindle e-reader.

set in PMN Caecilia 6,5/10

Vesper

Portez ce vieux whisky *au juge blond qui fume*
סימל יבצ תא ץחדש ,טק לזוג לע עפנ קסרתה רכ.
यह पहला कम्प्यूटर था, जिसमें सुंदर टाइपोग्राफी थी।

Leksa

Portez ce vieux whisky *au juge blond qui fume*
Эх, чужак! Общий съём цен шляп (юфть) – вдрызг!

Leitura

Leitura 1 Portez ce vieux whisky *au juge blond qui fume*
Leitura 2 Portez ce vieux whisky *au juge blond qui fume*
Leitura 3 Portez ce vieux whisky *au juge blond qui fume*
Leitura 4 **Portez ce vieux whisky *au juge blond qui fume***

Leitura News

Leitura News 1 Portez ce vieux whisky *au juge blond qui fume*
Leitura News 2 Portez ce vieux whisky *au juge blond qui fume*
Leitura News 3 Portez ce vieux whisky *au juge blond qui fume*
Leitura News 4 **Portez ce vieux whisky *au juge blond qui fume***

Adelle Thin → **Heavy**
Portez ce vieux whisky *au juge blond qui fume*

Chaparral Light → **Bold**
Portez ce vieux whisky *au juge blond qui fume*

Centro Slab XThin → **Ultra**
Portez ce vieux whisky *au juge blond qui fume*

Prensa Semibold
Portez ce vieux whisky *au juge blond qui fume*

Nexus Serif
Portez ce vieux whisky *au juge blond qui fume*

Marat Regular
Portez ce vieux whisky *au juge blond qui fume*

Bookish and multilingual
There is a whole new generation of
beautifully drawn text faces like
Novel, which are neutral enough for
immersive reading yet reveal a strong
personality when viewed at larger
sizes. As young designers are often
interested in non-Latin systems, these
fonts frequently come in Cyrillic,
Greek and Asian scripts.

set in Vesper 7,5/10 (Mota Italic)

Newsface systems
Newsprint is still a very singular
market, with its own technical
constraints. Presses are imperfect and
produce inequal results, which can be
compensated for with the right
choice of typeface. Specialist
newsface fonts often come in a range
of carefully balanced variants of the
regular weights, in order to fine-tune
the printing across the company.

set in Leitura 7/10 (DSType)

Heavy duty: legible slabs
PMN Caecilia represented something
of a breakthrough in thinking about
slab serifs: it suddenly seemed more
feasible to combine a humanist
construction with the low contrast
approach of a sans-serif. Many
type designers have followed suit,
devising new approaches to this
hybrid genre that lends itself so well
to on-screen typography.

set in Adelle 7/10 (Type Together)

Radical silhouettes
Inspired by Dwiggins's M-Formula
designers began experimenting with the
relationship between the character's
outside shape and the counter, drawing
abrupt transitions from one curve to the
next. Prensa by Cyrus Highsmith and
Nexus by Martin Majoor are striking
examples. Others, like Ludwig Übele with
Marat, explored the aesthetic possibilities
of inktrap-like incisions and unorthodox
silhouettes (→ p. 141).

set in Marat Pro 7,5/10 (Ludwig Fonts)

Optical size: tailor-made type

As users of digital type we can scale our fonts endlessly; we can make any typeface infinitesimally small, or infinitely large. While technically possible, this may not always be a good idea. One reason is that digital fonts are based on a *single master*: scaling a typeface means making a linear enlargement or reduction of one drawing. The result may be too coarse in large sizes, and too thin for comfort when set very small.

It hasn't always been like this. Typefaces used to be cut by hand at true size, so the detail was determined by what the punchcutter's eye could see and what his hand could do. Even if a type designer would cut compatible fonts in the same style to form a cohesive range, each size would be subtly different. Adjustments were made for proportion, weight, contrast and spacing to ensure that each typeface would be comfortable to read at its particular size.

These optical adjustments were abandoned with the advent of photocomposition and digital type. It was cheaper, and technically easier, to use one master for all point sizes. If the small print in old books is so much easier to read than in most recent books, blame single masters.

During the last ten years, type manufacturers have wised up. More and more fonts are designed for specific *optical sizes*. Each family in Adobe's Originals series has four different variants to cover the full spectrum of usage, from footnotes to large display settings. Families like ITC Bodoni or FF Clifford offer similar solutions. It is becoming more and more common to find type families that come with dedicated Text, SmallText and Display versions.

Herhaalde
Moderne

Amsterdam Type Foundry Garamond

Herhaalde
Moderne

Single-master digital Garamond

Herhaalde
Mode

↗ **Left: Scans from a specimen showing the Amsterdam Type Foundry's metal Garamond, based on ATF Garamond. The 72pt version and the 6pt version have been scaled to roughly the same x-height to show the remarkable differences. Right: a single-master digital Garamond does not offer these differences: it is a compromise. Not as subtle as the Amsterdam 72pt when used in large sizes, and somewhat too thin for comfortable reading in very small sizes.**

→ **Detail from a type specimen from the Voskens foundry in Amsterdam. In the seventeenth century, type designers (or punchcutters) did not cut a wide variety of designs. But although the range of weights was stylistically cohesive, there were functional differences in detailing and proportion between the various sizes.**

Augustijn Romyn
Quid si ad certum usum præfinitum tempus quis piam rem commodasset finitum tempore nec du m tamen sins usurem possit commodatario recip ere & optinuit comu commodatum repetere just um tempus quo usus repotui implerisit factum c
ABCDFGHIJKLMOPQ S T V W X Z

Augustyn Corcijf
Multa huius generis colligi possunt ex historiis quibus apparet dissimilitudinem humanarum obse rvationum non lædere unitatem fidei Quanquam quid opus est disputatione omnio quid sit iustitia fidei quid sit regnum Christi non intelligunt adue rsarij si indicant necessarim esse similitudinem sob

Mediaen Romein.
Responsum ad rivetum jam paratum est,ut edatur Maresiana exspectabo. Epigramma non displicet. epigramma quod rivetus suo libro addidit non esse Heinsii, pro certo habeo. miror Blavios ita lentos esse. De riveti scriptis legendis non sum follicitus, nimium mi-
ABCDEFGHIKLMNOPQRSTVWXYZJUÆ.

' Mediaen Romeyn.
responsum ad rivetum jam paratum est, ut edatur. maresiana exspectabo. Epigramma non displiciter. epigramma quod rivetus suo libro addidit non este Heinsii, pro certo habeo. miror blavios ita lentos este. De riveti scriptis legendis non sum follicitus, nimium mihi temdoris
ABCDEFGHIKLMNOPRSTVWXYZJUÆ 1245

Mediaen Romeyn.
responsum ad rivetum jam paratum est, ut edatur. Maresia-

Garmont Romeyn.
Multi mortates dediti ventri atque somno, indocti incultique Vitam sicut peregrinantes trans egere, quibus profecto contra naturam corpus voluptati, anima oneri fuit. Eorum ego vitam mortemque juncta æstimo: quoniam be utrapse sileut. veru me nimvero is demum mihi vivere, atque anima frui videtur, pui alicui negotio intentas præ-non displicet ÆABCDEFGHIJKLMNOPRSTVUWXYZ

Garmont Cursijf.
Multi mortates dediti ventri atque somno, indocti incultique vitamsicut pereginantes transegere,quibus profecto contra naturam corpus volupta ti,anima oneri,fuit.Eorum ego vitam mortemque juncta æstimo:quoniam de utraque siletur,verumen is demum mihi vivere,atque anima frui videtur,qui alicui negotio intentas præclari facinorū atque artis bonæ eamam quarit.ÆACDEGIJKLMNOPRST UVW XY Zffsfiæcat:

Garmont Cursyf.
Multi mortates dediti ventri atque somno, indocti incultique Vitam sicut peregrinantes transegere, quibus profecto contra naturam corpus volupta ti, anima oner, fuit. Eorum ego vitam mortemque junča æstime: puoniam de utrapse siletur verumen imvero is demum mihi vivere, atpue anima frui videtur, pui alicui negotio intentas præclari facinoris atpue artis bonæ eamam puerit. Æ.ABCDEFGHIKLMNOPRSTVWXYZ

Garment Cursf.
Multi mortates de diti ventri atque somno, indocti incultique vitamsicut peregrinantes transegere, quil us profecto contra naturam corpus voluptati, anima oner, fuit. Eorum ego vitam mortempue juncla est mo:puoniam de utrapue siletur, verumen imvero is demum mihi vivre, acpue anima frui videtur, pui alicui negotio intentas præclari facinoris atpue artis l on æ eamam

Galjard of groote Brevier Romeyn.
Jus bonorum possessionis introductum est à Prætore emendandi veteris juris gratia. Nec solum in intestatorum hereditatibus vetus jus eo modo Frætor emendavit, sicut supra dictum est: sed in eorum quoque qui testamento facto decesserint. Nam si alicnus posthumus heres fuerit instituter: quamvis hereditatem jure civili adire non poterat, cum institutio non valebat: honorario tamen jure bonorum possesior efficiebatur, videlicet cum à Prætore adjuvabatur. Sed & is à nostra constitutione hodie recte heres instituto-facto heredes instituti sunt, ABCDEFHIKLMNOPRSTVXYZUJÆ.

Brevier Romeyn.
Ius bonorum possessionis introductum est à Prætore emendandi veteris juris gratia. Nec solum in intestatorum hereditatibus vetus jus eo modo Prætor emendavit, sicut supra dictum est: sed in eorum quoque qui testamento facto decesserint. Nam si alicnus posthumus heres fuerit instituites: quamvis hereditatem jure civili adire non poterat, cum institutio non valebat:

Freight Big

Taking you
all the way
123456

Freight Display

Taking you
all the way
123456

Freight Text

Taking you
all the way
123456

Freight Micro

Taking you
all the way
123456

Freight
Superfamily for all sizes

With the Freight suite, Joshua Darden took a radical approach to designing for optical size. Letterpress' subtle differences between the various body sizes have been translated into boldly drawn, hugely different variants with pronounced size-related characteristics. Freight turns the traditional, 'natural' gradations of contrast and width into a conscious stylistic device.

Each of the sub-families comes in six weights, from Light to Black, with striking italics. Freight Text is the workhorse, designed for average body text sizes. Freight Display is fine-tuned for use in headlines and on book covers; for really large sizes, as in posters or page-size magazine headlines, there is the spectacular Freight Big. Freight Micro, designed for text in size 6pt and below, is the most radical of the lot. The contrast between the thick and thin parts was drastically reduced, making sure that the text stays clear in small sizes. The serifs are blocky, as in a slab serif. Deep cuts were made where curves join the stems to obtain a more open image. All this makes Freight Micro eminently readable in small sizes. But as it is so full of character, designers like using it for display purposes as well, see *Courrier International* on → p.105.

Les
typographes

m'excuseront de rappeler ici que les caractères typographiques consistent en primes rectangulaires dont l'une des extrémités porte en saillie la lettre, accentuée ou non.

Les
typographes

m'excuseront de rappeler ici que les caractères typographiques consistent en primes rectangulaires dont l'une des extrémités porte en saillie la lettre, accentuée ou non.

Les caractères typographiques consistent en primes rectangulaires dont l'une des extrémités porte en saillie la lettre, accentuée ou non.

Les
typographes

m'excuseront de rappeler ici que les caractères typographiques consistent en primes rectangulaires dont l'une des extrémités porte en saillie la lettre,

Les caractères typographiques consistent en primes rectangulaires dont l'une des extrémités porte en saillie la lettre, accentuée ou non.

Minuscule
Extremely small

Minuscule by the French designer, researcher and teacher Thomas Huot-Marchand was inspired by the work of Louis-Émile Javal, whose theories about the way we see and read are referred to in the first chapter of this book (← p.15). Minuscule was specially developed for setting texts at 6pt and smaller – down to 2pt, which is about the size of a footnote in a matchbox-size bible. Having thoroughly tested reading behaviour at these extreme sizes, Huot-Marchand realised that with each step down, legibility decreases so quickly that it was necessary to design a separate master (or basic drawing) for each point size. Huot-Marchand developed five versions, optimised for use in 6pt (Minuscule Six), 5pt (Cinq), 4pt (Quatre), 3pt (Trois) and 2pt (Deux).

All versions of Minuscule share the same characteristics: large x-height, robust slab serifs, vertical stress, open structure, big counters, low contrast. However, as the designated point size gets smaller, the forms become more pronounced and elemental. At two points size, the 'o' is just a tiny black square, as is the middle section of the lowercase 'g' ... and it works! Above, Minuscule Six, Trois and Deux are all shown at 60pt, 18pt and 6pt; the bottom lines of Trois and Deux were set in the body size they are meant for.

← How do we read? 14
→ Typographic detail 117
→ Small & narrow type 141

Choosing typefaces

For some designers one of the highlights of the design process is the moment when a project's typefaces need to be chosen. They spend days doing research and online tests, downloading PDF type specimens, comparing character sets. In contrast, other designers quickly pick a font from their familiar repertoire. The result is not necessarily better or worse.

There is no standard answer to the question which typeface is best for what kind of job. It all depends on context, constraints and personal taste. Everyone working with type will have to develop some sensitivity allowing her or him to select typefaces with confidence – forever different fonts, or always the same ones. It is useful to gain an understanding of what the market has to offer, the way a fashion designer can benefit from a knowledge of fabrics and haberdashery. In order to be able to narrow down the endless possibilities, it helps to understand what specific fonts can and cannot do.

'Safe choices': not necessarily best

Many web articles and books recommend classical typefaces from past centuries as safe choices for all types of layouts. Time and again we encounter the same names, from Jenson to Gill, from Futura to Frutiger, with a few recent fonts like FF Scala and Interstate thrown in for good measure. The message is always the same: well-known equals reliable. This is a useless simplification. As we've seen, there are many versions of each classic, and some really aren't that good. Often a relatively unknown, newly designed font may be better placed to do the job (← p. 96–99).

Make lists, ask questions

Choosing a typeface is not just about aesthetics and personal preferences. First and foremost, it is about choosing a face that suits the job, and therefore you'll have to ask yourself a few questions in order not to run into difficulties later.

- **Money** Does the project allow for investing in buying new fonts? Is it perhaps a nice excuse for getting some fonts which you can use for other jobs in the future? Can the client be convinced to at least share the extra cost with you, and if so, what's the budget?
- **Context: client** Do you have a complete overview of what the fonts will have to be able to do? Is there a chance that this little project is the beginning of something big, which will require more complex functionality in the future? A few examples. You may not need tabular figures now, but what if your client wants an annual report in six months' time? How about language coverage? Could your client be planning to conquer the Central European, Russian or Greek market soon? Or make brochures for the Turkish and Arab population in your town? He or she may also have special wishes regarding style. Some clients simply don't like oldstyle or bold type. Or they love everything geometric. Find out in time.
- **Context: target audience** If the target group is not like you (for instance: older, or more conservative) then some empathy is a sign of professionalism. Forcing your personal tastes upon those you design for is not always the best plan. Your prospective audience must at

Head of a Bald Young
Red crayon on paper
7⅛ × 5⅞ in

all times be convinced that whatever you designed is meant for them. On a more practical level – you wouldn't believe (if you are under 30) how fast eyesight deteriorates after 45. Sure, people have spectacles, but they don't get new ones every three years. So forget that extra-light sans-serif text font if you want to communicate with pensioners.

- **Function** What is the nature of the publication you are designing? Does it contain longer texts for immersive reading? Is there a need for subtle typography with a hint of tradition – in other words, do you want small caps, oldstyle figures, special ligatures? Will the text font double as a headline font, so that it needs to be interesting enough to view at large sizes? If you're designing for the web, or if the project is likely to include a website, the client may appreciate it if you propose a font that can be licensed for web through Typekit, Fontdeck or a similar service.

- **Taste, style and atmosphere** There are two diametrically opposed attitudes in type selection. The first is to always follow one's own predilection – set it in one's favourite face of the moment, whatever the nature of the job. The other is to slavishly adapt to the contents: if it's about the nineteenth century, then it has to be Didot or Clarendon; if it's about some Modernist subject, then it can't be anything but Futura or Akzidenz. Neither attitude is ideal. The former can result in absurd or silly combinations; the latter in a boring cliché of 'appropriateness'. Surprise us.

- **Your hidden agenda** But then again, you may have a plan of your own. A friend's font you want to try out. A secret typographic infatuation you want to indulge in. It can all become part of your design decision, as long as the result respects the reader.

- **Combinations** Often typefaces are not chosen individually, but as part of a typographic *palette* – a small system for one publication, a series, or an identity. Smart combinations are a key to typographic interestingness. More about this on → p.104

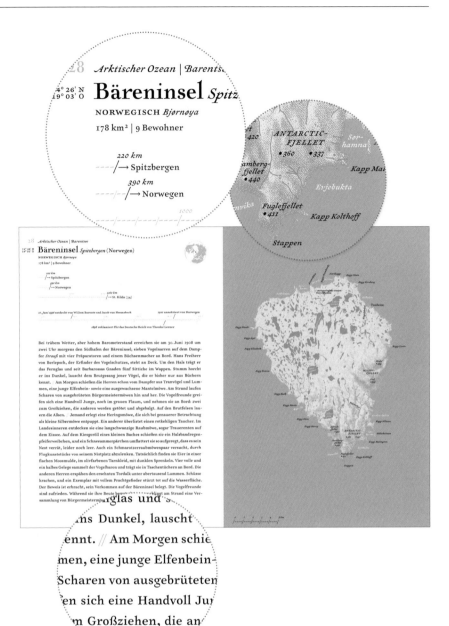

Atlas of remote islands

Berlin-based designer-author Judith Schalansky (she of *Fraktur mon Amour*) is a 200 percent double talent, and expresses herself in both her fields – literature and typography – with admirable verve and style. Her *Atlas of Remote Islands: Fifty Islands I Have Never Set Foot On and Never Will* (2010) is as much about language as about visual information. Each of the islands she describes is presented through a story, most of which are sad, even deeply tragic. But the misery and disappointment is described in such a wonderfully laconic tone, that despite it all it gets the reader into a good mood. Although the text, maps and other infographics are based on true facts, Schalansky's approach evokes a feeling of irreality. As she explains in the foreword, her detached view of faraway places has to do with her East-German past: when she was a child, the country was locked off from most of the world, and most countries were literally unreachable.

The unreal and melancholic atmosphere of the book is reflected in the choice of type: the baroque Sirenne family by Alan Dague-Greene is neither contemporary nor revival: it is splendid typographic fiction.

The page shown is from the original German edition, MareVerlag 2009.

Combining typefaces

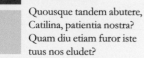

**High-contrast, complementary:
Futura Bold with Garamond**

**Keeping it within the family:
FF Absara Head with FF Absara Sans
and its small caps**

There are various reasons for choosing to use more than one typeface or family in a project: to break the monotony, emphasize parts of the text, identify recurring elements, establish a hierarchy. Mostly, combining typefaces is about increasing articulation to make the content more accessible, and/or enhancing the reading and browsing experience by building an interesting typographic palette.

Colours

The word 'palette' is telling: mixing typefaces is like matching colours. The main concern when building a palette is to find a balance between difference and 'sameness'. Combining Garamond Regular with Futura Bold is a bit like juxtaposing lime green and deep blue. The contrast is extreme, but the colours combine well because they are complementary. The same can be said of these two typefaces. In stylistic terms, the one does exactly what the other one doesn't; yet they work well together, possibly because they have similar proportions – both are related to the monumental alphabets of ancient Rome. A more modest strategy may be to combine typefaces from one family or superfamily, which resembles putting together related colours, like browns and reds.

While colour theory is a widely established discipline, there is no accepted theory for mixing type. This is partly because new fonts come out every day, and partly because typefaces have so many levels at which they interact – proportions, weight, shape, atmosphere, historical connotations – that decisions on 'good' combinations can become very subjective.

There are some rules of thumb, though. Don't use fonts that are too similar, such as two slightly different sans-serifs. When mixing fonts within a text, check that the x-heights are similar. Train your eyes to recognise stylistic affinities. And when in doubt, use fonts from the same superfamily.

Typographic palettes

6–8 ounces salt pork, cut into chunks
4 tbsp unsalted butter, divided
4 pounds trimmed beef chuck, cut into cubes
10–12 shallots, chopped
2 large peeled carrots, 1 chopped, 1 cut into chunks
4 garlic cloves, chopped
1 bottle Pinot Noir

Interview

**Lukt het je altijd om de mensen te laten geloven in d
beelden die in jouw hoofd bestaan?** Kunst is een
ijdel iets. Een enkele keer laat ik een plan
vallen, maar als ik ervan overtuigd ben dat
doorzetten. In haar bundel *On
Photography* bechrijft Susan
Sontag hoe de land-art werken
van Walter de Maria* in princip
bekend zijn geworden als een
fotografisch verslag, maar dat
dit ons niet terug leidt naar d

**WALTER DE MARIA
The Lightning Field**
*Commissioned by the
DIA Foundation in
the 1970s, this Land
Art project created
in a remote area of*

Four examples of how typographic palettes can be built according to different principles.

← **Elegance.** Both Didot Display and Brandon Grotesque are charming, personal interpretations of historical styles. They are very different, yet seem to have similar outlooks on life.

↙ **Friction.** A monospaced font for text (Simplon BP Mono) denotes contemporary, artsy design. Combined here with a bold, Helvetica-like font from the same foundry (Suisse BP Int'l) and a deliberately incongruous headline font, the contemporary blackletter Fakir.

↗ **Contrast in harmony.** Fonts from the Thesis superfamily combined: TheSans Condensed Black and TheSans Extra-Bold small caps are used for articulation with the text face TheAntiqua; the latter was designed as an oldstyle companion to the Thesis family.

→ **Fun.** Expressive American-style palette of contrasting fonts: the slab serif Archer, the sans-serif Breuer Text and the Bodoni-like Anne Bonny.

The migration movement

NETHERLANDS Most Dutch emigrants originated from vinces of Zeeland, Groningen and Friesland, whe clay soil had led them to specialize in crop growi: Emigrants were for the most part day labourers v on the farms. Another group consisted mainly of armers from the sandy soil areas in the east and t

NORDIC COUNTRIES The first Scandinavian immigrant the 19th century were relatively well off, mainly

Every week at
BONNY'S RESTAURANT
187 BREUER ST *next to Archer's*

Sunday Breakfast
UNTIL 2:30 PM

fruit toast, butter & conserves **$8**
seasonal fruit salad, natural yogurt & almonds **$12**
pancakes & blueberry compote **$10**
oasted turkish bread, scrambled eggs & truffle oil **$14**

Quirky personality, strong flavours

Courrier International

Designer Mark Porter selected an unusual combination of typefaces for his spectacular redesign of French political magazine *Courrier International*. He comments: 'I usually find that typographic decisions for redesigns or launches are based on a mixture of logic and instinct. Almost as soon as I had done my research on *Courrier International*, an image of bold black Omnes on a yellow background popped into my mind.

When I think of French type, I think of Roger Excoffon & Robert Massin – strong flavours. Omnes has an enormous amount of character and a degree of eccentricity, and it felt like it fitted into that tradition. *Courrier International* is also a unique and quirky publication with a lot of personality. When we started working with it, we found that French looked really good in the font – it's very important when designing in other languages to choose letterforms which suit the language.

I thought it would be interesting to mix the very distinctive sans with a classical serif, so we looked at various options.

Freight (← p. 101) was an obvious early choice because I often find that typefaces by a single designer combine well. There is no logical reason for this because weights, widths, x-heights etc. can vary a lot, but it did feel like there was a consistent sensibility in Joshua Darden's work which made for a harmonious mix between the two fonts.

The other advantage of Freight was that it comes in such a wide range of weights and grades. We loved the Display, but it was too elegant and not gritty enough for some of the hard news which *Courrier* covers. So we chose the Micro for news. This was originally designed for use at small sizes, and it therefore has a deliberate crudeness which made the headlines on the news pages feel more urgent and dynamic.'

Making 'type' without a font

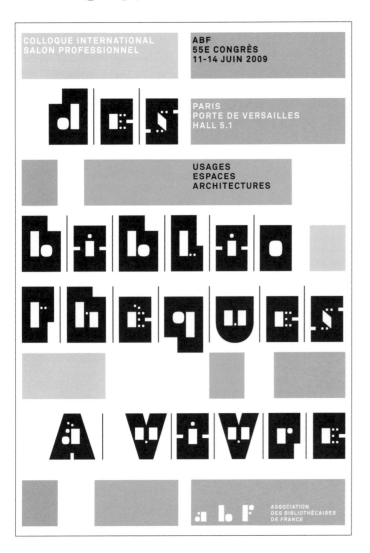

In typographic internet forums like Typophile or MyFonts' WhatTheFont Forum users often ask which font was used for a particular logo or shop sign, posting pictures that obviously show hand-rendered lettering. Apparently it is difficult for people to imagine that a designer is able (or inclined) to carefully draw letterforms for one-time use. But despite the abundance of available fonts that is precisely what happens, surprisingly often, and increasingly.

Designers can have good reasons to draw their own lettering – either on paper or in a program like Illustrator. Often it is purely for the pleasure of making things; using self-made alphabets can also be an effective way to put a unique signature on a design. At times a designer has an immediately vision of what would be the perfect font for a specific project – it just doesn't exist yet. The feeling of total control when drawing the ideal lettering yourself (outside your normal working hours if necessary) is hard to beat.

Paulette

↖ Philippe Apeloig, 'Des bibliothèques à vivre', poster for the 55th congress of the ABF, the French Librarians' Association. 2009, silkscreen, 118 × 175 cm. Apeloig personalises his posters, mostly for clients in the cultural field, by designing custom alphabets for each project.

↑ *Paulette* is a French magazine for readers who participate in visual and editorial choices. Designer Camille Boulouis visualised this close relationship in her design of the mag's nameplate – hence the hand-made look. Instead of a purely handwritten logo, Boulouis chose a form halfway between typography and handwriting.

← Dutch designer Letman (Job Wouters) is known for his organic, hand-made and improvised typography. Poster for a series of lunchtime theatre shows on a well-known theme at the Amsterdam Bellevue Theatre.

Organic lettering

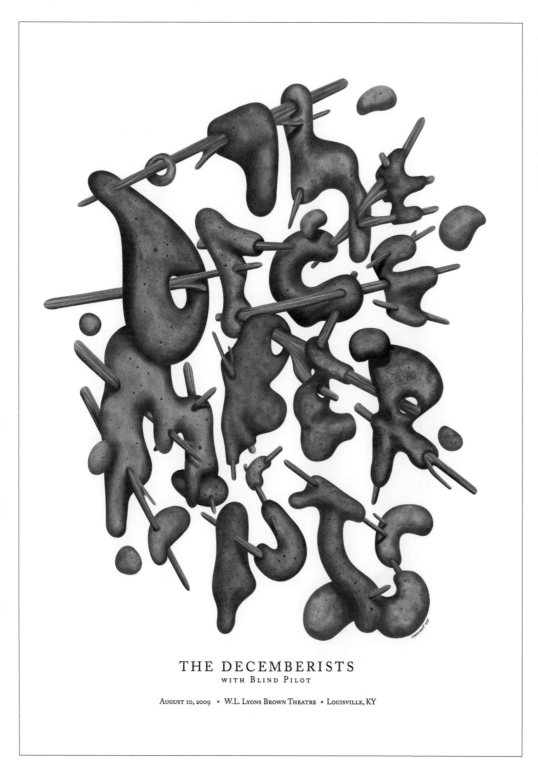

Barcelona-based designer Alex Trochut uses a combination of techniques to create witty and surprising lettering works in a eclectic mixture of styles inspired by Surrealism, psychedelic posters, Catalan graphic tradition and trash comics. This poster for a Decemberists concert at W.L. Lyons Brown Theatre in Louisville, Kentucky (client: Red Light Management, 2009) was done in a mixture of pencil drawing and digital techniques – mainly Photoshop.

← Book covers 30
← Modularity in type 92
→ Style & statement 146

Scripts: fonts or lettering?

That room had such an odd character

NORMAL BELLO SCRIPT

That room had such an odd character

BELLO PRO WITH AUTOMATIC OPENTYPE LIGATURES & ENDING SWASHES

SUDTIPOS PRESENTS

The Real Sign Painting

Lettering WITH Open Type SWASHES ALTERNATES LIGATURES

Based on calligraphy by A. Becker

ARGUABLY THE GREATEST AMERICAN SIGN LETTERING ARTIST OF ALL TIME

Until about 1960 hand-lettering was common practice: specialist designers and illustrators drew headlines for advertisements, posters and illustrated magazines. They were masters at inventing ever new letterforms. After thousands of display fonts became available in photo-type-setting and as dry transfer sheets in the 1960s and '70s, hand-drawing techniques gradually became obsolete. Recently, hand-lettering has made a comeback. Some designers use pencil, pen and brush, or create dimensional texts which are then photographed. Many others produce digital lettering using drawing programs such as Adobe Illustrator.

The vector outline technology used to produce these pieces of digital lettering is virtually the same as that used for drawing complete fonts. The result may have the same smooth finish. But as lettering artists create words and sentences rather than single characters, they have the opportunity to bend and shape each letter to adjust it to its context: one 'o' or 'n' may differ from another in order to better connect to the letter preceding or following it.

The difference between hand-drawn text and text made with an existing font is not always easy to see. It gets even more complex when a headline is set in a sophisticated OpenType font containing many alternates and ligatures: this gives the user a choice of multiple variants for each character, allowing him or her to create headlines that are virtually indistinguishable from hand lettering. Script fonts by Sudtipos and Underware are popular examples of such font magic.

Designing with fonts

Both the Bello typeface from Underware and Buffet by Ale Paul (Sudtipos) have been designed to convincingly mimic brush script lettering on handpainted signs and headlines. The spontaneous characteristics of hand-rendered text are emulated by using a wide array of alternate letterforms such as ligatures and 'swashes'.

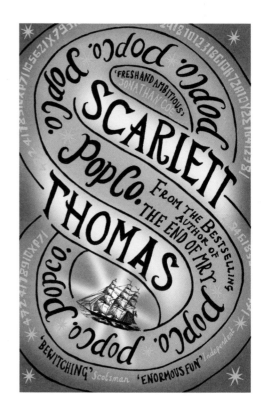

KING SIZE

tops 'em all for
TASTE and COMFORT!

Hand-lettering

↖ Book jacket by Boudewijn Ietswaart
for Querido publishers, 1966

↙ Today, an increasing number of
designers choose hand-lettering over
off-the-shelf fonts – either using digital
techniques or painting and drawing on
paper, or a combination of both. Magazine headline by Jessica Hische, made
with a vector drawing program.

↑ Anonymous 1950s headline for an
American cigarette advertisement.

↓ Hand-drawn book cover by Jonathan
Gray (Gray 318).

← Book covers 30
→ OpenType functions 130
→ Style & statement 146

Finding and buying fonts

A new computer or operating system usually comes with a collection of system fonts. So does design and office software from vendors such as Adobe or Microsoft. Yet there are plenty of reasons to build one's own collection of fonts. Personal taste, exclusivity or technical requirements can be motives for buying new fonts for one or more specific projects. Acquiring fonts via the web is a breeze; most vendors enable immediate downloading.

Licences and the EULA

Strictly speaking, fonts (like other kinds of software) are not *bought*. You can't own a font. What you acquire is a license to use it within well-defined restrictions, which are laid down in a document called *End User License Agreement*. EULAS differ from one foundry to the next. For instance, the number of computers that fonts may be installed on may vary, and so may the rules for embedding fonts in PDFs or websites. Special authorisation is usually required for modifying fonts – like adding characters.

A graphic designer who designs a logo using a font must possess a valid license. His or her client, who will receive the logo in the form of image files, will not require a license to use the font. Although some letters from the font are included in the logo, the font files themselves are not. The client cannot set any text in the font.

Things are very different if the client wants to be able to use the font(s) on their own computers for things such as correspondence, PowerPoint presentations or price lists. As it is generally prohibited to share fonts with third parties, giving your client a copy of the typefaces you bought for their job is illegal. Even sharing a license with fellow freelancers is a no-go.

Many professionals have a surprisingly relaxed attitude about these rules, and happily copy fonts to their business partners in co-productions involving editorial or corporate design. Whoever does this, is exposing the other party to a real hazard. Organisations such as the Business Software Alliance carry out audits, and infringements may result in costly legal proceedings.

To use the font legally, each company needs to buy a license for the appropriate number of computers. Many standard licenses allow for installing on five computers at the same location. An organisation wanting to use fonts on a larger number of computers needs a *group license*.

The Berlin-based Just Another Foundry (formerly in London) is run by Tim Ahrens and Shoko Mugikura. They offer their fonts through their own website as well as via the distributors MyFonts and FontShop. Ahrens also developed a series of design tools for type designers called Font Remix Tools.

Foundries and distributors. Where to buy fonts

On a world-wide level there are probably about a thousand independent foundries and type designers who sell their own fonts. Many have their own online shops where fonts can be viewed, ordered and downloaded (some will send you your wares by email or on a disk). Among the well-known microfoundries with their own online store are those of Lucas de Groot (lucasfonts.com), Eric Olson (processtypefoundry.com), Jean François Porchez (typofonderie.com), František Štorm (stormtype.com), Nick

Shinn (shinntype.com) and Underware (underware.nl). Several microfoundries have united under an umbrella called Village (vllg.com). There is a growing number of independent foundries whose library contains fonts designed by multiple designers. Well-respected publishers include Canada Type, Dutch Type Library, Emigre, The Font Bureau, Fountain, Hoefler & Frere-Jones, House Industries, Lineto, OurType, P22, ParaType, Primetype, Typotheque and TypeTogether.

Most users do not buy their fonts directly from the makers, but shop at the font world's supermarkets. The FontShop network represents, in addition to its own FontFont series, many other foundries. MyFonts represents the highest number of small, independent foundries, alongside some of the bigger players. Fonts.com (Monotype's online shop) and Linotype both represent their own collections alongside those of many other foundries. Veer is more of a boutique for specialists. Some countries

have type distributors with a more local customer base, such as Faces in the UK and Phil's Fonts in the USA.
Yet there are still a fair number of foundries that avoid distributors altogether and prefer doing business with their customers directly. To mention a few: Jeremy Tankard and The Foundry in the UK, The Enschedé Font Foundry in the Netherlands, and a handful of Swiss foundries including B+P Swiss Typefaces and Optimo.

Why pay for fonts?

A good font is a professional graphic design tool that allows the user to solve communication problems and help customers to differentiate themselves from the competition. So fonts do not only have technical and aesthetic value, but also provide exclusivity. It is only logical that this is paid for – just as companies pay for unique advertising or good seats in the meeting room. Clients may even accept paying for a font if the designer manages to explain the importance of personalised typography.

But distributing pirated copies of fonts is easy, and some do it out of a misplaced sense of idealism; they think all things digital should be free. Yet type designers are often self-employed and struggling to get by. Anyone distributing retail typefaces for free – especially a fellow designer – should realise that this implies a sincere 'screw you' to a type designing colleague.

The prices of digital typeface range from zero to about $/€200 per font, with most quality fonts in the $30–80 range (or cheaper for packages). But make no mistake: compared to the cost of strips of set text in the time of lead or photosetting, prices are lower than they have ever been.

So how about free fonts?

The web is a great source of free fonts. Using them for 'real' projects can be hazardous, though. Many consist of a single weight only, and have a very limited character set, lacking essential components such as accents, a Euro sign or other important symbols. As they may be badly produced by a beginner, they can cause technical problems and muddle up the production process.

The good news is that there are also excellent free fonts that are totally suitable for professional design work, and given away out of idealism or as part of a public relations strategy. Paratype's PT Sans and Vera from Bitstream were made freely available by these foundries. Aller Sans was designed by Dalton Maag for the Danish School of Media and Journalism, who offer it for free. Google has paid several designers to be able to distribute fonts for free. In addition, there are more and more designers and publishers who will make several weights of a family available free of charge in the hope that buyers will pay for other family members. Dutchman Jos Buivenga was a pioneer of this model with Museo.

Before releasing his first commercial typeface, Museo, Dutch designer Jos Buivenga developed several free fonts which were offered via his exljbris foundry.

Danmarks
Medie- og
Journalist-
højskole

Aller Sans

ȡɓÇɔĆȡȡƎƏɛFGǦȞȟɪKŁɯɲɳ
Ƥþ̦PΡꞄΣꜰTΤƲƱƲYYŻȜꞫɝƷƷƎAE
abcdefghijklmnopqrstuvwxyz
ɓ66ɗbʙçɗ̦ꬶ̦ɘꞔɗɖðəɵɛʒɜˀꞝfgɗ
ɦɦɣɥнɪɟjɟʃ̦ʄkꞣꞥ̦łłꞏɭɯꭑɰɳɳɲ
ɪøɸþþꝓꝒ̦ꝑꝹ̦ʀꞧ̦ɭ̦ꞃꞃꞟ̦ʃʆʒ̦ßʂtʈ̦ʈ̦ɬ̦ɥɯ

Gentium

ALEXANDER
WILLIAM
ALFONSO
VALDEMAR

AW Conqueror

Weimargefons
Weimargefons
Weimargefons
Weimargefons

Yanone Kaffeesatz

Fonts for free

Clockwise from top left: Aller Sans was designed by Dalton Maag for the Danish School of Media and Journalism; the school made the family's standard version available to the world at no cost. Paper company Arjo Wiggins commissioned Jean François Porchez to design this noble set of display fonts as part of their campaign to promote Conqueror papers. Kaffeesatz, the first font by German designer Yanone (Jan Gerner), became hugely popular as a free font. Yanone further developed the design into the more sophisticated FF Kava, released by FontShop International. Gentium by Victor Gaultney is offered free of charge by the idealistic organisation SIL as an extremely well-equipped multi-lingual 'typeface for the nations'.

Type on the screen: some hard facts

At the mention of the word 'typography' many people will still think of printed matter. However, on-screen reading is quickly becoming more common than reading on paper. We consume large amounts of text on monitors: e-mail, blog posts, news, entire books. In 2011, Amazon announced that for the first time more e-books than printed books had been sold. And when it comes to writing, the production and shaping of text is now taking place almost exclusively on the computer.

Many typographic principles developed for print roughly apply to on-screen typography as well. One thing that does make a considerable difference is resolution.

Resolution and dots-per-inch

In offset printing, the finest details can be made visible; even affordable laser printers now offer sharp detailing. On the screen the display is coarser. All information, whether images or letterforms, must be reproduced on a grid of square pixels. The smaller the individual pixels and the closer together they are, the finer and more detailed the image or text.

Most graphic designers are familiar with the unit DPI (dots per inch). We all know that for an image to print well in offset, a 300 DPI resolution is a safe minimum. When designing for screens, everything is relative. Inches don't really count: the only thing that is relevant are pixels. So how big is a pixel? That too is relative; it depends on

the size and resolution of the screen. Writers often mention 72 DPI as screen resolution. Don't be fooled. This was true in 1984 when the first Apple Macintoshes did indeed display 72 pixels per inch (PPI). Which was rather practical, because it meant that a single pixel corresponded with 1 pica point (= $^1/_{72}$ inch). So a typeface in a specific point size took up the same space on the early Mac screens as on a printed sheet of paper – but on a much coarser pixel grid than the one used for offset films or plates.

On-screen reading today

Monitors today have highly variable dimensions and resolutions. The pixel density of desktop monitors is typically somewhere between 70 and 130 PPI; laptops offer higher values. For comparison: TV monitors only display about 20 to 50 PPI. It is doubtful whether the average monitor resolution will increase dramatically in the near future. We are still waiting for scalable, resolution-independent operating systems; high-resolution displays are only offered in small-sized smartphones, such as the iPhone 4. Its Retina Display offers 960 × 640 pixels on a 3.5" diagonal, which corresponds to 326 PPI. Besides, what would be beneficial to the display of text might be problematic for bitmap files (the myriad existing photos and graphics on the web): these would simply look smaller.

The display technology used on Amazon's Kindle and Sony's Reader is an exception. It is based on E-Ink technology, which uses tiny, randomly distributed microcapsules roughly the width of a human hair that can be turned on and off (black/white). The result is a sharper-looking image that resembles printing more closely. E-Ink (from *electrophoretic ink*) also uses less energy because it doesn't rely on backlighting like LCD screens do. Some see this as a disadvantage, because the reader needs ambient light for reading. Nonetheless, the technology may be a harbinger of the future. Yet major limitations still have to be overcome: E-Ink cannot display colour or video.

↓ Emigre's Zuzana Licko was probably the first type designer to design typefaces that used low-resolution as an opportunity to make something genuinely new. Specially designed for the coarse screen resolution of the original Apple Macintosh, her 1985 typefaces Emigre, Oakland and Emperor treated the bitmap structure as a visual feature, not a handicap. Those early bitmap-based typefaces are now sold as a package under the font name Lo-Res.

How quickly daft jumping zebras vex
How quickly daft jumping zebras vex
How quickly daft jumping zebras vex
How quickly daft jumping zebras vex
How quickly daft jumping zebras vex
How quickly daft jumping zebras vex
How quickly daft jumping zebras vex
How quickly daft jumping zebras vex
How quickly daft jumping zebras vex

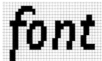

High-resolution
outline font

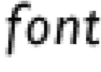

Screen font on grid,
no anti-aliasing

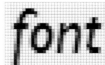

Greyscale anti-aliasing

Subpixel rendering

↑ Text fragment on a computer screen
with hinting switched off. Letterforms
are randomly deformed by the underlying, coarse pixel grid. Hinting helps
glyphs to fall onto the grid in a more
regular way.

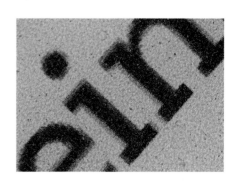

↑ Macro photo of a Kindle screen
showing the behaviour of E-Ink. Like
a stochastic screen in offset printing,
E-Ink does not use a regular pixel grid
but a random pattern. Yet here, too, the
letters' edges are slightly blurred using
greyscale values. Macro photography:
courtesy Jeffrey Hapeman.

↖ When a font is smoothed using greyscale anti-aliasing, the rasterising
software will calculate what percentage
of each pixel is being covered by the
letterform, translating the result into a
lighter or darker greyscale value. This
softens the 'jaggies' but it also makes
the text look less sharp. If, for instance,
a straight vertical stroke falls between
two pixels, then a sharp black line of
about 1 pixel width may turn into a 50%
grey two-pixel-wide stroke.

Rasterizing and hinting

For pixel-based screens, the basic problem
remains: to display text, shapes consisting of
lines and curves must be projected on a pixel
grid. This process, called *rasterizing* or *rendering*,
requires compromises. If a screen just displays
pure black and white, there are only two states: a
pixel is turned on (black) if it lies within the con-
tour, and off when it lies outside of it. If a detail
is too fine or 'drops off' the edge of a pixel, it will
disappear. Two identical shapes do not necessarily lie on the grid in the same way, so it can happen that two instances of the same character are
represented differently.

To avoid letters becoming deformed when
represented at small size on a screen, extra information can be packed into a font: *hints*. For
instance, a font can tell the rasterizer that a cross
bar should be at least one pixel thick and all
stems should keep the same width. As the letter
will look different for each pixel size, hints must
be included for each relevant size, e.g. 7, 8, 9 ... 24
pixels high. If done well, part of this is manual
work – a very costly job. Only very few fonts are
manually hinted for all relevant sizes. This has
been meticulously done, for instance, with core
system fonts such as Arial, Verdana, Georgia and
Courier – that is why these fonts often look best
on any screen, especially on Windows machines.

Anti-aliasing, subpixel rendering

Even with good hinting, a black-and-white
pixel grid would result in visible 'jaggies': jagged
edges on round and diagonal shapes. These can
be smoothed by adding greyscale – a technique
known as *anti-aliasing*. To put it briefly, this is a
way of making type on a screen seem smoother
by slightly blurring it. A more sophisticated
form of anti-aliasing is *subpixel rendering*. It
makes use of the fact that on a regular colour
LCD screen each pixel consists of three tiny 'colour lamps' – red, green and blue. By controlling
these coloured subpixels individually, a better
resolution can be simulated by adding coloured
halftone values.

The behaviour of fonts on screens varies
greatly across platforms, especially when comparing Windows-based systems to the Apple
Mac. This is because these two have developed
such radically different principles for rendering
type on the screen.

For designers – especially web designers – this
basically means one thing: every page designed
for viewing on multiple platforms should be
tested in all relevant operating systems and
programs. Designers must be aware that what
looks good on their screen (usually a Mac) may
look lousy when viewed somewhere else.

← Type on the web 30
→ Webfonts 114
→ Kinetic typography 158

The year of web fonts

One thing that web designers have learned to accept is that the end result can never be completely predicted. A web page takes its definite shape on the user's screen, and many variables are unknown. What size is the area? What is the resolution? How do the colours appear?

Until recently, this 'open' character of web design also applied to type: designers had very little freedom when choosing fonts, and had to limit themselves to so-called *web-safe fonts*: Arial, Times, Georgia, Verdana and a handful of other system fonts installed on virtually all computers. This is because a website had to use fonts installed on the viewer's computer for rendering text. Web designers who wanted a different typeface needed to convert the text into an image file (gif, jpeg or png) or Flash movie. As we have seen, a text that is saved as an image cannot be read by computers any longer: it is invisible to search engines, it is not possible to select and copy it, and for every text change a new image has to be provided (← p. 36).

@fontface

The solution, of course, would be to deliver the fonts together with the website's HTML code. This became possible when the @fontface rule was introduced. It allows a link to a font on a remote server to be built in, similar to embedding an image or sound file located anywhere on the Web. The @fontface rule is part of the CSS (Cascading Style Sheets), which efficiently lay down typographic style sheets for an entire website. What was still lacking was consensus about format and standardisation among browser vendors. Microsoft, for instance, introduced Embedded OpenType (EOT) but this font format, which is still in use, was only supported by their own browser, Internet Explorer.

There was another party that wasn't happy: the type designers and foundries. A font file that is downloaded with a web page's content can easily be saved on the harddisk and converted into a usable font by any clever hacker. While font vendors and type designers were aware that the web was an important new market, they regarded font embedding as an invitation to piracy. Security measures were called for.

WOFF: the built-in watchdog

A workable solution was provided by independent designer-programmers Erik van Blokland and Tal Leming, working with Jonathan Kew, developer at Mozilla (the makers of Firefox). Their new font format, WOFF (Web Open Font Format) was introduced in 2009 and accepted as a new standard by both the type and web worlds the following year. WOFF compresses fonts, allows for making *subsets* (i.a. using only that portion of the character set that is needed) and for adding meta information, such as info on copyrights and permitted use. For most typefoundries, the wrapper that is WOFF provides assurance that illegal use of webfonts is sufficiently discouraged. Theoretically it is still possible to crack a WOFF font, but several hurdles must be overcome, making malicious intent blatantly obvious.

Renting fonts

As of 2010 the future of web typography has looked considerably rosier: finally the same diversity has become possible in web design as in print. Hosting and embedding webfonts, however, is relatively complicated. Therefore several specialist service companies for hosting webfonts were set up in 2010–2011. Typekit, Webtype, Fontdeck, WebINK, Monotype and others each

↓ Typekit, the de facto market leader in the webfont domain, hosts webfonts made available by several prestigious foundries, including FontFont, Exljbris (Jos Buivenga) and TypeTogether. The latter two also participate in MyFonts' webfont program, which offers webkits for sale instead of the subscription service proposed by the competition.

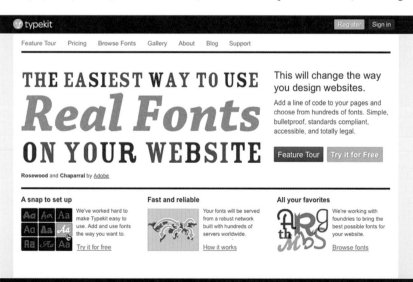

provide fonts from various foundries with different hosting models whose pricing depends on the way the fonts are used, taking into account the bandwidth, page views and/or number of domain names. As these are subscription-based systems, using these services is like renting fonts. Some foundries, including Typotheque in the Netherlands, have their own program providing webfont hosting. Even Google now offers a webfont service, providing a growing library of fonts for free. MyFonts is the only distributor that, for now, does not offer a hosting service but offers webfont kits at the price of a normal font.

The solution to the font format problem is only the first step. Meanwhile new problems have become manifest. Many of the fonts offered as webfonts turn out to be less useful than hoped. Many are fine to set headlines but look spectacularly bad at text sizes. Others, such as the script fonts from Sudtipos and others, need OpenType support to use the sophisticated ligatures and alternates, and the web doesn't offer that functionality yet. The most common problem is poor hinting: while non-system fonts usually look good on the web designer's Mac, they look brittle on Windows machines, especially when using Internet Explorer. In addition, loading webfonts can make a site slower. This is being addressed by experimenting with limited character sets (subsets) and the delivery of fonts in small packages.

In other words: web typography is still in its infancy.

→ The website for digital branding agency GOOD/corps (goodcorps.com) uses typography as a key component of its visual style, not only mixing different fonts but also the services that provide those fonts: Webtype provided Monotype Sabon, Typekit hosted FF Bau and Fonts.com's webfont service supplied Trade Gothic. According to the designers, using three different sources was still easier on page loading times than equivalent Flash or image replacement techniques.

← Type on the web 36
← Buying fonts 110
← Type on the screen 112

Index of the book *Philippe Starck* by
Pierre Doze, Sophie Tasma-Anargyros
and Elisabeth Laville. Designer Mark
Thomson used the alphabet as a kind of
horizontal spine running across the
optical middle of the spread, creating an
immediately accessible index.
Functionality is not compromised by
the unusual formal solution – quite the
contrary: it is enhanced by it.

A B C D E F G H I J K L M

Typographic detail

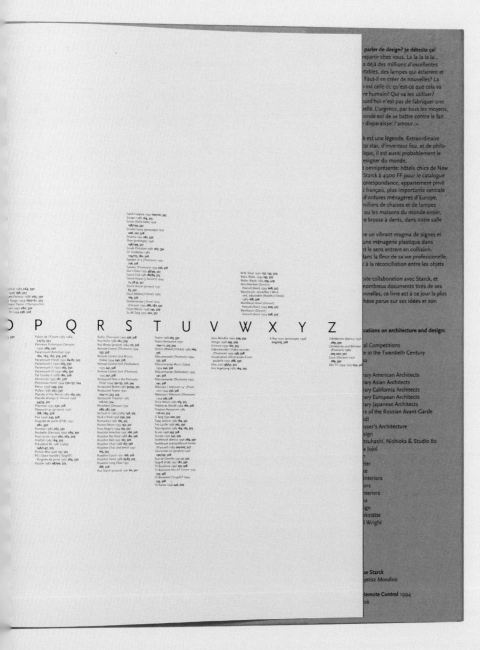

Making text look right

Beauty is in the eye of the beholder, and whether a book or magazine 'looks good' is, to a large extent, a matter of taste. But beyond personal preferences, it is certainly possible to recognise quality; to get a feel of whether a piece of text is harmoniously set, to pick out typesetting flaws (and correct them), to notice whether a text looks bland because that is what the designers wanted, or because they never looked beyond the default settings and fonts beginning with 'A'.

'The devil is the details,' the architect Mies van der Rohe is reported to have said – and although the details will not be noticed by everyone, any professional who deals with the shaping of text should be sensitive to them. There are several factors on which the appeal, functionality and accessibility of a piece of (typo-)graphic design may depend:

- **Text formatting** Choice of type and body size in relation to other decisions: column width; various levels of headlines; appearance of secondary texts such as introductions, pull quotes, footnotes and captions.

- **Paragraph formatting** Line length in relationship to line spacing (leading) and body size; indents and outdents; alignment (left, right, centred, justified); word spacing, etc.

- **Microtypography** The fine art of adjusting each devilish detail to achieve typographic excellence on the smallest level.

In this chapter we will gradually zoom in on the details that make a text hum.

Book jacket and detail of a page from *Unconcealed: The International Network of Conceptual Artists 1967–77 – Dealers, Exhibitions and Public Collections* by Sophie Richard. Designer Mark Thomson used only one type family, Arnhem by Fred Smeijers, to set a complex book full of footnotes, lists and tables, creating clarity and articulation by painstakingly fine-tuning point sizes, weights, numeral styles, column widths and line lengths.

paper drawings, *Relaxing. From Walking, Viewing, Relaxing* (1970). The artists performed a 'Living Sculpture' during the opening.[45]

Fischer first met Gilbert & George at the opening of *When Attitudes Become Form* at the ICA, London, in September 1969.[46] The artists performed an informal 'Living Sculpture' at the opening; at the end of the evening Fischer asked them to show with him.[47] The dealer first arranged performances elsewhere in Germany to build their reputation before their show in Düsseldorf.[48] Gilbert & George performed the *Singing Sculpture* during Prospect 69 (September–October 1969), although not as part of the official programme.[49] Their work was also included in *Konzeption/Conception* in Leverkusen (October–November 1969) and in *between 4* at the Kunsthalle Düsseldorf (February 1970).[50] Thus Gilbert & George's work had already been presented in various contexts that associated them with Conceptual art before their first solo show with Fischer in Düsseldorf.

between two official exhibitions. See: Jürgen Harten (ed.), *25 Jahre Kunsthalle Düsseldorf*, Städtische Kunsthalle, Düsseldorf, 1992, unnumbered pages. See also the recent exhibition *between 1969–73 in der Kunsthalle Düsseldorf, Chronik einer Nicht-Ausstellung* at the Kunsthalle in Düsseldorf from 27 January to 9 April 2007.

51 See: Database 3, Section Gilbert & George (Appendix 1.3).

52 *Gilbert & George, Art Notes and Thoughts*, Art & Project, Amsterdam, 12–23 May 1970. See: *Art & Project Bulletin*, no.20, 1 March 1970. This bulletin was sent from Tokyo because Art & Project temporarily moved their activities to Japan from February to April 1970. Via their bulletin, the gallery functioned as easily in Tokyo as in Amsterdam.

53 *Gilbert & George, Underneath the Arches, Singing Sculpture,*

Galerie Heiner Friedrich, Munich, 14 May 1970. See the organised by Heiner Friedrich, in Urbaschek, *Dia Art Fo op. cit.*, p.233.

54 Letter from Fischer to Gilbert & George dated 15 D in Korrespondenz mit Künstlern 1969–70, AKFGD.

55 *Idea Structures*, Camden Arts Centre, London, 24 J 1970. Artists: Arnatt, Burgin, Herring, Kosuth, Atkinson Baldwin and Hurrell.

56 Charles Harrison (ed.), *Idea Structures* (exh. cat.), S Borough of Camden, London, 1970.

57 *Art-Language*, vol.1, no.2, February 1970 (contribu Atkinson, Bainbridge, Baldwin, Barthelme, Brown-Dav Hirons, Hurrell, Kosuth, McKenna, Ramsden and Thom

Typographic evil

'Type crimes', 'typographic sins', 'things you should never do with type': judging by the books, websites and meticulously silkscreened posters dedicated to the horrors of imperfection in type-setting and layout, typographers must be an intolerant bunch. And to a degree, they are. They care about detail, and in their zeal to convince the world of its importance, they sometimes lose sight of the bigger picture. Many graphic designers who are less obsessed with the finer points of typography and prefer concentrating on concept and communication simply shrug, ignoring the admonishments about inverted apostrophes and missed opportunities for ligaturing, and get on with their work. Admittedly, they do get the odd apostrophe wrong at times.

Etiquette

So how important is typographic correctness really, and how unforgivable are those crimes against the 'laws' of typography? One way to look at typographic rules (most of which are more like conventions or habits) is as a kind of etiquette. In many countries, people take off their shoes when they enter a private home. This is regarded as polite, and it is also practical: less dirt, less wear. In other countries, taking off your shoes at a first visit may be seen as disrespectful. No lives will be lost if those habits are ignored, but it may be regarded as boorish, and so it's good to be aware of the local etiquette. It is always more sensible to break a rule for a reason than to do it out of ignorance. Of course, just like rules in etiquette, some conventions and habits make more sense than others from a functional, practical or aesthetic point of view.

This author does not necessarily agree with all the typographic 'laws' advocated on the afore-mentioned silkscreened posters. But several of the ones cited here definitely make sense. On the following pages you'll find a few arguments in favour of good typographic manners – as well as some valid reasons for trespassing.

Don't mix up straight marks and 'smart quotes' or apostrophes. Pay attention to international habits. → p. 136

Don't use an opening quote or 'inverted comma' instead of an apostrophe. → p. 136

Observe the differences between hyphens, en dashes and em dashes. → p. 137

The rule: Never use **MULTIPLE WAYS OF EMPHASIZING!** The reality: it used to be seen as silly, but became fashionable a decade ago.

The rule: Prevent ascenders and descenders from touching! Spiekermann's advice: It is a rule that allows for exceptions. → p. 127

The rule: Eliminate orphans and widows. The practice: single words or half lines at the top of a column or page are disturbing; a single word on a bottom line, less so. → p. 123

Never try to adjust lines by squeezing or stretching the tracking. Go for the subtle solution: adjust word space instead. → p. 123

Don't combine small caps with lining figures, or all-caps with old-style figures. → p. 138

Do not create pseudo italics/bold/small caps. ← p. 68 → p. 132

The rule: Never stretch or compress type! The reality: it usually looks dumb or blunt, but in the hands of a master it can be an effective stylistic trick. → p. 172

Use real fractions when available. Know your dots and commas in foreign languages. → p. 139

Avoid proportional figures in calculations or financial listings. Don't make a mess of your tables. Use tabular figures. → p. 138–139

Government "shocked" by new details.

The summer of '87

Works 1965-1998

I feel so GREAT!!!

Party People!

...ut there is no greater mistake than to suppose that a man who is a calculating criminal, is, in any phase of his guilt, otherwise than true to himself, and perfectly consistent with his whole character. Such a man commits murder; this is the natural culmination of his course; such a man will outface murder with hardihood and effrontery.

Such a man will commit murder, and murder is the natural culmination of his course; such a man has to outface murder, and he will do it with hardihood and effrontery. It is a sort of fashion to express

CRIMES COMMITTED IN 1998
CRIMES COMMITTED IN 1998

Having such CRIME upon his conscience, can so brave it out.

fashion VICTIM

Pour 1/2 pint of milk
Utilisez 0.5 litre de lait

```
 156
4238
7900
+ 211
```

Formatting the paragraph

Although the choice of the font is an important factor, the look and readability of a text depend largely on decisions taken on the paragraph level – on choices regarding type size, alignment, line width and line spacing (=leading).

It is virtually impossible to provide specific values for leading or line width. The 'ideal' solution depends on a complex interplay between the characteristics of the typeface (size, width, x-height, overall clarity), word spacing, column width and more. In a program like InDesign, the default setting for auto leading is 120% of the type size, which means that at 10pt type size the leading (more precisely: the baseline shift) is 12pt. Yet most typefaces look better with some extra leading. When the typeface has a large x-height, the 'Auto' value is certainly not ideal.

Line length

Lines should not be too long: the reader's eye may have difficulty finding the beginning of the next line, especially when linespacing is tight.

Contrarily, very short lines offer little flexibility for adjusting word space especially in justified texts, which may result in white 'holes' appearing between words, or in excessive hyphenation.

As a crude rule of thumb, 45 to 70 characters per line are good average widths for paragraphs with not much extra leading. For multi-column layouts like the present one, narrower columns are appropriate – say, 35 to 55 characters per line.

Een letter heeft twee soorten tegenvorm: de ruimte binnen en de ruimte tussen de letters. Ervaren letterontwerpers proberen iedere mogelijke combinatie van twee letters te voorzien en te zorgen dat de verhouding tussen vorm en tegenvormen harmonieus is. Het doel is niet om een

Chaparral 9/9

Een letter heeft twee soorten tegenvorm: de ruimte binnen en de ruimte tussen de letters. Ervaren letterontwerpers proberen iedere mogelijke combinatie van twee letters te voorzien en te zorgen dat de verhouding tussen vorm en tegenvormen

Chaparral 9/10,8 (Auto)

Een letter heeft twee soorten tegenvorm: de ruimte binnen en de ruimte tussen de letters. Ervaren letterontwerpers proberen iedere mogelijke combinatie van twee letters te voorzien en te zorgen dat de ver-

Chaparral 9/14

Een letter heeft twee soorten tegenvorm: de ruimte binnen en de ruimte tussen de letters. Ervaren letterontwerpers proberen iedere mogelijke combinatie van twee letters

PMN Caecilia 7/11

Een letter heeft twee soorten tegenvorm: de ruimte binnen en de ruimte tussen de letters. Ervaren letterontwerpers proberen iedere mogelijke combinatie van twee letters

FF Seria 10/11

↑ Changing the leading at a fixed point size changes the typographic colour of the text – the denser the line spacing, the 'darker' the colour. '9/12' means: 9pt type size at 12pt baseline shift i.e. with 3pt leading.

↖ As we've seen before, Caecilia and Seria have very different x-heights. This implies that a relative line spacing of only 110%, which works well for Seria, would never do for Caecilia. Not only does Caecilia need a relatively small point size for text settings, it also needs generous leading.

Een letter heeft twee soorten tegenvorm: de ruimte binnen en de ruimte tussen de letters. Ervaren letterontwerpers proberen elke mogelijke combinatie van twee letters te voorzien, en te zorgen dat de verhouding tussen vorm en tegenvormen harmonieus is. Dat is voor de gebruiker van die letters een goede reden om bewust en zorgvuldig met letterspatiëring om te gaan.

Helvetica Neue 8/11

← Three examples of long lines. The first block has around 100 characters per line, which makes for strenuous reading in longer texts as the eye has difficulty finding the beginning of the next line. In the second sample, a line width of 80+ characters is compensated for in two ways: by choosing a bolder and wider font and by adding extra leading. The third sample uses Bell Gothic, a rather narrow sans-serif. It works because the type is large, and the line spacing is generous.

Een letter heeft twee soorten tegenvorm: de ruimte binnen en de ruimte tussen de letters. Ervaren letterontwerpers proberen iedere mogelijke combinatie van twee letters te voorzien, en te zorgen dat de verhouding tussen vorm en tegenvormen harmonieus is. Dat een goede reden om bewust om

Helvetica Neue Bold 8.5/15

Een letter heeft twee soorten tegenvorm: de ruimte binnen en de ruimte tussen de letters. Ervaren letterontwerpers proberen iedere mogelijke combinatie van twee letters te voorzien, en te zorgen dat de verhouding tussen vorm en tegenvormen harmonieus is.

Bell Gothic 10.5/18

Playing with line length, distance and density

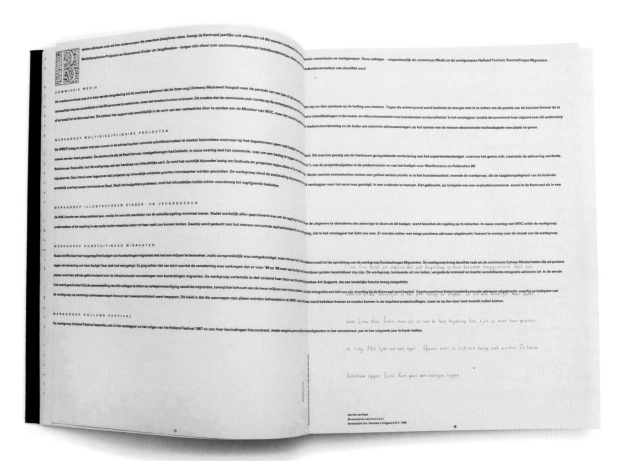

↗ Extremely long lines in a design by Irma Boom. This is acceptable because the texts are short, the type is dark in colour and the line spacing is generous. Besides, the audience (the addressees of the Annual Report of the Dutch Arts Council) were part of an elite that was interested in experiments.

→ Negative linespacing (i.e. a baseline shift that is smaller than the body size of the typeface) is impossible in typesetting with physical metal or wooden letters. Digital production has now made this possible. Designs by Pierre Vincent, Paris, France, and Stéphane De Schrevel, Ghent, Belgium.

Alignment

↓ In justified text the remaining word space in each line is evenly divided between the words. The example has been deliberately exaggerated: it has more gaps than necessary. Below, the same paragraph, flush left. The word space is always the same, resulting in a more even text but an irregular column shape, ragged right.

Een letter heeft twee soorten tegenvormen: de ruimte binnen en de ruimte tussen de letters. Ervaren letterontwerpers trachten iedere mogelijke combinatie van twee letters te voorzien en te zorgen dat de verhouding tussen vorm en tegenvorm

Een letter heeft twee soorten tegenvormen: de ruimte binnen en de ruimte tussen de letters. Ervaren letterontwerpers trachten iedere mogelijke combinatie van twee letters te voorzien en te zorgen dat de verhouding tussen vorm en tegenvorm

↓ Hand-lettered title page designed by Boudewijn Ietswaart. The centred layout, in combination with the Roman numerals, lend the page a tongue-in-cheek classicist atmosphere that befits the book's memoire-like character.

IsaacFaro
DE KNAGENDE
WORM
Uit de papieren *van*
Jacobus
NACHTEGAAL
Œ
Q
AMSTERDAM
Em. Querido's Uitgeverij n.v.
MCMLXIV

A paragraph of text can be set *justified* – as a solid rectangle – or *ranged left* (also known as *flush left* or *ragged right*). All other settings are the exception rather than the rule, which is not to say that there can't be good reasons to set a particular piece of text ranged right, centred or in a shape of your choice.

Justified setting

Justified setting (ranged left and right) was the default procedure in letterpress. A logical choice, as the text area had to be firmly adjusted within the 'forme', and a rectangle was the most stable unit for this. Justified setting is still the norm in texts for immersive reading (such as novels).

In order to create a justified paragraph or text block (i.e. ranged left as well as right), the width of the word spaces will be different in each line, but equal within one line.

This becomes clear when comparing a justified paragraph with the the same text set ranged left: the remaining white space at the end of each line varies, while in a justified setting this space must be distributed between the words. In short lines especially this can lead to annoying irregularities, gaps and, when various gaps occur in consecutive lines, *rivers* of white space running through the text, see opposite page.

Centred text

There is nothing inherently wrong with centred text. As with ragged right or fully-justified text alignment, what works for one design might be totally inappropriate for another. There are simply fewer situations where centred text is appropriate. Longer settings of centred text are harder for the reader because the starting position of each new line changes.

When in doubt, don't centre it. It lends a formal appearance to text, which is why it is often used in formal wedding invitations, certificates and on plaques.

Justified

Ranged left / flush left

Ranged right / flush right

Centred

Irregular

Hyphenation & justification

Justified text is easily generated by the computer, but it needs the human eye to make necessary corrections. The type has to be checked paragraph by paragraph to find irregularities and other chances for improvement.

Hyphenate and justify

Layout applications such as InDesign and Quark XPress allow the user to optimize typesetting using the control panels for justification and hyphenation. With more compact word spacing, there's less risk of visible gaps in the text. Compact setting is a matter of exploring where the limits are – below a certain minimum value, words stick together.

The other key to good typesetting is a sensible hyphenation policy. Rules for hyphenation can be set in the program, but some manual final processing is always recommended.

- Try to avoid a sequence of more than two hyphenated words.
- No hyphenation dictionary is complete or error-free. Watch out for weird proposals, especially when foreign words pop up.
- Select those word breaks that make most sense considering the meaning: type-setter is preferable to typeset-ter.
- Try to avoid hyphenating names.
- Check that the right language and dictionary are selected for the text at hand.

Family affairs

Widows and *orphans* are single words or groups of words separated and isolated from the rest of their paragraph. There is some confusion and contradiction as to which is which.

- The last word(s) of a paragraph at the top of the next page (this is usually called a *widow*).
- A single word on the last line of a paragraph.
- The first line of a new paragraph at the bottom of a page.

Of these dramas, only the first results in an objectively annoying layout flaw – the other two are often tolerable. Widows and orphans can be removed by adjusting word spacing and hyphenation, and forcing line breaks. In extreme cases, text edits can be proposed to the editor or author.

The punchcutter begins his work of practical design by drawing a geometrical framework on which he determines the proper position of every line and the height of each character. A small

of the face to prevent the touching of a descending letter against an ascending letter in the next line, as well as to prevent the wear of exposed lines cut

↑ The wordspacing in this justified column is too loose, resulting in gaps that distract the eye. In last six lines additional tracking (letterspacing) has been used to justify the text – resulting in a text image that is even more distracting.

The punchcutter begins his work of practical design by drawing a geometrical framework on which he determines the proper position of every line and the height of each character. A small margin

of the face to prevent the touching of a descending letter against an ascending letter in the next line, as well as to prevent the wear of exposed lines cut flush to an edge

↑ In this column, lower word spacing values have been set, resulting in a more compact setting with no conspicuous gaps. In the long run, it will save space as well. Letterspacing is set to zero.

	Minimum	Desired	Maximum
Word spacing:	85%	100%	133%
Letter spacing:	0%	0%	0%
Glyph scaling:	100%	100%	100%

↑ Layout programs allow users to set the limit values for spacing. Always set letterspacing to zero. For most fonts, setting the 'Desired' word spacing to a somewhat lower value than the default 100% is a good idea; in unjustified text settings the program observes only the 'Desired' value. Also, the idea to allow for variations in glyph scaling is simply ludicrous. Always set to 100%.

L'ipotesi dell'omonimia non è però da scartare senz'altro; né deve impressionare troppo, perché il fenomeno non è certo infrequente nel Trecento: si conoscono, ad esempio, un Dante Alighieri padre di un Gabriello e un Dantino Alighieri di poco posteriore al poeta. Anche ammettendo un terzo Dante Alighieri, è assai improbabile che ciò generi confusioni rilevanti nella biografia del poeta, perché bisognerebbe

← From line five, this fragment shows spaces lining up in five consecutive lines, causing a so-called *river* to flow through the text. Re-flow by adjusting a line break or by subtly adjusting word spacing a few lines above.

Distinguishing sections and paragraphs

Most texts of some length are divided into paragraphs. If a sentence expresses a single coherent thought, then a paragraph represents a string of these thoughts, often with an internal resolution. A paragraph can be several sentences long or, increasingly in online contexts, just one sentence.

It is helpful if readers notice that a new paragraph is beginning. They can be alerted to this in various ways, but the most common method for immersive reading is the first-line indent. The paragraph you are now reading lacks an indent. In this case it is not a problem because the preceding line is very short – but if the line is fuller, the beginning of the next paragraph may happen unnoticed.

So if indenting is a good idea, how large is the ideal indent? It can be done with restraint; a common solution is to use a space roughly equal to the em – the point size of the font used.

For a more pronounced effect, using an indent equal to the leading height will create a neat square at the start of the paragraph. In longer line lengths, more generous or exaggerated indents can be used – turning this practical device into a stylish design element.

The type of text being set will determine what strategies are appropriate for marking paragraphs. We've explored a few on these two pages, but many more possibilities exist.

First-line indent

The most common method, suitable for extended immersive reading in books and journals as well as the shorter line lengths found in newspapers and magazines.

Line break

Line breaks or white line spaces between paragraphs are the norm in correspondence – letters and emails – and increasingly in web pages, where a long block of continuous text is considered off-putting to the user.

Running indent

Setting a whole paragraph deeper than the preceding and following paragraphs marks it out for special attention. If this text is a long quote, the type size is usually one or two points smaller.

Outdent

A more dramatic way to mark a new paragraph would be to extend the first line outside the main text block.

Paragraph marks

An unusual but surprisingly old method to mark a new paragraph without starting a new line is by inserting some sign. This could be any *dingbat,* or a short coloured bar or, as shown here, the traditional paragraph mark: the *pilcrow.*

---

lijk merkwaardig dat hij zo gespannen liep te zoeken naar een ventje, waar hij nog maar zo kort achteraan gelopen had. Anderzijds was hij nu ernstig ongerust wat het eten betreft.

Op de vestibule sloot een restaurant aan, dat propvol geur was. Aan bijna alle tafeltjes zaten mensen bedreven te kauwen. Dian liep er met grote passen langs, maar niemand gaf hem iets. Af en toe werd er door luidsprekers geschreeuwd en dan stonden van sommige tafeltjes ineens mensen op, die maakten dat ze wegkwamen.

Er was een kind dat Dian aan een papieren servetje liet ruiken, wat hij langdurig bleef doen.

Het station was in vol bedrijf. De onverstaanbare stemmen van de luidsprekers plonsden rukkerig in het gewoel en het benenwoud reageerde op rauwe kreten die doorgaans getallen inhielden. Kleine stoeten trokken soms één richting uit, maar het woud vulde zich onophoudelijk aan door de draaideuren, als het zich op die manier had uitgezeefd.

Waar ruikt het woud naar? De straat, de huizen en kaas; damp van auto's, soms naar een hond ineens en onmiskenbaar, maar drukkend en met walm schuivend vooral naar mensen. Naar mensen en hun geslacht, dat ze meevoeren op reis. O zo gehoorzaam aan achttien uur zeven en veertig, vierde; achttien acht en vijftig, zevende.

Dian heeft honger. Ontstellend. Hij is het ventje vergeten, maar soms staat hij opnieuw bij de draaideur, die het woud aanzuivert. Hij is er héén doorgelopen, maar men laat

68

← Experimenting with indentation. In his typography of Anton Koolhaas's book *A shot in the air* (1962 Dutch Book Week Gift) designer Charles Jongejans specified indents the same length as the previous line, minus (approximately) an em. He allowed for exceptions; in this page, for instance, the first full paragraph follows a filled line and is therefore 'normally' indented.

Initials

Initial capitals are enlarged characters usually found at the beginning of a chapter or section. Their use results in a looser and more decorative design and a slightly old-fashioned look and feel. An initial can be set in the same font as the main text, but it can also be a way to bring color and decoration to an otherwise plain page. Even a dry technical manual can be made more attractive by a large initial capital in a different colour.

It is customary to place initials on a baseline of the main text; if they are 'built in' (*drop caps*) it may be a good idea to adjust the size by hand to optically align the top with the main text. A technique to create a natural transition from the initial capital to the main text is to set a few words in small caps, as Marian Bantjes did in the example shown on the right.

Make sure that the enlarged character is not repeated in the first word.

↑ Mediaeval manuscripts were often status symbols, whose cost and value depended in part on the ingenuity and beauty of the illumination. Initials were an excuse to indulge in lush ornamentation. Early printed books such as Gutenberg's bible, shown here, imitated the hand-written book. As coloured illuminations could not yet be reproduced, it was up to the owner of the printed book to commission artists to fill the white spaces left open for initials.

↓ Detail from Marian Bantjes's book *I Wonder*. This article is about stars; its design was inspired by the celestial-themed jewelry used in a 150-foot timeline of the universe at the Griffith Observatory in Los Angeles. The design of the piece ties in with one of the book's themes – our need to honour contents by decorating it. And as we just saw, a sumptuous initial is one of the most effective and oldest ways to honour a text.

B Drop caps are normally aligned to the top of the first line and stand on one of the subsequent lines. Adjust the initial's height manually by adjusting its point size.

W Drop caps are usually nested in a rectangle, but not always. They can be allowed to protrude from the main text; some typographers let the text wrap around the shape of an 'A', 'O', 'V' or 'W'.

K Raised caps stand on the baseline of the first line. Ensure that the rest of the letters of the first word are spaced so that it remains legible.

Y Hanging initials allow for a more theatrical approach: the initial cap may occupy the entire height of the column; and the typeface or hand-lettering can be ornamental or illustrative.

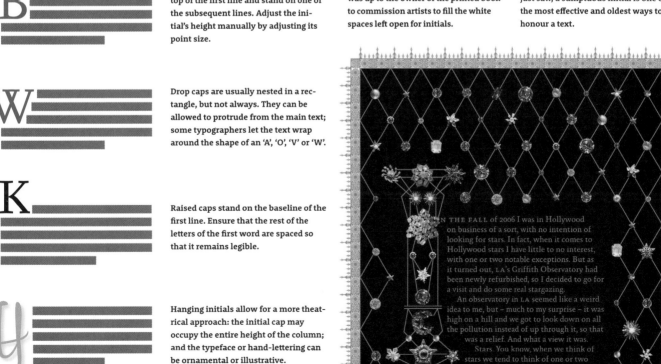

Letter and word, black and white

Whoever designs something to be placed in an environment contributes to the design of that environment itself as well. Buildings, furniture and accessories all have two forms: their shape, and the space they enclose or help to define: a street, an entrance hall, a cosy sitting area, a car interior – the *counterform*.

In graphic design, something similar happens. In the layout of a book, poster or web page, the *negative space* between the elements is as crucial to the reading and viewing experience as the (positive) texts and images themselves.

On the level of words, sentences and paragraphs the tension between form and counterform plays a decisive role. Typographers often speak of *black* and *white*: the black of the letter, the white of the page. These don't literally have to be black and white – they can be coloured, too. And when the text is reversed (light on a dark background or image) then the 'white' of the letter is the darkest colour.

Some specialists are convinced that it is not the text itself but its negative space that helps us most to identify letterforms. Many type designers have stated that when drawing letters they are usually not looking at the black shapes. What they actually design is the white shapes that are enclosed within these forms.

In an interview with the present writer, American type designer Cyrus Highmith related that his mother, a painter, taught him to look at counterforms. 'The lesson came one day when I was frustrated that my drawings of trees never really looked like trees. They just looked like a bunch of lines. I could not get a feel of the shape or structure of a tree. She taught me to draw the shapes between the branches instead of the branches themselves. When you do that, you quickly come a lot closer to actually drawing something that resembles a tree. When I am drawing letters I use the same approach. I am drawing the white shapes, not the black strokes.'

Each letter has two counterforms: the space within, and the space it shares with the preceding and the next letter. Experienced type designers try out every possible combination of two letters to make sure that the relationship between form and counterform is always harmonious. For the users of these fonts, that is a good reason to treat the letterspacing with caution and respect.

The balance between black and white shapes of the same form is a basic principle of Japanese graphic art – *no-tan*, light and dark. The famous yin-yang circle illustrates this principle: each part is what the other is not.

The white of the word

A piece of text looks most harmonious when the space *between* the letters is tailored to the space *inside* the letters. This implies – and to some designers this may be a surprise – that thin letters look better when a bit further apart, and bold ones look better in a tight setting. When a typeface is well-designed, this has been taken into account. When used normally, no further correction (kerning) is needed. One exception: if a normal or light text face is used at a large size, then the distance may be too large and some negative tracking might help improve the word image. See the next page.

Mengvorm

Mengvorm

→ In their teachings at the Royal Academy of Arts in The Hague (KABK) the painter Hermanus Berserik and the typographer Gerrit Noordzij used a playful system to teach students to look at the white of the letterforms. The shapes of letters were constructed with pieces cut quickly from white paper.

Fine-tuning headlines

When setting display type, the default settings can (and sometimes must) be tweaked to obtain the best result. Lines in all-caps – which have no extenders – can be set very tight: the leading can be inferior to the point size. This may even work with lowercase – see below.

There is a rule saying descenders and ascenders must never touch.

There is an exception to this rule: touching is allowed if it looks better.

MONDAY I'VE GOT FRIDAY ON MY MIND.

MONDAY I'VE GOT FRIDAY ON MY MIND.

← Wisdom from Erik Spiekermann. The quote is from his 1987 'typographic novel' *Rhyme & reason*. The typeface is Spiekermann's revival of the 1914 Louis Oppenheim original Lo-Type.

↓ Fonts designed for a broad range of sizes usually have their letterspacing optimised for use at c. 12–24pt body size. At smaller sizes, some subtle extra tracking may help readability. At large display sizes, some negative kerning helps to tie the word together. The font is Museo Slab 100.

↑ Taz UltraBlack and Taz UltraLight by Luc(as) de Groot. Both faces are shown here at standard setting, with no adjustments to the tracking: De Groot made the lighter weight's letterspacing a lot looser to match the inner counterforms. These all-caps settings allow for lines to be stacked with very little leading, although the light weight needs some more linespacing than the heavy one to match the horizontal spacing. At 40pt size, UltraBlack has 30.5pt leading, while 40pt UltraLight looks better with 37pt leading.

Living in space
7pt, +20 units

Living in space
11pt, +6 units

Living in space
18pt, standard spacing

Living in space
36pt, -5 units

Living in space
48pt, -10 units

Living in space
60pt, -20 units

Spacing: tracking and kerning

In a font, the space between letters is controlled in two ways. The *tracking* sets the default spacing between letters, each letter existing within its own free area (the *bounding box*). Therefore, in many combinations of letters there is a well-balanced distance from the preceding character to the next. But not always! In a surprising number of combinations, the type designer still has to tinker with the distance between two letters. This is done with *kerning*. Most fonts contain hundreds, even thousands, of kerning pairs – letter combinations generated in part automatically and sometimes by hand to achieve the best optical result. These kerning tables are part of any sophisticated typeface designer's *font metrics*.

→ Even something that seems as objective in principle as tracking is still subject to trends and fashion. Magazine adverts of the late '70s and early '80s are notable for their extremely tight letter spacing. 'Tight, not touching' was the adage often heard in art direction departments, even though in many cases the setting was so tight that letters *were* indeed touching if not actually colliding.

Each glyph has its own 'free zone' – its bounding box. Kerning set at 0 in the character controls will override both the font's metrics and any optical kerning used by the software, causing the setting to default to the unsophisticated tracking defined by those free zones.

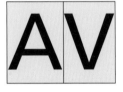 

Metric kerning uses the pairs the font designer has specified in the kerning table, created either by hand or automatically in the font design software.

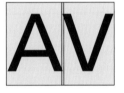 

Page layout and typesetting software such as InDesign have their own optical kerning features, which should only be used when a font's kerning is faulty. It often sets text tighter than the metrics established by the type designer.

Improving kerning

When using a carefully designed font, the rule of thumb for tracking is: don't change the standard setting – in other words, trust the font's metrics.

If there are indications that a font has not been well kerned, then there are three options. If a font's overall letterspacing is too tight (this does happen), make a paragraph style with a bit of extra tracking. To correct small bits of text, layout programs like InDesign have a rather intelligent 'optical' kerning function. Select the text and check 'Optical' in the Control Panel. If that doesn't improve matters, then use your eyes. With the cursor inserted between two letters, choose better kerning values for any weak pair.

↓ When a word is set in a combination of letters from two different fonts, the kerning pairs won't work and the user must correct manually – especially if the point sizes differ as well.

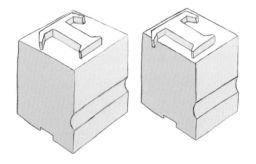

← Kerning has become a general term for adjusting the spacing between two individual letters. In cold metal typesetting the word had a more specific meaning: a kerned letter was a letter of which the face protruded from the body and rested on the next letter's body in order to avoid awkward gaps between the two letters.

Adjusting optical alignment

Please remove all your unused BICYCLES as soon as pos

26pt **Please remove all your unused**

29pt **BICYCLES**

24pt **as soon as possible**

Sometimes software is smart, sometimes less so. When shaping text, it is seldom a good idea to accept blindly what the computer proposes. A pair of trained eyes is the perfect complementary tool. Here are some ways to improve on the defaults by trusting what you see.

Vertical alignment

↑ A block of display text set in a single font at a constant point size (this is 24pt Helvetica Condensed) does not necessarily look best with the same leading value for each line. If the letters in a line are optically higher, for instance because it contains several ascenders or words set in all-caps, then it is no crime to tweak the linespacing a bit until a better result is achieved.

Horizontal alignment

→ When a headline contains punctuation marks such as dots, commas, dashes and quotation marks, optical correction is a must. In centred text, the layout software will include the punctuation when calculating the middle of lines, while the eye mainly takes the text itself into account. To restore the balance, try setting the 'naked' text first, then copy the frame on top of itself and add punctuation while keeping the text in the same position. When using InDesign, its 'Optical margin alignment' function (well hidden in the Story palette) may also help.

Aligning margins

→ In many fonts, especially sans-serifs, there is a small space between the left edge of the frame and the first letter – notably when the left side of the letter consists of a straight vertical stroke. In small or long texts this gap is inconspicuous and even helps in creating a harmonious left margin, but if successive display lines are set in very different point sizes, shifts may occur. Some manual correction is called for. Use separate frames or insert a space with negative value.

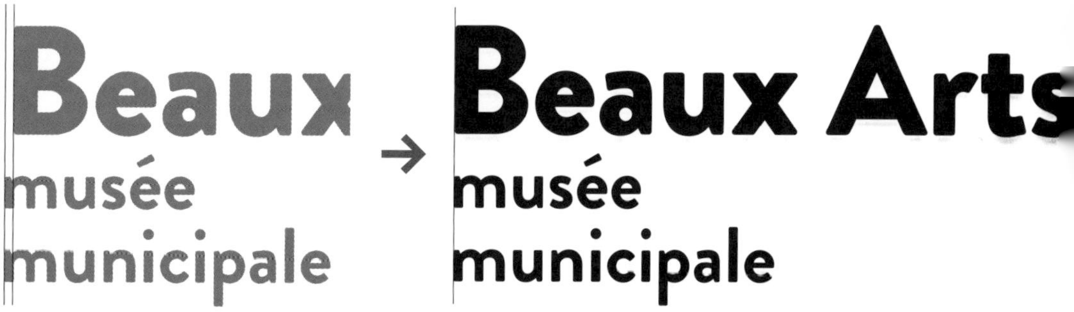

'You should believe me' → You should believe me → 'You should believe me'

Where could she be... → Where could she be → Where could she be...

Beaux musée municipale → Beaux Arts musée municipale

OpenType functions and features

As we've seen (← p. 65), the obsolete digital font formats PostScript Type 1 and TrueType have gradually been replaced by one universal font format, OpenType. Although the standard has been in use since 2001, most type foundries have needed a lot of time to convert their old fonts to OpenType, and many still aren't done. Today, ten years later, most distributors still have a lot of fonts with the old structure on offer. Converting typefaces into OpenType usually implies a lot of work beyond the simple technical task of changing the format – the new standard offers many new possibilities that foundries cannot ignore.

Unfathomable

Many users find the implications of OpenType hard to fathom. This is, at least in part, the fault of the people who make and market the design and word processing software in which these fonts are used. Microsoft's Office suite still ignores most OpenType features; and in Adobe programs such as InDesign, many features are hidden deeply within palettes and submenus. And these, mind you, are the two companies that jointly developed the OpenType standard.

Here are some key OpenType characteristics:

● **Platform-independent** The same font will work on Windows, Mac and Linux. In the past, each platform had its own fonts – although since the advent of Mac OS X, TrueType works well on both Mac and Windows systems.
● **Room for expert characters** An OpenType font can contain all the special characters that used to be contained in separate 'expert fonts': small caps, ligatures, decorative capitals, alternate letters, various types of figures, dingbats and more.
● **All languages in a single font** OpenType fonts can accommodate 65,535 glyphs, including diacritics (accented characters) for all languages that use the Latin script, as well as other scripts such as Greek, Cyrillic, Arabic and Chinese.
● **Unicode** OpenType fonts are based on Unicode; each sign has its fixed position and name. See opposite page.

Working with OpenType

When a typeface is marketed as an OT font, this does not necessarily mean that it comes with any OpenType features. It may simply be a converted PostScript font with little or nothing new added. But it may also be chock full of special characters and offer 'advanced OpenType functionality', in which case it is programmed to perform typographical tasks to facilitate and partially automate the typographer's work. But the advent of OpenType has also brought with it new kinds of errors. If, for instance, you hope to activate small caps at the push of a button and your font doesn't include any, your layout program will automatically generate ugly, 'fake' small capitals. You need to train your eye to spot those.

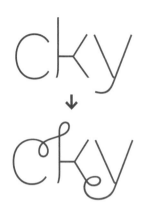

Activating Discretionary Ligatures in Brownstone Sans Thin from Sudtipos.

OpenType some features and functions

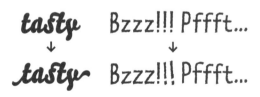

Automatic glyph substitution

In certain character combinations chosen by the type designer, the individual glyphs are replaced by specially designed combinations. The font is Covergirl by Trine Rask.

- -

Contextual glyph substitution

Here, too, glyphs are automatically replaced; but how and where depends on the context. This function enables complex typographic constructions, including the simulation of hand-lettering. In a different use, a font like Kosmik loops through a number of variants of each letter, so that no two identical characters ever stand side by side.

Bello: beginning and end characters

Kosmik: Alternating versions of each glyph

- -

Stylistic sets

Some OpenType fonts contain multiple stylistic variations of a number of characters, which may significantly alter the atmosphere of the font; sometimes complete alternative alphabets are included. These stylistic variants can be activated by checking off one or more Stylistic Sets in the OpenType palette.

Pluto: limited set of alternates

Studio Lettering Slant: 'national' variants

● more on OpenType → p. 135 ff

Unicode: mapping the world... once more

The characters of a font are stored in the computer as numbers: each character has its own code. Until recently there existed separate encoding standards to structure character sets for each computer platform and language – dozens of systems used in parallel, resulting in chaos and, when exchanging files between various platforms, in messages being mangled and misunderstood. In order to address this Babel-like confusion and make an inventory of the languages of the world and their writing systems, a new standard was created – Unicode.

The Unicode Standard is managed by the Unicode Consortium, a non-profit organisation that evaluates and implements proposals for corrections and extensions. The standard's first version (1991) contained 7,085 characters, the second (June 1992) 28,283; twenty years later Unicode has grown to contain 109,242 signs. Unicode has now been incorporated in virtually every modern operating system, program and browser. Thanks to Unicode, data can now be transported across different systems without corruption, regardless of the hardware, programs or languages that were used to create them.

From hieroglyphs to emoticons

Unicode contains the scripts of virtually every living language, including huge systems such as Chinese ideograms and relatively obscure ones such as the script used by indigenous peoples of Canada. It also contains a number of dead scripts, like Egyptian hieroglyphics and cuneiform. Researchers appreciate these developments; when the ancient scripts they investigate are encoded, they can enter 'living text', which allows them to compare ancient documents via search functions.

Unicode accommodates non-linguistic and even somewhat frivolous systems as well. Symbols for mapping and transport; signs for chess, checkers, mah jong and domino; alchemist and astrological symbols; pictograms and emoticons: all these and more can be found in Unicode and can therefore be effortlessly transposed from one font to another – provided that these fonts contain the signs in question – and sent via e-mail, text messaging or as text files.

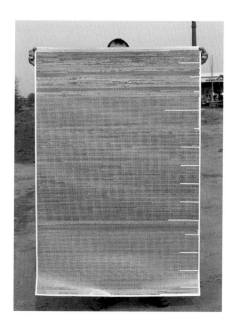

Where to find all these signs

Characters that are not on the keyboard can be entered in several ways.

- An ideal method is to use a virtual keyboard like those installed on smart phones and tablets. The signs from the script system selected in the settings appear on the keys; the computer looks for a font that contains this script.

- Macs have a Character Palette, Windows has the Character Map tool, and many graphic programs come with a Glyphs Palette in which each character in the active font is shown and can be selected.

- A character's Unicode number, if known, can be entered directly into many Windows programs by typing it while holding down the Alt key; on a Mac the same can be done by ticking off the option 'Unicode Hex Input' in the System Preferences (Language & Text) and then selecting it in the menu bar. A utility like PopChar shows which Unicode characters are available in a font and allows each sign to be entered directly into the text by clicking it.

- The decodeunicode.org website has a sophisticated and extensive search function. Finally there is shapecatcher.com, built to recognise your hand-sketched Unicode sign.

decodeunicode.org

Designer-researcher Johannes Bergerhausen of Mainz University is the initiator of 'decodeunicode.org', a project that aims to help professional and non-professional users understand Unicode from a typographic point of view. Its first publication was a poster. The first edition from 2004, shown here, contained more than 65,000 characters. The group then created a sophisticated, beautifully designed website that now (mid-2011) lists 98,884 characters, in other words, the complete Unicode 5.0 standard, along with background information on specific signs. And since 2011 there is also a book, published by Hermann Schmidt Mainz, that shows the complete collection of Unicode signs (all 109,242 of them), plus a wealth of information about languages, scripts, digital text and the development of Unicode. Most of the information on this page is based on this book.

← Character set 65
→ Alternates 135
→ Numerals 137
→ Small caps 138

Small capitals

Until the nineteenth century book designers did not have bold or sans-serif faces to set subheads, intros or fragments of special interest. All typefaces were in one basic weight (which we'd now call Regular, or Book); they only had different sizes of romans and italics to articulate the text. And they had small caps.

Small capitals have been around since the sixteenth century as tertiary type besides roman and italic. Small caps are relatively wide; they have the same height as the lowercase 'x,' or slightly higher. Their proportions are sturdier and wider than those of capitals – otherwise they would look narrow and thin. Small caps were (and are) often given generous tracking.

Small caps and OpenType

Before OpenType, small caps were accommodated in special fonts that were called 'SC' or 'Expert'. The large character maps of today's OpenType fonts have plenty of room for small caps but don't always contain them. Many typefoundries have two versions of their text faces: a standard version without small caps and other extras, and a more expensive professional version that is fully equipped.

As it is not always clear what a font contains and what it doesn't, do not assume it is all in there. When selecting Small Caps in the toolbar of the Character palette, check to see that what you get looks like real small caps (narrow and skinny = not good), or check the Glyph palette. Electronically reduced caps are seldom an acceptable alternative.

→ 'Fake' small caps, above, and real ones, below. The electronically reduced caps are skinny and narrow; the real ones are sturdy and wide and, in the case of FF Quadraat, shown here, have some built-in extra tracking.

You always wonder: ARE THEY REAL?
You always wonder: ARE THEY REAL?

Using small caps

Small caps are basically used in two ways. They substitute all-caps words and acronyms inside body text, in order not to disrupt the visual flow of the lowercase. Or they are adopted as a stylistic device to add another colour to the typographer's palette without having to add a different font. Small caps can be combined with uppercase initials, or the initials can be omitted altogether (it is important to stick to your decision throughout the text). In InDesign, the option All Small Caps allows a selected text to be set in small caps with no uppercase initials without converting the underlying text to all-lowercase first.

The opinions expressed in this publication are not necessarily those of UNESCO/IBE and do not commit the Organization.

Acronyms longer than two or three
letters are less disruptive in small caps.

FLANDERS, J.R. 1987. 'How much of the content in mathematics textbooks is new?' *Arithmetic teacher* (Reston, VA), vol. 35, P. 18–23.

Small caps for diversification in information-
rich texts such as bibliographies.

MACBETH [*aside*]
    If chance will have me king, why, chance may crown me.

In theatrical plays, the names of the
characters are traditionally set in
small caps.

A GIGOLO'S THOUGHTS ON PERFUME

Sans-serif small caps with generous
extra tracking are an elegant companion
to exuberant display and script faces.

SMALL CAPITALS HAVE BEEN AROUND since the sixteenth century as tertiary type besides roman and italic. They were relatively wide

In traditional book typography, chapters
often start with a few words in small caps.

UNFATHOMABLE Many users find the implications of OpenType hard to fathom. This is, at least in part, the fault of the people who made

Small caps in a contrasting font are a
possible way of formatting subheadings.
Use extra tracking.

Articulation and hierarchy in the 17th century

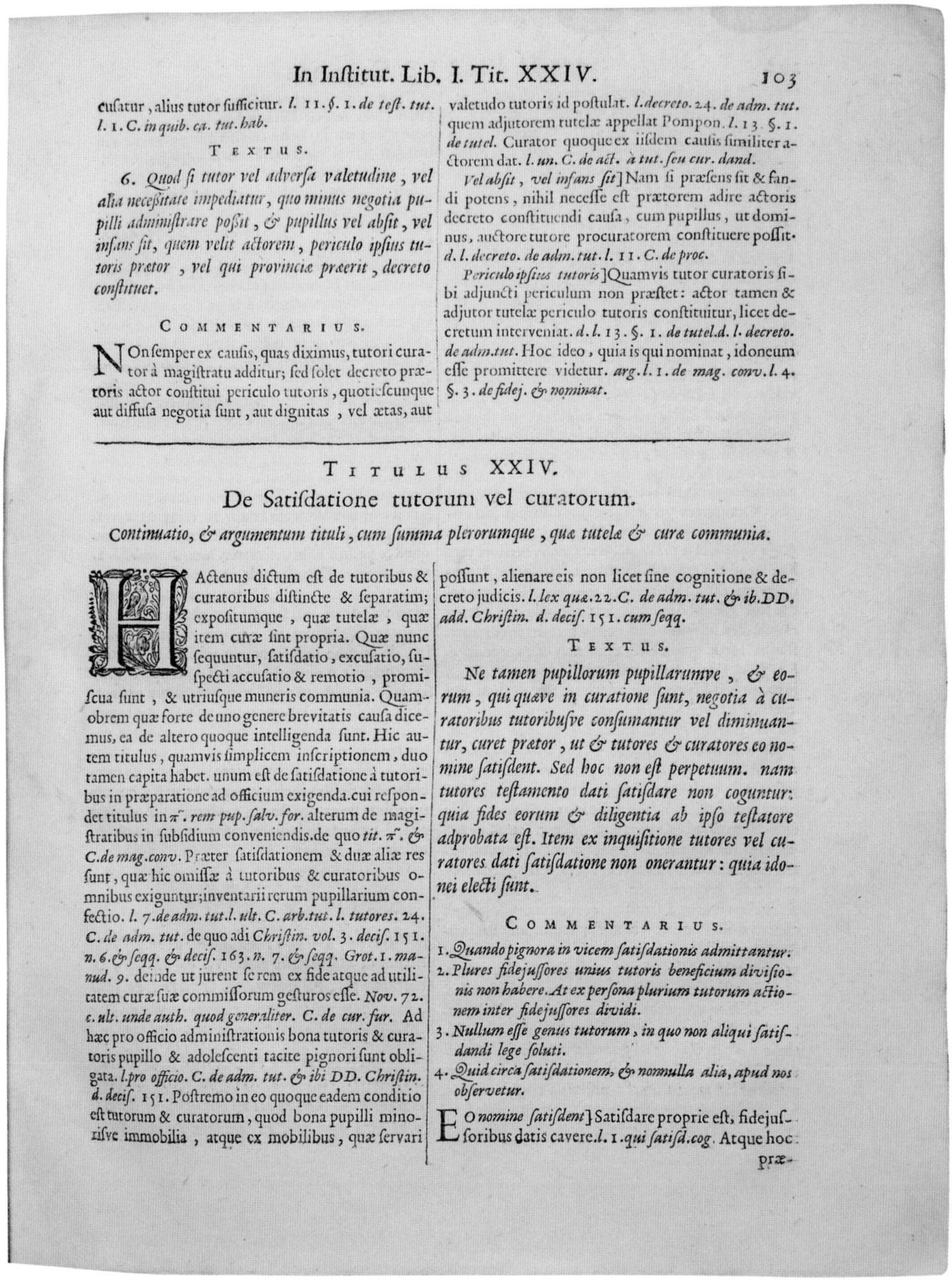

In Inſtitut. Lib. I. Tit. XXIV. 103

cuſatur, alius tutor ſufficitur. *l.* 11. *§.* 1. *de teſt. tut. l.* 1. *C. in quib. ca. tut. hab.*

TEXTUS.

6. *Quod ſi tutor vel adverſa valetudine, vel alia neceſſitate impediatur, quo minus negotia pupilli adminiſtrare poſſit, & pupillus vel abſit, vel infans ſit, quem velit actorem, periculo ipſius tutoris prætor, vel qui provinciæ præerit, decreto conſtituet.*

COMMENTARIUS.

NOn ſemper ex cauſis, quas diximus, tutori curator à magiſtratu additur; ſed ſolet decreto prætoris actor conſtitui periculo tutoris, quotieſcunque aut diffuſa negotia ſunt, aut dignitas, vel ætas, aut valetudo tutoris id poſtulat. *l. decreto.* 24. *de adm. tut.* quem adjutorem tutelæ appellat Pompon. *l.* 13. §. 1. *de tutel.* Curator quoque ex iiſdem cauſis ſimiliter actorem dat. *l. un. C. de act. à tut. ſeu cur. dand.*

Vel abſit, vel infans ſit] Nam ſi præſens ſit & fandi potens, nihil neceſſe eſt prætorem adire actoris decreto conſtituendi cauſa, cum pupillus, ut dominus, auctore tutore procuratorem conſtituere poſſit. *d. l. decreto. de adm. tut. l.* 11. *C. de proc.*

Periculo ipſius tutoris] Quamvis tutor curatoris ſibi adjuncti periculum non præſtet: actor tamen & adjutor tutelæ periculo tutoris conſtituitur, licet decretum interveniat. *d. l.* 13. §. 1. *de tutel. d. l. decreto. de adm. tut.* Hoc ideo, quia is qui nominat, idoneum eſſe promittere videtur. *arg. l.* 1. *de mag. conv. l.* 4. §. 3. *de fidej. & nominat.*

TITULUS XXIV.
De Satiſdatione tutorum vel curatorum.

Continuatio, & argumentum tituli, cum ſumma plerorumque, quæ tutelæ & curæ communia.

HActenus dictum eſt de tutoribus & curatoribus diſtincte & ſeparatim; expoſitumque, quæ tutelæ, quæ item curæ ſint propria. Quæ nunc ſequuntur, ſatiſdatio, excuſatio, ſuſpecti accuſatio & remotio, promiſcua ſunt, & utriuſque muneris communia. Quamobrem quæ forte de uno genere brevitatis cauſa dicemus, ea de altero quoque intelligenda ſunt. Hic autem titulus, quamvis ſimplicem inſcriptionem, duo tamen capita habet. unum eſt de ſatiſdatione à tutoribus in præparatione ad officium exigenda. cui reſpondet titulus in π. *rem pup. ſalv. for.* alterum de magiſtratibus in ſubſidium conveniendis. de quo *tit.* π. & *C. de mag. conv.* Præter ſatiſdationem & duæ aliæ res ſunt, quæ hic omiſſæ à tutoribus & curatoribus omnibus exiguntur; inventarii rerum pupillarium confectio. *l.* 7. *de adm. tut. l. ult. C. arb. tut. l. tutores.* 24. *C. de adm. tut.* de quo adi *Chriſtin. vol.* 3. *deciſ.* 151. *n.* 6. *& ſeqq. & deciſ.* 163. *n.* 7. *& ſeqq. Grot.* 1. *manud.* 9. deinde ut jurent ſe rem ex fide atque ad utilitatem curæ ſuæ commiſſorum geſturos eſſe. *Nov.* 72. *c. ult. unde auth. quod generaliter. C. de cur. fur.* Ad hæc pro officio adminiſtrationis bona tutoris & curatoris pupillo & adoleſcenti tacite pignori ſunt obligata. *l. pro officio. C. de adm. tut. & ibi DD. Chriſtin. d. deciſ.* 151. Poſtremo in eo quoque eadem conditio eſt tutorum & curatorum, quod bona pupilli minoriſve immobilia, atque ex mobilibus, quæ ſervari poſſunt, alienare eis non licet ſine cognitione & decreto judicis. *l. lex quæ.* 22. *C. de adm. tut. & ib. DD. add. Chriſtin. d. deciſ.* 151. *cum ſeqq.*

TEXTUS.

Ne tamen pupillorum pupillarumve, & eorum, qui quæve in curatione ſunt, negotia à curatoribus tutoribuſve conſumantur vel diminuantur, curet prætor, ut & tutores & curatores eo nomine ſatiſdent. Sed hoc non eſt perpetuum. nam tutores teſtamento dati ſatiſdare non coguntur: quia fides eorum & diligentia ab ipſo teſtatore adprobata eſt. Item ex inquiſitione tutores vel curatores dati ſatiſdatione non onerantur: quia idonei electi ſunt.

COMMENTARIUS.

1. *Quando pignora in vicem ſatiſdationis admittantur.*
2. *Plures fidejuſſores unius tutoris beneficium diviſionis non habere. At ex perſona plurium tutorum actionem inter fidejuſſores dividi.*
3. *Nullum eſſe genus tutorum, in quo non aliqui ſatiſdandi lege ſoluti.*
4. *Quid circa ſatiſdationem, & nonnulla alia, apud nos obſervetur.*

E*O nomine ſatiſdent*] Satiſdare proprie eſt, fidejuſſoribus datis cavere. *l.* 1. *qui ſatiſd. cog.* Atque hoc præ-

Page from a juridical handbook published by Daniel Elsevier in Amsterdam, 1659. The tools for creating typographic hierarchy and articulation are slightly different from those we use today – but not that much. Small capitals play a starring role.

← Navigation 24
← OpenType 128
→ Numerals 136

Ligatures &c.

Ligatures are very much in fashion and few new typefaces that take themselves seriously come without a truckload of them. So let's briefly dwell upon the question of what ligatures are good for.

A ligature (from the Latin *ligare*, 'to bind') is, technically, the joining of two or more letters into a single glyph. Ligatures are quite old – they were among the tools Gutenberg used to make his books look more like manuscripts. For centuries, scribes had joined letters and abbreviated words to speed up their work, use less space and justify columns of text. → p. 162

Once printing acquired an aesthetic of its own, ligatures in text typefaces had two functions: firstly, to fuse letters that would otherwise clash or leave a gap (such as an overhanging 'f' with an 'i' or 'l'); secondly, to make text prettier by adding a little flourish to common letter combinations such as 'st' and 'ct'.

The first use is functional. It becomes unnecessary when there is no clash, as when the 'f' has no long flag or hook. The second is ornamental, and should be used with caution. A piece of body text full of arbitrary 'ct', 'ck' and 'st' ligatures risks looking mannered and can be annoying to the reader. In OpenType fonts, a distinction is made between 'Standard' and 'Discretionary' ligatures, although these do not always correspond exactly to these functions.

ff	→	ff
fi	→	fi
fl	→	fl
ffi	→	ffi
ffl	→	ffl

Standard ligatures

sk	→	sk
ct	→	ct
ity	→	ity

Discretionary ligatures

fi fl ff

FF Profile

fi fl ff

Optima

fi fi
fl fl

Futura ND

fi fi
fl fl

Menlo

The purpose of ligatures changes when they are used in fonts that mimic some kind of fancy lettering: calligraphy, brush script, hand-rendered headlines or letters cut in stone. In those cases ligatures, like alternate forms of single letters, become an instrument to create diversity within a text and enhance the illusion that the letters have been drawn one by one. See the opposite page.

↖ **Standard ligatures are selected for those pairs of lowercase letters where a collision would otherwise take place. Discretionary ligatures are optional, and give the text a fancy look. Right: When the f has no overhang, ligatures aren't necessary. In this version of Futura, they look very exaggerated; in a monospace like Menlo, it is rather useless to put two letters into one box.**

↑ **Foundry type: Bodoni fi-ligature.**

ß or Eszett exclusively German

Berlin illustrator-designer Nadine Roßa (pronounced 'Rossa') likes the ß: it is part and parcel of her name. She designed these ß earrings.

It looks a bit like a capital B or a Greek beta (β) but is pronounced as 's'. It is used only in German, but the German-speaking Swiss abolished it ages ago, replacing it with ss. Sometimes referred to as 'Eszett' (S–Z), this character is the ß or 'sharp s'.

The ß is a bit of a controversial letter in German culture. There are several theories about its origin, most suggesting it is

a kind of ligature between the mediaeval 'long s' and the normal 's'. Some scholars, however, insist that it has its roots in a combination of (long) 's' and 'z', which would justify its nickname as well as the z-like form in some of its designs.

What is even more vividly discussed is whether a capital ß is desirable, or even legitimate. As the ß comes from two lowercase letters, it reverts to SS

when set in caps or small caps: *weiß* becomes *WEISS*. People (and towns) whose name contains an ß aren't happy about this – part of their identity somehow gets lost in caps. Individual campaigning to get the capital ß accepted has been successful in that it has now officially been added to the Unicode standard, to the dismay of purists. As of April 2008, capital ß has Unicode U+1E9E.

Swashes, flourishes, beginnings & endings

With OpenType, type designers have endless possibilities to add alternative characters. Some fonts, such as Underware's Liza or the Studio Lettering series from House Industries, have three different versions of each character for the various positions within the word: beginning, middle and ending – just like the standard Arabic alphabet. Script fonts such as Memoriam come with dozens, if not hundreds of alternates – mostly swashy and flourished versions of letters.

Moderation

While beginning and ending alternates make a lot of sense in fonts that emulate handwriting and signpainting – forms of typographic expression where a bit of overstatement is in order – they are not a necessity in text fonts, or in less ornate display fonts. Type designers have fun inventing exuberant varieties of their characters; but it is up to the graphic designer to use these frills with moderation – unless you deliberately go for excess and, let's face it, kitsch.

Also, do refrain from using swashed or otherwise fancy capitals in all-caps settings.

↖ Liza: contextual alternates provide each word with beginnings, endings and other alternative forms.

↑ Memoriam (Canada Type) offers up to seven alternates for each letter.

← Jos Buivenga's Geotica has a full load of fancy ligatures, swash caps, beginnings and endings; it also comes with a 'Fill' version which allows for layering in different colours.

Ampersand simply 'and'

It is easy to see why many type designers like doing an ampersand. Of all the standard glyphs there is probably no other that gives them so much freedom and such a wide choice of *bona fide* historical models.

The ampersand developed from the Latin *et* ('and'), as is still discernible in some of its incarnations. While the sign developed further under the influence of writing speed and stylistic conventions, its various historical variants have been revisited by type designers, so that many different forms are in current use today and many designers offer more than one variant in a font. The Thesis family is a case in point.

Traditional typographers like to use ampersands for 'and' in body text. Imitate them with moderation. It soon looks pretentious.

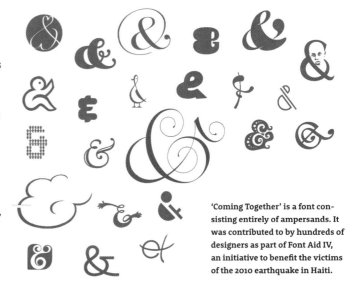

'Coming Together' is a font consisting entirely of ampersands. It was contributed to by hundreds of designers as part of Font Aid IV, an initiative to benefit the victims of the 2010 earthquake in Haiti.

Punctuation at home and abroad

'Quotes'

Like power sockets and computer keyboards, quotation marks – 'quotes' – are different wherever you travel. When typesetting international publications, it is highly appreciated if you respect each region's habits. The list below is far from complete. Many languages use more than one system; more importantly, they also have rules for 'quotes "within" quotes'. The Oxford system uses double quotes within single quotes, in the US it is the other way around.

"Typewriter"
'British English (Oxford style)'
"American English"
« French »
«Spanish + Portuguese»
"Brasilian Portuguese"
„German + Slavic languages"
»German – elegant«
«German – Swiss»
«Russian, Ukrainian»
„Polish"
„Dutch – traditional"
'Dutch – Oxford style'
„Danish" »Danish«
"Swedish + Finnish"
«Norwegian»

Smart quotes, dumb quotes, primes

A common error in DTP is using 'straight quotes' or 'dumb quotes' instead of curly typographer's (aka 'smart') quotes. Those straight marks are intended for several other purposes – see below. Using them for quotation marks is a leftover from the era of mechanical typewriters – typists had to make do with a very limited character set on their machine. These marks are often called *primes* although, strictly speaking, traditional primes aren't straight but skewed.

Layout programs have a function for automatically substituting typographers' quotes when inserting these 'typewriter primes'; they are adjusted for the language specified. It's a handy feature, but switching it on also results in an opening quote when hoping for an apostrophe after a space (*summer of '67*).

3' • **prime**
feet (ft)
arcminutes (am), ⅟₆₀ of a degree
minutes (min)

45" • **double prime**
inches (in)
arcseconds (as), ⅟₆₀ of an arcminute
seconds (s)

'98 • **apostrophe**
omissions in dates (*'67, '90s, 'twenties*)
omissions in words (*'hood, rock'n'roll, it's*)

BOOM! Palm Springs Plans a Wacky, $250m Old Folks' Community for Gays

Dumb quote!

BOOM! Palm Springs Plans a Wacky, $250m Old Folks' Community for Gays

v Roman`, Times, serif;">
;margin:12px 0px 15px 8
Old Folks’ Commu

Smart quote!
(apostrophe, really)

Getting it right on the web

Contrary to popular belief, the web supports both 'curly quotes', as web designers like to call them, and real apostrophes. No need to make do with primes or double primes. A good way to obtain the sign that is typographically correct is by inserting its html code. The naming is based on a simplistic description of the British/American system of quoting, for instance: “ = *left double quote*, and ’ = *right single quote* (equals apostrophe).

Hyphens, dashes, spaces – ¡and more!

Hyphens and dashes

Hyphens, en dashes and em dashes are all short lines used for formatting text, each with a different function, with some small variations of use in different countries.

Hyphens (the shortest kind) are often mistakenly used instead of dashes, possibly because dashes can't usually be accessed directly from the keyboard. In e-mail, using a double hyphen to make an en or em dash is fine, in more formal documents it should be replaced with the proper character.

Several spaces

Sophisticated layout programs such as InDesign and Quark XPress offer spaces of various fixed widths, allowing a designer to fine-tune the text. For instance, the designer can choose to use a Thin Space or Sixth Space on either side of the en dash if a full space creates gaps in the text – or a hair space before a question or exclamation mark, if it appears to 'stick' to the text.

Spaces are also something to observe when setting texts in French. As shown in the list of international quotation marks, the France like some air around their punctuation marks. This is why there are also spaces before colons and semi-colons:

C'est français ; c'est différent !

¿Qué?

In Spanish, interrogative and exclamatory sentences (or clauses) are preceded by an inverted question or exclamation mark. There is a good reason for this: Spanish is one of those Latin languages where the order of the words usually remains the same in interrogative and exclamatory sentences, so that the reader – and, more importantly, those who read a text aloud in public – can use an extra directive. In private communication, such as e-mail and text messages, inverted question marks are now often omitted; but in more formal situations, these opening marks are not optional.

- -

She's not so very different from her brother

A clear-cut break

Catherine Zeta-Jones

● **hyphen**
Used to split words onto the following line, and to join two separate words together to make a single concept. Also for double names, in which case the typesetter may decide to use a *non-breaking space* in order to keep the second part of the name on the same line.

- -

Monday–Friday

1983–1994

I took a – rather brief – break

● **en dash**
Roughly the width of the letter N. Indicates a duration or a transition, usually between dates or numbers. In British English and most European languages it is also used to interrupt the sentence with a related thought or clarification, with a space on each side.

- -

They decided to take a—rather long—break

● **em dash**
Roughly the same width as the letter M. Found mainly in American English, performing the same function of marking digressions as the en dash in European languages; most official handbooks use no spaces on either side.

- -

¿Qué estás comiendo?
¡Un pincho de atún!

Spanish inverted question and exclamation marks as conceived by a Spanish designer: Rumba by Laura Meseguer.

Numerals, figures, digits, numbers

Many new fonts today come with more than one set of numerals (or figure sets). Well-equipped OpenType fonts may offer up to ten or more different kinds of numerals. When working with an OpenType-enabled program, the user can activate the style that fits the context best through OpenType functions.

Proportional lining	0123456789 xX
Proportional oldstyle	0123456789 xX
Small caps	0123456789 SC
Tabular lining	0123456789 xX
Tabular oldstyle	0123456789 xX
Fractions	01234/56789
Subscript & superscript	123456789 xX 123456789

• •

Avoid uppercase with oldstyle figures. Use lining figures instead.

UPPERCASE 0123456789

With lowercase body text, use oldstyle figures when available.

Lowercase 0123456789

All good combinations. With small caps, both oldstyle figures and small caps figures (bottom) are fine. Few font families offer small caps figures, but their number is on the rise.

UPPERCASE 0123456789

Lowercase 0123456789

SMALL CAPS 0123456789

SMALL CAPS 0123456789

Oldstyle figures vs. lining figures

Lining figures (LF) or *caps figures* stand firmly on the baseline and all have the same height. This strict order brings regularity to a page full of numbers and combines well with words or units set in allcaps. However, within a lowercase text, a group of lining figures (e.g. in dates) stands out, just like a word in all-caps would.

In running text, this effect is usually undesirable. This is what *text figures* are for. They dance around the base line: the 5 below, the 6 above, 7 below, the 8 above. Their form is historically older; therefore they are called *mediaeval* or *oldstyle figures* (OSF). Which kind of numeral is set as the default depends on the particular font.

Tabular figures

We read letters horizontally in sequences of words. With figures there is also another possibility. In lists and invoices, there is a vertical reference. It is easier to compare or add up numbers if the ones, tens and hundreds are vertically aligned – i.e. if all the digits occupy exactly the same width. Figures that do this are *tabular figures* (TF); all characters are equally wide, as opposed to the *proportional numbers*, where 1 is narrower than 8. Recent fonts often provide both oldstyle and lining sets, each in a tabular and a proportional version.

Superscript and subscript

Superscript and subscript numbers are figures with a specialist purpose. They are typically used for footnote references, square or cubic units such as km² or in chemical formulas like H_2O. These characters are not simply scaled-down normal numbers but are made especially: they have the correct line width and are generally drawn a little wider. They are not ideal, however, for mathematical fractions. For this purpose, another type is used, the fractional digits. They are a less extreme sub- and superscript, so that the entire fraction is visually displayed on the baseline.

Formatting numbers

Long sequences of figures can be hard to decipher. Unlike letters, any combination of numerals can indicate meaning. In order to identify each single figure, splitting numbers into groups can be beneficial. Numbers of more than three digits can be divided using non-breaking spaces, starting from the right in groups of three. For sums of money, a comma is the normal practice, with a point separating the decimal positions. Note: In many other languages, including Spanish, French and German, it is the opposite: commas before decimals, points between thousands.

Sometimes it is not clear from the context whether we are dealing with a letter or a number – for example, in programming code, serial numbers or British postal codes. When typesetting such a code it is important to choose a font where there is no likelihood of confusion. The usual suspects for ambiguity are the serifless 1 (don't confuse with lowercase l), the oldstyle 1 (may look like small caps I) and zero (looks like uppercase or lowercase o). Some fonts contain a special slashed zero (Ø) to prevent ambiguity.

Thousands and decimals

34,281.50   ← The English-American notation

34.281,50   ← The European notation

Jan Tschichold
præceptor typographiæ

2 Penguin Lane
West Drayton
UB7 0HI
+44 (0)20 8962 2155
+44 (0)79 2402 1874

Numerals and style

In phone numbers, the area code and number can be separated in many ways: spaces, dots, slashes and hyphens are all common, and preferences depend on the country. When designing for an international audience, do pay attention to the local habit. The selection of a specific kind of numeral and way to separate numbers can be a stylistic decision as well — witness these examples designed by Florian Hardwig in two contrasting styles, both practised and recommended by Jan Tschichold in the course of his long career.

1000+500+100+100+(100-10)+1+1=1792

Roman numerals

Our numbers are often called Arabic numerals because they arrived to Europe through Arabia during the Middle Ages – but in fact they come from India. For some purposes, we use a second system: the one invented in ancient Rome. It uses capital letters (I = 1, V = 5, X = 10, L = 50, C = 100, D = 500, M = 1000) and is suitable for the numbering of anything official: levels, popes, world wars, Olympic Games. We also find them on antique-looking clocks and in dates on buildings. In book design, they are used for outlines, for the pagination of forewords and identifying multi-volume editions.

For those who don't remember how they work: the trick is to add up numbers when in increasing order, but subtract a small number when it precedes a bigger one.

Equal-width table figures

Fonts that were designed with an eye to financial communications may come with a range of table figures in which all numerals have equal width in all weights, from light to bold or black. This allows for highlighting individual rows of numbers without breaking the column (weight duplexing).

Among the foundries that have included this feature in part of their fonts are OurType, FontFont and Hoefler & Frere-Jones (shown below: the Archer typeface by H&FJ).

NET RESULTS 2011	
Profit before taxation	34,283
Taxation	12,617
Profit for the year	*21,666*
Attributable to	
Shareholders	21,157
Minority interest	509
Total	**21,666**

Adjusting to circumstances

There are many circumstances in which a text has to work hard to be read. Bad printing, lack of space, cluttered environments, low-resolution screens, distance: each of these less-than-ideal conditions presents an interesting challenge to type designers and graphic designers.

ExtraLight *negative*	Light *positive*
ExtraBold *positive*	**Bold *negative***
SemiBold *neg. back-lit*	**Bold *reflecting light, etc.***
Extra Bold *back-lit*	**Bold *reflecting light, etc.***
Regular *reading size*	SemiBold *XSmall size*

↑ Before designing TheSans and the other members of the Thesis typeface family, Dutch type designer Luc(as) de Groot worked at BRS Premsela Vonk, an Amsterdam design firm specializing in information design projects, including administrative forms and signage. In many such projects, balancing positive and negative type is part of the graphic designer's job. Remembering his frustration about never finding the perfect typeface for a job well done, de Groot gave Thesis eight weights, allowing its users to play with the subtle differences in stroke thickness.

→ The missing horizontal crossbar of the Dutch road signage font (orange) makes C and G harder to distinguish. In Ralf Herrmann's Wayfinding Sans (blue) the difference is more pronounced.

↘ Erfurt: the first line shows the German road sign font DIN 1451 and the result when blurred by bad lighting or rain; in Wayfinding Sans, second line, the more pronounced shapes result in better recognisability of the letters.

→ Top to bottom: The road signage typeface used in Spain and Italy; Transport Bold (United Kingdom); Wayfinding Sans.

Positive and negative

Text is perceived differently when shown in black on a light background (positive), or the reverse (negative). Negative type – white letters on a dark background – seems to lighten up and therefore looks slightly bolder than dark letters on a white background.

This is not only true for ink on paper, but also for lettering in signage systems. It becomes all the more apparent when type is used in light boxes. When a text is *backlit,* the light beams make the edges blur and negative type seems bolder, while positive type appears decidedly thinner. Type designers can compensate for these heavy-duty circumstances by designing typefaces that come in a high number of closely calculated weights. It allows specialist information designers to fine-tune the colour of the text for each use and each combination.

Speed, haste, rain

In wayfinding systems for public motorways, the legibility of signs is vital to the safety of road users. Their clarity may be hampered in different ways: speed, distance, lack of attention, and especially the weather. In the quest for the best possible (and potentially life-saving) road sign, the ideal typeface plays a pivotal role.

German designer Ralf Herrmann travelled across Europe for three years documenting road signage systems and found that no system was perfect. He decided to design 'the ultimate way-finding typeface'. He first wrote the Legibility Test Tool for Mac to simulate the conditions motorway signs are subject to. In Herrmann's words, 'to increase the viewing distance of my design I needed to experience my typeface in this blurry state where it is just about to become readable and I needed to test it when visibility decreases, for example by an overglow effect through the headlights of a car.' His typeface addresses the flaws that even the most familiar signage faces display. Instead of uniform shapes, Hermann stressed the individual character of each letter. Instead of geometric engineer's skeleton, he drew open forms that are almost humanist.

Wayfinding Sans will soon be ready for retail.

Small and narrow type

Inktraps: fun follows function

Printing technology has made considerable progress: even high-speed rotation presses now offer excellent quality. This wasn't so a few decades ago, and type designers were among the technicians whose job it was to minimise the damage of mediocre printing of small type on cheap stock. Among the areas most affected were daily newspapers and phone books.

A type design trick used to avoid the clutter of ink in sharp corners is the *inktrap*: an extra nick cutting into the shape of the letter where the excess ink can go. Exaggerated inktraps were used, for instance, in Matthew Carter's Bell Centennial, specially designed for use at very small sizes in phone books.

Although printing is now usually so razor-sharp that hardly any ink gets cluttered at all, inktraps still make some sense as an optical correction – in small sizes, our eyes seem to need that extra incision to perceive the letterform as it was meant to be.

More importantly, inktraps have now become a stylistic feature. Graphic designers began using Bell Centennial for headlines because they liked the quirky effect of its inktraps, which then suggested to type designers to use those deeps cuts as stylistic features.

Bell Centennial Adress · 919 Madison Ave #16

Bell Centennial Name & Number · 617-5224-12

Bell Centennial Sub Caption · Brooklyn Heights

BELL CENTENNIAL BOLD LISTING · CARTER & CONE

Sharper **Knives**

↑ Bell Centennial, designed by Matthew Carter in 1975–78 as a space-saving face for AT&T's telephone directories. Ink traps were used to improve legibility at small sizes.

← Christian Schwartz's Amplitude uses exaggerated inktraps as a stylistic device.

Condensed type and how to save space

Here's a test: Hold up a page of small text in front of you, so that you can only just read it. Tilt the page 45 degrees on the horizontal axis (top half backwards). The letters appear less high, but remain readable. Now turn the page 45 degrees on the vertical axis instead. The letters look narrower ... and you'll hardly be able to read a word.

What this test from Emile Javal may teach us is that the condensed type is not a great space-saving solution. Even well-designed condensed versions of fonts need a larger point size to have the same legibility as the normal version. Electronically condensed fonts are worse: they distort the design. The better option is to simply choose a smaller size. You may even want to select a well-designed wide font and use it at a very small size.

Some designers will use digitally condensed fonts to create funky headlines – but it takes talent and judgement to get away with that.

I here present you, courteous reader, with the record of a remarkable period in my life: according to my application of it, I trust that it will prove not merely an interesting record, but in a considerable degree useful and instructive. In that hope it is that I have drawn it up.

AMPLITUDE COMPRESSED REGULAR 7.5/11

I here present you, courteous reader, with the record of a remarkable period in my life: according to my application of it, I trust that it will prove not merely an interesting record, but in a considerable degree useful and instructive. In that hope it is that I have drawn it up.

AMPLITUDE REGULAR 7.5/11 – 65% CHARACTER WIDTH

I here present you, courteous reader, with the record of a remarkable period in my life: according to my application of it, I trust that it will prove not merely an interesting record, but in a considerable degree useful and instructive. In that hope it is that I have drawn it up.

AMPLITUDE REGULAR 6/8

I here present you, courteous reader, with the record of a remarkable period in my life: according to my application of it, I trust that it will prove not merely an interesting record, but in a considerable degree useful and instructive. In that hope it is that I have drawn it up.

AMPLITUDE WIDE REGULAR 5/7

I here present you, courteous reader, with the record of a remarkable period in my life: according to my application of it, I trust that it will prove not merely an interesting record, but in a considerable degree useful and instructive. In that hope it is that I have drawn it up.

AMPLITUDE REGULAR 7.5/11

↑ Text set in 7.5pt Amplitude, itself a rather narrow typeface.

← Four drastic attempts to save space. Both Amplitude Compressed and an electronically condensed Normal have mediocre legibility at unchanged size. A smaller point size at normal width is more readable. Amplitude *Wide* set in an even smaller size turns out to be the winner: maximum space-saving and good legibility. One red square = 1mm.

← How do we read? 14
← Information design 34
← Optical size 100

At the Hochschule für Gestaltung (Design College) of Offenbach, Germany, Berlin video artist Rotraut Pape curated a series of lectures and performances on 'Media archaeology'. One of the project's underlying themes was the loss of data stored by means of obsolete media. The poster concept developed by Offenbach professor Klaus Hesse was a clever translation of this aspect of media theory and history. The sequence of posters illustrated the deterioration and dissipation of information as the announcements were gradually covered and made invisible, overwritten as they were by new information.

erkki huhtamo. lost but not dead media.
30 10 01. 19.30_vortrag. verlorene, nicht tote medien. ausflüge in die logik der medienkultur. in englischer sprache. hochschule für gestaltung offenbach am main, schlossstraße 31, raum 101

hfg

christian scheidemann. wie haltbar ist video-kunst? 2011 01. 19.30_vortrag. zur erhaltung eines historischen mediums. hochschule für gestaltung offenbach am main, schlossstraße 31, raum 101

hfg

diedrich diederichsen. die stimmen der satelliten hören. 04 12 01. 20.00_vortrag. die welt des joe meek. zwischen wahnsinn und studiotechnologie. hochschule für gestaltung offenbach am main, schlossstraße 31, raum 101

hfg

Design strategies and concepts

mike hentz. digitale steinzeit.
18 12 01. 19.30 _vortrag. eine lost media performance. hochschule für gestaltung offenbach am main, schlossstraße 31, raum 101

hfg

uta brandes. vom *wer-bin-ich* zum
wo-bin-ich. 22 01 02. 19.30 _vortrag. hochschule für gestaltung
offenbach am main, schlossstraße 31, raum 101

hfg

stelarc. zombies und cyborgs.
19 02 02. 19.30 _vortrag. überflüssige, unfreiwillige und automatisierte körper.
hochschule für gestaltung offenbach am main, schlossstraße 31, aula

hfg

Typography and good ideas

As soon as typography is more than an 'invisible' conduit for a text, the designer's task becomes directive. His/her decisions about how a text is shaped affect the way the reader experiences and interprets its content. To some extent, the designer becomes a co-author. At times the design may reinforce and underpin the text, at other times it may take up a position of its own by providing critical comments or by putting the content in a new context.

The designer as author has been a key concept in discussions on the role of graphic design during the past fifteen years. The new concept of the graphic designer as a creator who actively and critically contributes to the content is a response to the traditional view of the designer as passive and neutral service provider.

There are many degrees of graphic authorship. Ever more graphic designers manifest themselves as editors, writers, publishers, curators, filmmakers or photographers. Some operate on the borderline between art and design and mainly create self-initiated projects; some work exclusively with clients who allow them great autonomy. This is not the place to elaborate on this trend. For our purpose, it is interesting to reflect on the opportunities typographic designers have, especially in the context of day-to-day assignments, to make a substantive mark on the result simply by reflecting on their decisions regarding structure, form and production – in other words, through a strong typographic concept.

Years ago, *Emigre* issued a mouse mat on which they had printed a sentence that is delicious in its simplicity and ambiguity: *Design is a good idea*. Design starts with a good idea – which does not necessarily mean a complex intellectual concept. The second meaning of the phrase is that it's a good idea to design things in the first place – a better idea, for instance, than *not* designing them and relying on the default solutions put in place by software engineers.

A concept may result from content (reading a text before you design it is *also* a good idea) or from context. A concept can be complex and multi-layered, or have childlike simplicity. The ways in which designers can make reading and looking more interesting are endless.

Tambo festival poster

During a prolonged stay in Mozambique, Portuguese designer Barbara Alves was asked to design a poster for the annual festival of the Cultural Association Tambo-Tambulani-Tambo. Tambo wanted a poster that reflected the theme of the festival, which focuses on Mozambique's art and tradition, while simultaneously communicating a sense of youthfulness, 'a new way of looking at the world and change through empowerment'.

Alves suggested that the text be silk-screened in white on the local *capulanas*, pieces of fabric the Mozambican women use as clothing, hats, bags, towels, for carrying babies, and more. She invited local people to help her choose the patterns. With the capulanas as a traditional-style backdrop, the lettering and image provided a contemporary touch. The posters were produced with sustainability in mind: they can be saved and reused next year.

An exercise in transparency

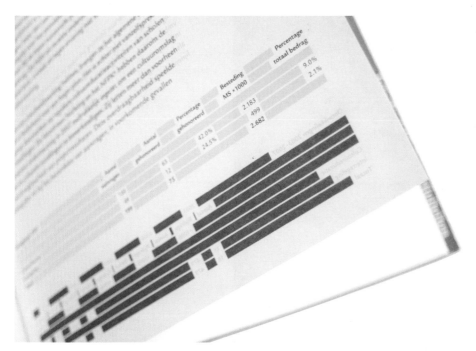

Mondriaan Annual Report

The Mondriaan Foundation is the major Dutch government-funded foundation for the arts. Its Annual Report is one of the organisation's chief tools to make its decision-making and finances public – in other words, to show that the foundation's way of spending public money is based on openness and transparency. For the 2007 edition, designer Ingeborg Scheffers took her cues from precisely those two themes. She took an ironic approach to the idea of openness by presenting each chapter as a closed signature, to be cut open before reading. Transparency played a major role in the layout, using coloured bars on the reverse side of the page to accentuate the rows in tables. Her choice of typeface was equally outspoken: Sibylle Hagmann's Odile is the opposite of the business-like font one expects in annual reports; so the type selection was as much about making adventurous choices as the foundation's policy was itself. Photos by Eva Czaya.

Style and statement

When, in 1917, a group of Dutch artists and designers founded a magazine to propose a radically new approach to all things visual, they called it 'Style': *De Stijl*. Back then, style was a powerful concept that could be the pivot of an artistic programme. The red, yellow and blue rectangles and black lines in the paintings of Piet Mondriaan – one of the group's main artists – were not simply a cool new way of filling a canvas. They represented a revolution of the mind.

Countless '-isms', style wars and lifestyle magazines later, the concept of style has become virtually meaningless. Worse, it is now suspect among artists and designers striving for authenticity. Many have come to associate the term with superficiality; style seems to have become a thing to avoid when concerned about substance, depth and integrity.

So is it possible to make work that is devoid of style? Hardly. One of the famous axioms of communication theoretician Paul Watzlawick is 'One cannot not communicate.' Likewise, you cannot *not* design. In the 1930s and 1960s, functionalist designers passionately looked for ways to make design that was neutral – as objective and unexpressive as possible. When we see those works now, they look to us as typical expressions of the 1930s or 1960s: examples of a style.

Style awareness

If you're relatively new to the business of shaping text, it is a good exercise to explore different styles, simply to find out what the tricks are; how to convey a message in different tones of voice and addressing different audiences. Most of all, it is important to become aware of the wide array of possibilities that designers have at their disposal to convey somebody else's message or create a message of their own. A good jazz musician will master different styles and genres in order to feel in control in various formations or in jam sessions. A professional graphic designer, too, will have to improvise and find ways of communicating all kinds of contents in all kinds of circumstances. Having explored a wide array of stylistic choices provides a designer with a bigger and better kit of visual tools – so that avoiding or embracing a style, any style, becomes a conscious choice and not the outcome of some kind of prejudice, or the prejudices of one's teachers.

Proposal by Paris designer Pierre Vincent for a series of posters for a performance festival, with photography by Maxime Lemoyne. The technical-looking alphabet that Vincent drew specially for this purpose, nicely ties into the festival's title, Anti-codes. The proposal was rejected.

A personal signature

Immediately after graduation, Mexican designer Rebeca Durán landed a job as art director of *Twist*, a magazine for teen girls. Being only slightly older than her readers she came up with a cheeky, style-conscious approach, borrowing elements from grunge, punk and pulp magazines. Sound typographic choices (the main typefaces being Underware's Bello and Auto) completed an eclectic, in-your-face mix that was just right for the target group.

Design proposal for the Jerusalem cultural weekly 24/7 by Israeli designer Moshik Nadav. While the scarcity of content and the generous use of white space may betray the fact that this is a student project, there is a remarkable confidence in the choice of stylistic and rhetorical means. There are strong references to 1920s Constructivism – the vertical type, use of red and black, bold bars and cut-out image – yet the overall effect is not that of a stylistic exercise or pastiche but of a thoroughly contemporary and functional design.

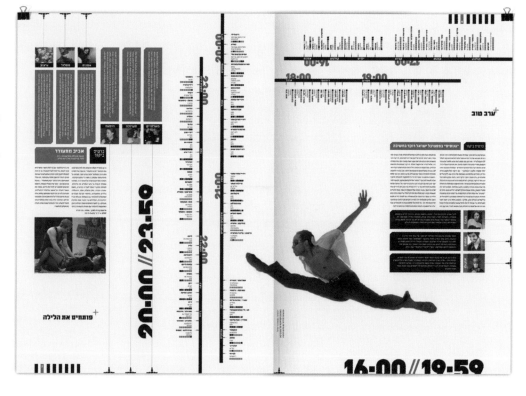

Reference, pastiche, parody

In all the arts there are various ways of dealing with styles and inventions from the past. Many contemporary creations incorporate aspects from the past; the degree of originality, integrity, virtuosity and intelligence with which this is done can vary greatly.

Think of pop or rock. When a young band of today plays a rock'n'roll song as if it's 1957, then this is an *imitation*. If done as a respectful homage to the rock greats of the past, it could pass for a *tribute*. If they play a song of their own in which stylistic characteristics from the old days blend with modern elements, the band is simply *inspired* by the past (though admittedly this is a much-abused word). If elements of an original are exaggerated with the aim to ridicule, you can speak of a *parody* or *caricature*.

Imagine our band presents a number as their original composition, while in truth they have nicked melodies and riffs from others; this can be a case of *plagiarism*, unless it is totally obvious and clearly done with humour and/or respect for the original – then you can conclude that those riffs are *quotes* or *references*. And when a literal quote is lifted from a recording as a sound clip and mixed into a new song, whether or not in a repetitive loop, then we speak of *sampling*.

The same degrees of stylistic dependence apply to visual disciplines such as graphic design; we use roughly the same terms. Some experience is needed to be able to discern thievery from intelligent hints, but great pleasures lie ahead for those who learn to appreciate visual puns, references and *double entendres*. You could compare it to the films of Tarantino, whose movie-fan humour is wasted on anyone who doesn't get the director's myriad references to great (and obscure) moments from film history.

Pastiche

Pastiches are a particularly interesting and ambiguous category in this family of 'derivatives'. A pastiche is a kind of parody without satirical motives. Stylistic characteristics of existing works are imitated and filled with new content, but not with the intent to mock the original – more like a tribute. Pastiches are at their best when an approach from the past is translated to our time with humour and intelligence; when the formal references to the original are spot-on while at the same time something new happens. A degree of virtuosity certainly does not hurt.

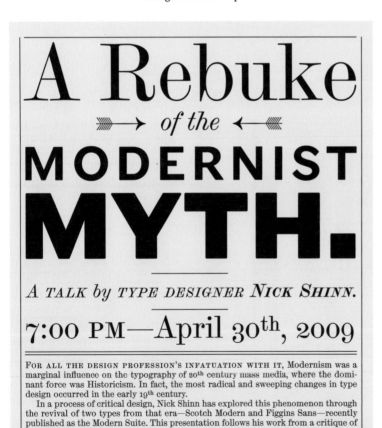

A Rebuke *of the* MODERNIST MYTH.

A TALK BY TYPE DESIGNER NICK SHINN.

7:00 PM—April 30th, 2009

FOR ALL THE DESIGN PROFESSION'S INFATUATION WITH IT, Modernism was a marginal influence on the typography of 20th century mass media, where the dominant force was Historicism. In fact, the most radical and sweeping changes in type design occurred in the early 19th century.

In a process of critical design, Nick Shinn has explored this phenomenon through the revival of two types from that era—Scotch Modern and Figgins Sans—recently published as the Modern Suite. This presentation follows his work from a critique of conventional wisdom to the discovery of new relationships between culture, technology, and designed form. Following the talk, Nick will be signing copies of his book, "The Modern Suite".

the URBAN GALLERY

☞ #401 Richmond Street (*beside Swipe Books*), Toronto

Advertisement designed by Nick Sherman for a lecture by Nick Shinn, using typefaces from the latter's Modern Suite: Figgins Sans and Scotch Modern. As these typefaces refer to mid- to late-nineteenth-century styles, it seems very appropriate for the ad to reflect the same period. The design is a witty pastiche of late nineteenth-century newspaper and magazine layouts; this also ties in nicely with the lecture's theme.

Mannerist window-dressing

Saks Fifth Avenue: 'Want It!'

Designer Marian Bantjes: 'Making typography look like the thing it described was both challenging and amusing. Some came together easily, others took many rounds of revisions. The Saks creative team did an amazing job of using the artwork in pretty much every way imaginable.' Art direction by Pentagram's Michael Bierut, and Terron Shaefer of the Saks Fifth Avenue creative team, 2007.

↓ Page from *Spieghel der Schrijfkonste* (Reflection of the Art of Writing) by Dutch writing master Jan van den Velde, 1605. This classic manual of mannerist calligraphy showed a wide array of styles but was most remarkable for van de Velde's virtuoso figurative flourishes. While not copying any specific shapes or ideas, Bantjes has clearly taken cues from this style of formal writing.

Logo strategies

A logo must be unique; only then can it emit a strong identity. However, that is not the only reason. When a new logo bears too many similarities to an existing one, this is morally and legally problematic. Many logos are registered trademarks. Therefore a crucial aspect of developing logos is research. The logo on the right (intended as a stylized 'Q') was launched in 2007 by a renowned software company. As bloggers pointed out almost immediately, not only was the sign the spitting image of the Scottish Arts Council's stylized 'a' (left), it also resembled elements of about half a dozen other logos. Within no time, the logo was withdrawn and replaced by a new one.

In the 1960s and 1970s specialist agencies developed a host of new logos which often consisted of abstract geometric symbols, often based on letters. This resulted in a number of memorable vignettes but also in numerous meaningless constructions of circles and lines. And the larger the number of abstract logos that appeared, the harder it was to recognize or remember them.

Too much simplicity can be problematic – witness the example on the left. In recent times, designers have devised several strategies for stronger branding through logotypes, making sure that the logo has substance – that it has a story to tell about the brand, event or organisation it represents. A logo does not need to be a single, static entity. It can take several forms, it can be animated for screens, it can even be automatically generated in infinite variations, so that it appears a little differently each time.

↑ Lettering artist, type designer and BMX fan Seb Lester drew a logo in four variants for a new BMX frame designed by Emer Bicycles. 'Emer said they wanted a logo that conveyed speed and dynamic energy,' says Lester. He translated the Swift's flight into dashed curves, adding an *inline* to enhance the suppleness without making the design look in any way nostalgic.

↓ The name of this Finnish company means 'unique'. Saku Heinänen, using a stencil font, designed the logo in multiple versions, allowing each employee to choose a unique variant of it for his or her business card.

Peter Biľak's History is a typeface in a multitude of variations, in which different historical styles can be identified. Italian agency FF3300 chose the letter for their identity for Index Urbis, a celebration of architecture and urbanism. A randomising script allows an infinite number of variants of the logo to be automatically generated, each with different colour and style combinations in several layers.

Reflecting the product

Tolix is a French brand of high-quality metallic furniture. When asked to revamp the company's identity, Pierre Delmas Bouly and Patrick Lallemand of the Lyon-based studio Superscript[2], decided to give the classic logo a facelift instead of proposing a more drastic redesign. They simplified the logo by removing the somewhat naive dimensional effect and articulated it by introducing details referring to the visual idiom of the furniture. They added a

small library of abstract shapes based on the company's signature chair. The corporate identity programme also included a colour scheme (relating to the basic colours of Tolix furniture) and a corporate typeface with industrial connotations – National by Kris Sowersby. Templates were developed for all printed matter for the brand.

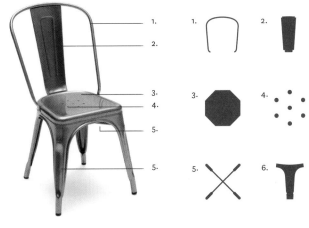

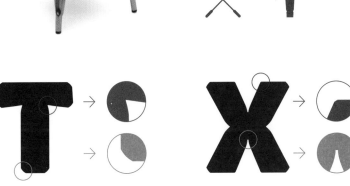

Typographie
Typographie
Typographie
Typographie

Typographie
Typographie
Typographie
Typographie

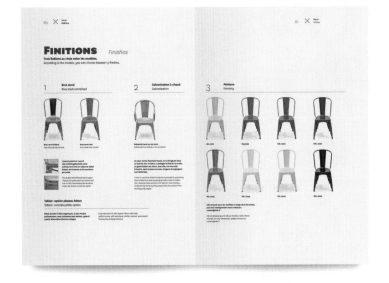

Corporate typefaces

In most corporate identity projects the type-faces play a key role. There are cases in which the corporate typeface is a single display font that matches the logo and is used exclusively for headlines and slogans; in other cases there is a complex system of different type families needed to cover the full spectrum of visual communication – a collection of compatible fonts with which the complete range of brochures, annual reports, advertising, stationery, lettering on buildings and vehicles, internal signage, videos and websites can be designed.

If the identity is developed for a large organisation, then it is conceivable that the design agency recommends having a custom font or family designed. It can be a customised version of an existing typeface, which can often be ordered from the original designer or foundry. It can also be a whole new font family which, depending on the agreement with the type designer, is used by the organisation on an exclusive basis for a limited or unlimited period of time.

In 2008 there existed over two hundred departments, bureaus and agencies within the Dutch government, which all used different logos, colour schemes and typefaces for their corporate iden-tities. In a bid to simplify this situation, the Dutch government held a pitch that was won by Studio Dumbar in Rotter-dam. It introduced a single new logo and a brand identity based on a pre-cisely defined colour scheme. As part of this new identity, type designer Peter Verheul was invited to develop a cus-tom font family for all forms of visual communication. Based on his earlier typeface Versa, Verheuls typeface is a binding element of the nationwide government house style.

Corporate type

Having a bespoke font designed is not cheap. Yet it can be the most interesting and economical solution for several reasons, especially for large organisations. For those working in big business or administration on either side of the table (or aspiring to), here are some advantages of having corporate typefaces custom-made.

- **Uniqueness** A typeface or type family with its own personality can lend a stronger impact to an organisation's communication. Even non-specialist audiences are sensitive to this, as proven by the fierce reactions when a popular newspaper changes its typeface.

- **Language and technology** An organisation that decides to have its own type family designed or customised can take the opportu-nity to specify precisely what they need: the languages of its market, the special signs used in its industry, bespoke arrows, icons or numerals. Specially hinted versions can be ordered as office fonts for optimal on-screen readability. The designer or foundry can pro-vide webfont versions to personalise the organisation's websites.

- **Royalties and economy** An organisation that has many computers needs the correct number of licenses for each font. If an exist-ing commercial font family is selected, acquiring licenses for hundreds or thousands of employees can be quite costly and is not easy to manage for a fast-growing company. In these cases a custom typeface with an unlimited license can provide an efficient alternative.

Typographic placemaking

Opened in 2008, Wiels is a centre for contemporary art in Brussels, housed in a former brewery. The 1930 building by architect Adrien Blomme, one of the few remaining modernist/Art Deco buildings in Brussels, was beautifully restored. The competition for the centre's visual identity was won by London-based Belgian designer Sara De Bondt. She quoted the brief in a presentation: '...Wiels does not want to play a part in any longing for retro or nostalgia...' commenting: 'Their biggest worry at the time was to become known as "that amazing heritage site with a bit of art in it," rather than "Wiels, the centre of contemporary art which happens to be housed in a beautiful listed building."' Although this implied that a logo that made reference to art deco shapes was 'a big taboo', De Bondt ended up referring to the building's silhouette after all – but in a very subtle way.

The logo then became the point of departure for a bespoke typeface, which was seen as a good way to firmly put the Wiels stamp on everything designed for the centre. In a lively dialogue with De Bondt, type designer Jo De Baerdemaeker developed Wiels Bold, a striking font in one weight. In its deliberate ruggedness it is reminiscent of the national road signage alphabet: a very Belgian, decidedly non-decorative engineers' font.

↑ Photo of the pre-restoration Wiels building and superimposed sketch showing the rationale behind the Wiels logo. The E in the final version has normalized proportions; the letters were given subtly rounded corners to obtain a friendlier overall feel. Photo by Guy Cardoso.

↑ Sponsors wall of fame in the hallway of the Wiels art centre, set in Wiels Bold; the embossed nameplates are a perfect match for the industrial-looking font, and vice versa.

→ Poster for an exhibition featuring the design studios that participated in the competition for the Wiels visual identity.

↑ Badge and tri-lingual brochure designed with the Wiels Bold typeface.

Materiality and the third dimension

Letters can have many meanings when placed in an environment – they can confirm a superpower, define or claim an area, impose, impress or entertain. When the Roman empire began propagating its monumental alphabet it was much more than a series of texts in well-proportioned shapes. It was a political statement – as Fred Smeijers has said: the world's first corporate typeface – and it had the materiality that fitted a symbol of power. It was an alphabet hewn into stone and marble, made to last for centuries to come. We don't need marble today to make dimensional type that may last a lifetime or longer. New technologies and materials allow us to take digitally created shapes into the third dimension at the push of a button; we have digital photography and video to document more ephemeral structures.

Letters are designed to be two-dimensional signs. When carved into marble with a chisel (or pressed into soft clay tablets with a stylus, as in cuneiform script) then the result is somewhere between two- and three-dimensional. It is still writing, and is still text meant to be read.

When letters take on a sculptural form, they enter a different realm. Communicating language, the alphabet's core task, may not be the main function of the object they constitute. The text becomes a pretext, so to speak. But there are also cases in which a text becomes larger than life while retaining its function as a 'machine for reading'. As we move away from material media to ever smaller and more disposable screens for our daily reading, environmental typography may help remind us of the material aspect of letters.

↑ Alphabets constructed using straight lines only were part of the Modernist quest for simplicity – be it in Russia, the Netherlands or Italy. Not only did these letterforms represent an ideology, they were also quite practical to use in three-dimensional constructions. The Italian Futurist Fortunato Depero designed this Pavillion of the Book for the publisher Bestetti-Tuminelli-Treves on the occasion of the third International Exhibition of Decorative Arts in Monza, 1927.

→ Modern technology enables designers to convert the subtle curves of digital type into sculptural shapes. The curvilinear forms of a modern Thai font have been converted into exhibition furniture by the design company Cadson Demak, Bangkok.

Monumental reading

'Vai com Deus' was a temporary installation on the façade of the former convent Ermida Nossa Senhora da Conceição in Porto, Portugal. Designers Liza Ramalho and Artur Ribero (R2) collected dozens of Portuguese expressions using the word deus ('god'), to recall the building's original function

The Erholungspark Marzahn is a recreational park in a Berlin suburb that has become widely known for its Gardens of the World project. Among the gardens created within the park are Chinese, Japanese and Balinese gardens, a Labyrinth and a Renaissance garden. In 2011 the Christian Garden was inaugurated as a new addition to the park. The project by Relais Landschaftsarchitekten used the model of the cloister, using a cast aluminium typographic fence to wall the corridors. The texts were taken from the Old and New Testament as a reminder that Christendom is a religion of the word. Typographic designer Alexander Branczyk of xplicit designed a typeface in multiple widths in order to create a sturdy support for the vertical structure. The resulting 'Written Garden' is a structure with a surface measuring c. 20 × 20 meters , probably the largest building completely made out of type.

Spatial illusions

Type and lettering offer infinite possibilities to create illusions of volume and perspective. In digital typography, the ease with which a hint of dimensionality can be added to type on the printed page or the screen has made 3D type into a cliché; only when executed with superb wit and attention to detail, does dimensionality add value and not banality to a typographic solution.

Anamorphosis

Our brain has great capabilities of correcting what the eyes see in order to construct a more 'normal' or acceptable picture. Optical illusions play with this tendency to unconsciously rearrange visual data. Perspective is, to a certain extent, a means of creating an optical illusion – a powerful tool to suggest volume and distance on a two-dimensional canvas. But it can also be used to do the opposite: to create the illusion of a two-dimensional picture or text in a spatial setting. Anamorphosis is a technique brought to perfection by renaissance painters; their method of fooling the spectator by stretching or condensing the image has been put to use for artistic as well as practical purposes (as in stop signs or bicycle pictograms painted on road surfaces to enable identification from a distance). Practical considerations and playful experimentation are now often combined to create eye-catching effects in signage and placemaking projects.

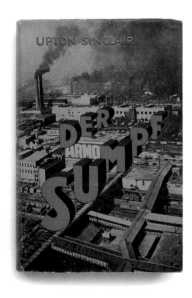

Der Sumpf was the German translation of Upton Sinclair's 1906 *The Jungle*, a novel describing the conditions in the American meatpacking industry. This 1922 design by John Heartfield (born Helmut Herzfeld), who later became famous for his anti-Nazi photomontage, effectively uses a combination of photography and three dimensional lettering that was unique at the time.

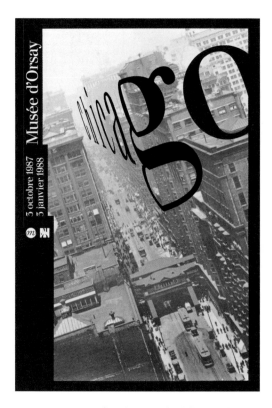

↑ In this poster by Philippe Apeloig the idea of the twentieth-century metropolis with its grid of perpendicular streets is translated into a typographic simulation of a 90-degree angle. Poster for the exhibition *Chicago, naissance d'une métropole, 1877-1922*, Musée d'Orsay, Paris 1987.

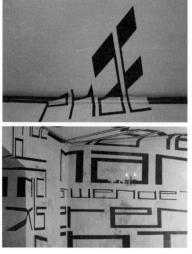

← Much like the wayfinding project described on the following page, this piece by Felix Ewers with fellow students at the Folkwang Hochschule in Essen, Germany, uses anamorphosis, the visual trick of 'correcting by distorting' also found in paintings by Leonardo da Vinci and Hans Holbein. The German text reads: 'Phenomena that are not used don't exist.' No ready-made font was used: the lettering was specially designed for the project.

Anamorphosis for wayfinding

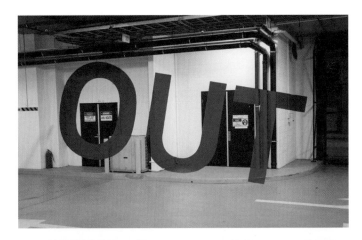

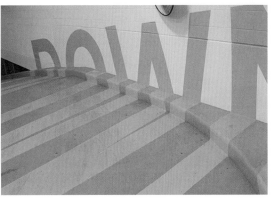

Wayfinding project by Emery Studio at the Eureka Tower Parking in Melbourne. Instead of mounting conventional signs, designer Axel Peemöller proposed to use the entire space as a canvas. The site's irregularity, with curves, curbs and pillars standing in the way of a 'clean' image, was taken advantage of by using anamorphosis: a distorted perspective that allows viewers to see the key words magically floating in space when observing them from a specific point.

The fourth dimension

For decades after the invention of the 'talkies', type in film meant a sequence of static titles at the start and a credit roll at the end of a movie. Designer-illustrator Saul Bass was instrumental in changing that with his cutting-edge graphic film title sequences. Bass's animations from the mid- to late 1950s are particularly striking, using shifting, simple cut-out images and type to hit their point home. Ten years later, title sequence type was about as sophisticated as it would ever get in the pre-digital era: the opening sequence of 1968's *Barbarella* showed Jane Fonda getting undressed with equally gorgeous, free-floating

kinetic type emanating from her spacesuit and body. Many animated type sequences for film and TV have followed suit, made photographically or drawn by hand, but Maurice Binder's *Barbarella* animation still stands out.

Once digital tools had become widely available, layering, dimensionality and interactivity brought new possibilities for exploring meaning and adding depth to kinetic type, both visually and conceptually. Some of the earliest examples of kinetic type were seen in art installations. In 1988 Amsterdam-based Australian artist Jeffrey Shaw created *Legible City*, an interactive piece

↗ *Barbarella* titling sequence

↓ **In many pieces of motion design in which the typography plays a major role, the choice of type and the subtleties of typesetting take a back seat to motion and concept. This is not the case in the video made by designer Jarrett Heather for Jonathan Coulton's song 'Shop Vac'. Each typographic reference is spot-on, each fake logo a perfect parody or pastiche.**

that allowed the viewer to take a bike ride through a virtual city made of type. The piece was echoed, possibly unwittingly, in a video made by French design group H5 for 'The Child' by Alex Gopher. The clip tells of a wild taxi ride to a city-centre hospital, replacing all buildings, objects and characters by two- and three-dimensional words describing those things. It became one of the most-watched clips on YouTube.

Deconstructing

In the course of the 1990s, styles that were first pioneered in print came alive in time-based pieces. Designers such as Tomato, Jonathan Barnbrook and David Carson made typographic videos in the layered, eroded, deconstructed style we have come to know as 'grunge'. Kyle Cooper, in his title sequence for the movie *Se7en*, drew his lettering directly on film to obtain a 'scratchy' effect.

Animated type is now part of many a designer's portfolio and many a graduate design course. Word-for-word visual readings of rock lyrics are now a genre of their own. These pieces can only fully succeed if the designers are as savvy about type and typography as they are about the more obvious aspects of motion design. Animated type is at its best when visual effect and rhythm go hand in hand with typographic sophistication.

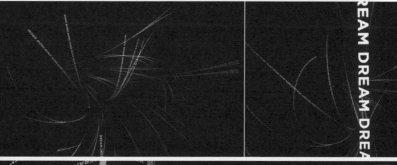

Kinetic typography for the TED 2009 event by Trollbäck + Company. Created using Maya® 3D software, it took two designers two weeks to create the basic design and two CG animators about a month and a half to produce it, resulting in 'a seamless animation which only had a few cuts'. The biggest challenge was to 'get the ribbons to turn and twist in a precise and flexible way.'

The allure of the hand-made

For about twenty years, virtually all typographic design has been done on a computer. More and more work remains permanently intangible: websites, newspapers, season's greetings, even complete books are both produced and consumed on the screen. A rapidly growing group of designers are unhappy about this. They miss the tangible aspect, and they miss the lack of craftsmanship – handling materials, tools and machines. Just like low-fi recording and acoustic instruments have brought a fresh ear and innovation to rock music, the typographic world has rediscovered pre-digital graphic techniques as a way to find new routes and reopen old ones.

No nostalgia

All this has little to do with nostalgia. Take Sam Arthur and Alex Spiro, for instance. These two London designers gave up their careers in digital filmmaking and animation to found Nobrow, a publishing platform and screen-print workshop for limited-edition hand-made books and prints. 'We don't have any problem with technology,' they say. 'We simply don't want to be slaves to what is easiest or most efficient ... We try to incorporate analogue processes into the digital framework of our world.' Screen printing is a favourite technique, because of 'the tactile nature of it, the way the ink is slightly raised off the paper, the vitality of the colours, the beautiful mistakes that simply cannot be replicated with any process of mass production.' Also in London, Alan Kitching's Typography Workshop showed how letterpress printing (often with large-size wood type) could be used to create innovative graphic design; Kitching has been hugely influential within and outside of the UK.

Letterpress printing has become truly mainstream in the United States and Canada, where a lot of jobbing printing such as invitations and keepsakes is done by preparing digital files, then converting these into polymer plates to be printed on a proof press. Also, more and more graphic designers get interested in working with metal and wood type. The successful film *Typeface* paints a portrait of the Hamilton Wood Type Museum in Wisconsin, showing how young designers work there to get inspired by the limitations and surprises of artisanal printing.

Both in Europe and North America mechanical printing techniques have come out of the somewhat stuffy corner of *private presses* and literary editions. Getting your hands inky: yes, it's back.

← Poster for a letterpress conference at London's St Bride Library. Design and printing by Helen Ingham, owner of Hi-Artz Press, who is also Letterpress Tutor and Workshop Facilitator at St Bride Foundation Print Workshop.

→ Poster by Nick Sherman for the film *Typeface*, made with wood type from the Hamilton Wood Type Museum, the organization that is the movie's hero.

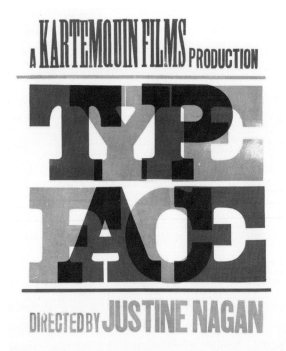

Letterpress updated

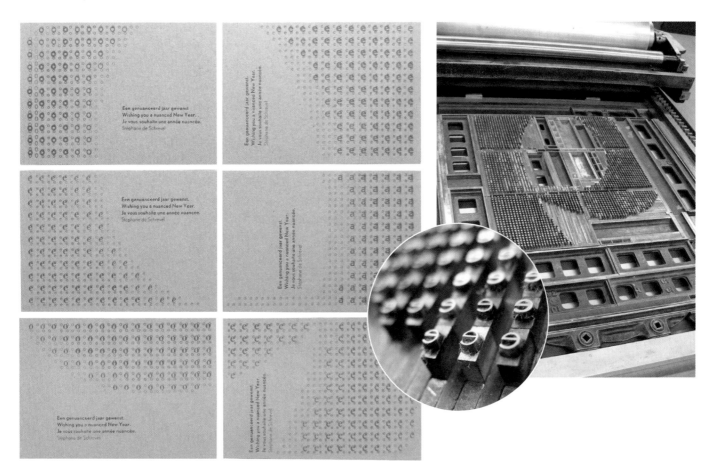

↘ Armina Ghazaryan, an Armenian designer based in Ghent, Belgium, mixes analogue and digital technologies in this wedding invitation. The process is popular in North America and has caught on in Europe as well: digital files are processed into letterpress plates made from polymer, magnesium or zinc, then printed on a flatbed proof press or platen press. It allows designers to use contemporary digital fonts like the one in this work, Reina by Lián Types, and still lend their work the aura of something hand-made. Today, part of the allure of luxury letterpress work is the debossing effect caused by the impact of the press on the soft paper – a thing letterpress printers tried hard to avoid in the old days.

↑ Stéphane De Schrevel is a Flemish book designer also based in Ghent, who uses both digital and analogue techniques, and sometimes mixes the two. For his 2009 New Year's greetings he simultaneously printed six different cards that form a '9' when put together (a rare sighting). The process was letterpress in three colours from foundry type, a total of 2.879 sorts, all hand-set.

The Linotype linecaster, introduced in 1886, was the first mechanical system for casting fresh lines of type. It was also the first commercially viable typesetting machine, and became a worldwide success despite the fact that it required constant maintenance – it had thousands of parts that needed cleaning, adjusting and, at times, replacing. Each and every part is listed in this catalogue from Mergenthaler Linotype, New York 1934.

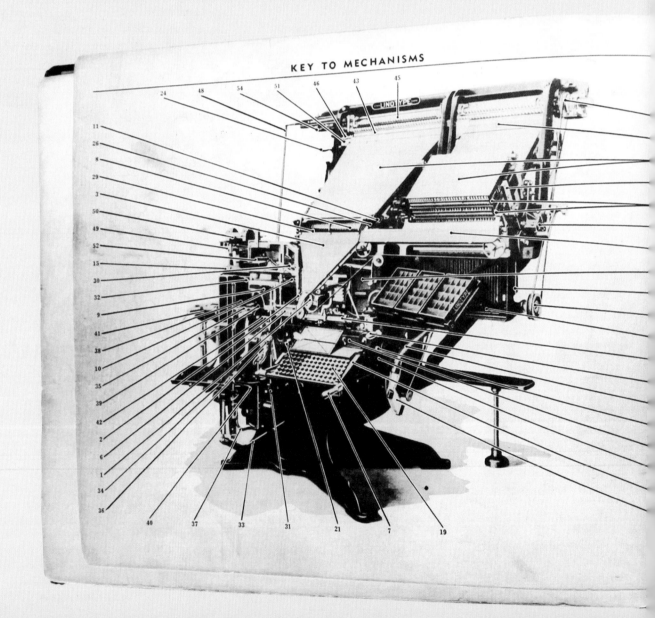

KEY TO MECHANISMS

Type and technology

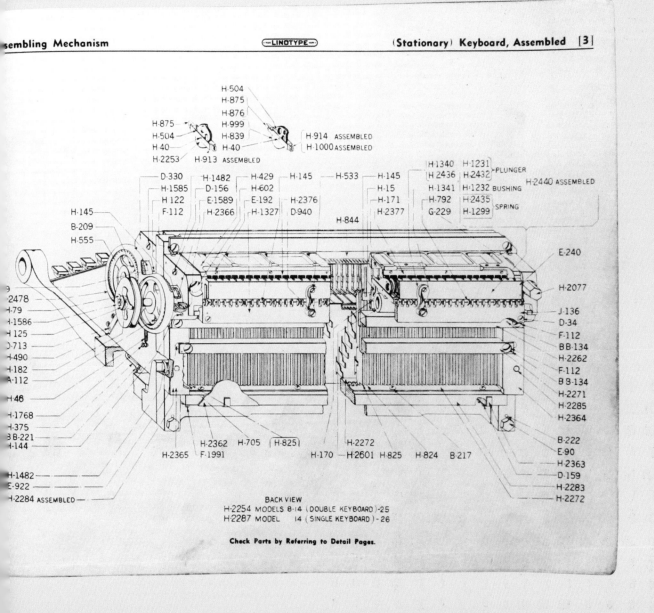

H-504
H-875
H-876
H-875 — H-999
H-504 — H-839 — H-914 ASSEMBLED
H-40 — H-40 — H-1000 ASSEMBLED
H-2253 — H-913 ASSEMBLED

H-1340 H-1231
H-2436 H-2432 PLUNGER
D-330 H-1482 H-429 H-145 H-533 H-145 H-1341 H-1232 BUSHING H-2440 ASSEMBLED
H-1585 D-156 H-602 H-15
H-122 E-1589 E-192 H-2376 H-171 H-792 H-2435 SPRING
F-112 H-2366 H-1327 D-940 H-2377 G-229 H-1299

H-145
B-209
H-555

H-844

E-240

H-2077
J-136
D-34
F-112
BB-134
H-2262
F-112
BB-134
H-2271
H-2285
H-2364

2478
79
1586
125
713
490
182
112
46
1768
375
B-221
144

H-2362 H-705 H-825 H-2272
H-2365 F-1991 H-170 H-2601 H-825 H-824 B-217

B-222
E-90
H-2363
D-159
H-2283
H-2272

H-1482
E-922
H-2284 ASSEMBLED

BACK VIEW
H-2254 MODELS 8-14 (DOUBLE KEYBOARD)-25
H-2287 MODEL 14 (SINGLE KEYBOARD)-26

Check Parts by Referring to Detail Pages.

A brief history of typographic technology

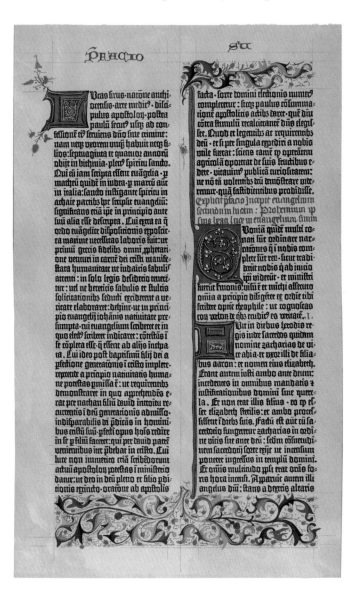

The art of printing with moveable type was developed around 1450 in the German city of Mainz. It is very likely that the former goldsmith Johann Gensfleisch zur Laden zum Gutenberg (usually referred to as Johannes Gutenberg) was the inventor of the process. It is certain that it was his workshop that produced the 42-line Bible – the first masterpiece made with the new technology. Production took place between 1452 and 1455; of approximately 180 original copies, twenty-one have been fully preserved. Gutenberg did not only print books. Apparently, he financed his experiments partly by printing indulgences commissioned by the Catholic Church – letters of spiritual credit which credulous believers could buy to redeem their sins.

Media revolution

From southern Germany the art of printing spread to Italy, Switzerland, France and the Netherlands. In the 1470s it progressed at an impressive pace, with printing presses being set up in almost a hundred European cities. Where the impact of the media is concerned, only the advent of television, almost five hundred years later, has had a comparable impact. To mention only one aspect: without the art of printing, the ideas of Luther and Calvin would never have spread so quickly. The Reformation, the icono-clastic fury and subsequent religious wars of the 16th and 17th centuries would have taken place more slowly – or perhaps not at all.

↖ Page from Gutenberg's magnum opus, the 42-line Bible. Only the red and black text was printed, the illuminations were applied by hand after the work was pur-chased. Each copy is different.

← To smoothly introduce the new tech-nology, Gutenberg did his utmost to approach the hand-written book. For his Bible, he used 299 different characters, including many abbreviations developed to save space by scribes in monasteries. Gutenberg's successors rigorously sim-plified the character sets. It wasn't until the advent of OpenType, 570 years later, that such a wealth of alternate charac-ters would be available again.

Punchcutting and typefounding

The art of printing was developed into a mature craft in the first decades of its existence. Once in place, there were no substantial changes for almost 400 years. We don't know exactly how the first printers worked. The newly invented art was cloaked in an air of mystery: the pioneering work involved huge investments and nobody was eager to give competitors insight into what exactly they had discovered by writing something about it down. It wasn't until 1683 (after almost 250 years) that the first handbook on printing was published – *Mechanick exercises* by the Englishman Joseph Moxon.

What we do know is that making letters soon became a speciality. The punchcutter became a freelance provider of punches or matrices to printers and type-founders. Thanks to Moxon's book and to publications like Pierre Simon Fournier's *Manuel typographique* from 1764 we know with some accuracy how moveable letters were cut and cast – and had been, to all probability, from the late 15th century onwards.

This is how:

↑ This seventeenth-century print by Abraham van Werdt paints a clear picture of how printing shops worked for several centuries. Women and children were (sometimes) put to work as typesetters. The printing was done by two men – working the hand press required muscle as well as coordination.

    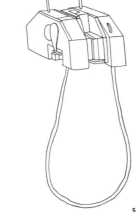 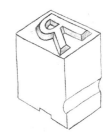

| 1 | 2 | 3 | 4 | 5 | 6 |

↑ A stamp of basic shapes (counterpunch) is cut from a piece of unhardened steel with a sharp knife (fig. 1). After being hardened by heating and quickly cooling, it is used to strike the counterform of a letter into another piece of steel (fig. 2). This resulting steel stick is then cut and filed into a mirror image of the letter – the punch (fig. 3).

→ A punchcutter at work.

↑ The steel punch is then used to make a matrix (fig. 4) by hardening it and striking it into a block of copper – a softer metal. This hollow, 'readable' mould will be the mother of all the letters of its kind, hence the word 'matrix'.

↑ The casting is done in the hand mold, fig. 5, which has been constructed in such a way that, together with the letter, a block of standard height is cast (the body) with a standard groove and notch, so that it can be combined easily with other characters on the press, and the typesetter can discern top and bottom without looking. One such metal character is called a *sort* (fig. 6).

→ Demonstration by Dutch type designer Fred Smeijers, the author of *Counterpunch* (1996), the definitive book on punchcutting.

Five centuries of typesetting

Fig. 1ᵉ

← Each sort (character, glyph) has its fixed place in the case so that the typesetter can find it blindly. The capitals (and small caps) in the top case, the minuscules below. For that reason, the former are called 'uppercase' and the latter 'lowercase' to this day. Type case layouts differed from country to country, partly because each language needs different amounts of each letter. This is a French case, where special ligatures and diacritics were also accommodated in the upper case.

↑ A medium-sized composing room around 1900. Each typesetter works at a typecase, a flat box placed on a rack with a sloping top. After each use the case is placed back into the rack like a drawer and another font pulled out.

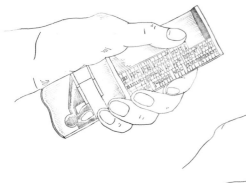

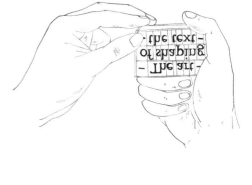

↓ Hand-setting was a lot of work, and *distribution* (returning type to the case) was a separate, time-consuming task. That is why the set pages of books were often stocked up with a view to a possible reprint. Called 'standing type', 'live matter' or 'standing matter', the stuff took up a lot of space.

↑ Setting it straight. First set a few lines of text in the *composing stick*, letter by letter (reverse: from right to left). To justify each line, add word spaces of equal width. Having set a few lines, lift the type from the composing stick and transfer it to the *galley*, a kind of baking tray. When the complete text is on the galley, the page is ready for *make-up*: adding line-spacing (leading) if needed and *blocks*: lines, ornaments, halftones. The type is then secured by binding it up with page cord.

→ Finally, the type is *locked up* in a steel frame (or chase); it is *imposed* (put in position) using wooden and metal *furniture* and the resulting *forme* is ready for the press. Photo: Annette C. Dißlin of the letterpress workshop bleiklötzle Buchdruckatelier.

Lithography, the mother of offset printing

From around 1800, innovations in printing happened in rapid succession. The first machine for paper production (1798), the Stanhope iron press (1800), stereotyping – a method for cheaply copying entire pages of metal composition (1805), the König steam cylinder press (1811), the first letter casting machine (1822).

Of all the inventions of that era, lithography ('stone printing') is probably the most relevant today. Alois Senefelder, an unsuccessful German playwright, was looking for a way to reproduce his own work. Between 1796 and 1798 he devised a way to make prints from smooth limestone, making use of the repulsion of oil and water. A drawing with crayons or greasy ink on a stone, when dampened, will hold the oily ink while the rest of the stone repels the ink.

Lithography freed the designer from the limitations of letterpress: the rectangular grid, the dependence on prefabricated characters and ornaments. Moreover, it was quick. Nimble craftsmen would copy a design onto the stone in no time. Today, when thinking of lithography we tend to picture impressionistic artworks drawn with coarse chalk and printed in pastel shades. Often, however, old lithographs are at first sight hard to distinguish from copper engravings – so fine and precise are the drawings.

↑ Lithographic stone and printed result. As lithography allowed great freedom in designing ornaments and patterns, it was a common technique for any papers of value. Lithographic print had the additional benefit that once a stone had been imaged, very high runs could be printed – up to several million. To reuse a lithographic stone it must be re-sanded, which is laborious – the drawing penetrates deeply into the porous stone.

Mechanisation

In the course of the nineteenth century lithography became a common technique primarily for advertising, stocks and shares, and maps. To speed things up, automated lithographic presses were developed – hulks weighing several tons, powered by steam and later by electric engines. From about 1840 chromo- or colour lithography made it possible to combine multiple colours, but as a separate stone had to be prepared for each colour, the process was quite laborious. This changed in 1870 when French poster artist Jules Cheret devised a method allowing a range of colours to be created by overprinting transparent inks using just three stones.

Lithography is still a widely used technique in graphic art. Interestingly, a better type of stone has never been found than the Solnhofer limestone with its fine pores that inspired Senefelder's invention.

Offset

Based on the same principle, offset printing was developed for non-artistic high circulation production; today, it is by far the most common printing technique. Here, too, the central principle is the repulsion of oil and water. The stone has been replaced by plates made of metal or polyester that are bent around cylinders. Transferring the image onto the plate is now done by means of photographic exposure and some chemistry. For decades, offset plates were created photographically from transparent films, but today the plate imaging usually happens directly from the computer – the *computer-to-plate* (CTP) process. The new technology has reduced cost and production time and improved print quality.

Speeding things up

The nineteenth century was the age of industrialization. The advent of the steam engine led to the mechanisation of production processes which until then had relied on human and animal muscle power. In the printing trade, mechanisation went hand in hand with new construction principles for machines. In newspaper printing for instance, flat 'formes' were replaced by cylinder shapes. Metal, hand-set pages were pressed into papier-mâché slabs, resulting in molds from which plates could be cast – a process known as *stereotyping*. As the papier-mâché was flexible, the slabs could be bent to form hollow molds from which semi-circular metal plates were cast that fit around the cylinders.

The Times in London had a scoop with its rotary press that was built in 1866 on the instructions of the newspaper's owner, John Walter III. Not only was this machine equipped with cylinders, it also made use of kilometre-long ('infinite') rolls of paper instead of single sheets.

↑ Smiling, the workers of the *Illustrated London News* carry out their slave labour on the 1843 *steam printing machine*.

← The Kastenbein machine was the most successful typesetting machine until the invention of the Linotype.

↓ Paige's typesetting machine, a cause of much misery.

Mechanical typesetting

While printing speeds increased, typesetting by hand became a bothersome bottleneck. And so, from the early nineteenth century onwards, dozens of inventors and charlatans were looking for the ultimate composing machine. Many tried mechanising the task of the typesetter – picking individual sorts (letters) from the type case – but this proved impractical. Operating Young & Delcambre's Pianotype from 1840, for instance, required seven men, although a later version made do with a crew of three.

The same number of operators was sufficient for the Kastenbein machine from 1869, a 'letter sorting machine' with 84 keys that was relatively successful. A quite complicated contraption that consisted of 18,000 parts was Paige's compositor: it drove two officials at the Patent Office crazy, and ruined the writer Mark Twain, who had invested a considerable sum in Paige's typesetting robot.

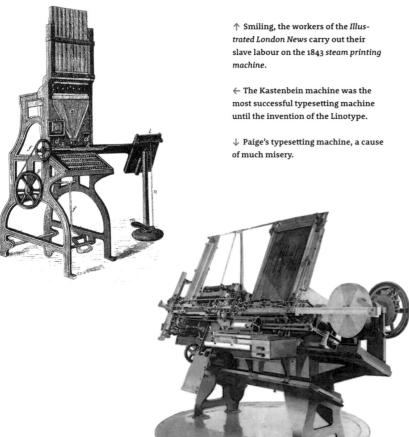

Hot-metal typesetting

Linotype: a line of type

The first technician to build a successful type-setting machine was Ottmar Mergenthaler, an instrument maker of German origin who worked in Baltimore. Mergenthaler's breakthrough invention was to have the machine typeset not letters, but individual matrices. In 1886 he completed an ingenious machine that produced newly cast lines-of-type. Hence: Linotype (operators call these lines *slugs*).

Linotype machines, with production facilities established in England, Germany and the US, caused a revolution in the newspaper business. A daily paper was now so much quicker and cheaper to produce. The linecaster remained in production until the year 1960.

After the advent of phototypesetting, Linotype became a pioneer of the new technologies, but the breakthrough of DTP brought deep trouble. The German branch survived as a relatively small company that owns major typographic trademarks such as Helvetica and Frutiger.

The workings of a linecaster

Brass matrices for single letters (pros call them *mats*) are drawn up in array via a keyboard until the line is full. The line of mats is pressed against a concave shape which is then filled with liquid metal that instantly solidifies. Less than a second later a line of type is dropped into the galley. One of the machine's most brilliant features is the system for distribution: each mould has a pattern of indentations, as unique as the teeth of a key, allowing the machine to automatically take each character back to its proper place in the magazine. Thus the mats circulate through the machine in an endless cycle.

Monotype

Almost simultaneously with the introduction of the Linotype, Tolbert Lanston invented the Monotype, which was first seen in 1887. On a Monotype machine, typesetting and casting are separated. The typist makes a punch tape, which is fed into the caster. Thus the work of several compositors can be processed by the typecaster, which can be in a different room. As the name suggests, the Monotype doesn't cast lines but individual sorts (letters), which are also put in the correct order. This makes it more sophisticated than the Linotype. In case of corrections it is possible to replace single sorts, while for the Linotype a complete line has to be re-cast. In addi-tion, it is possible tho re-use Monotype sorts as foundry type.

Like all typesetting systems, Monotype had its own specially designed typefaces, which were of unparalleled quality. While the Monotype was 'the grand piano of typography', the Linotype was more manageable: a real workhorse.

The company's current incarnation, Monotype Imaging, is one the world's biggest players in digital typography. In 2006 the company acquired its former competitor, Linotype; and in November 2011 it was announced that Monotype was buying MyFonts, its largest competitor in font distribution.

← Monotype keyboard.

Typesetting with light

After World War II offset printing began replacing letterpress. Printing from flexible plates brought practical advantages for the reproduction of pictures: letterpress had required the production of separate blocks for each image and each colour. However, reproducing text in offset printing was initially cumbersome. Lead type was printed on special paper and photographed, then combined with the halftone images on films, which in turn served to expose the offset plate. The advent of phototypesetting put an end to this laborious method.

In the course of the 1950s, one manufacturer after another brought out photocomposition systems. Typeset texts were no longer 'stamped' mechanically by means of high pressure, but photographed. Phototypesetters worked with glass or plastic plates and disks full of letters that were exposed one by one at lightning speed.

The earliest phototypesetters looked like transformed hot-metal machines: the keyboard and matrix case of the Monophoto, for example, were virtually identical to that of the old Monotype casting machines.

As early as the 1960s, electronically controlled phototypesetters became common. The various machines were not compatible. Each manufacturer had their own system, which required specially adapted fonts. One major difference with most metal type was that all type sizes were now derived from one single original using lenses; sometimes the italics (more precisely: obliques) and even semibold versions were obtained by optically or electronically distorting the projection of a 'Regular' negative.

↑ Bram de Does's Trinité was originally produced for Bobst Graphic and Autologic phototypesetters. In this system, eight versions of the font could fit on to a single disk.

← Glass plate for the Berthold system with Hermann Zapf's Optima Normal.

Display type for everyone

↑ Letraset: instructions for use

↓ As late as 1987 Letraset brought out a new catalogue of dry transfer sheets. Otmar Motter was one designer who specialised in spectacular display type.

From the late 1950s onwards, innovations followed in rapid succession. One thing remained unchanged: typesetting equipment and fonts required huge investments, resulting in high bills from the typesetting shop. A strip containing a few lines of display text (for instance for a poster or book cover) would easily cost the equivalent of 30 to 50 dollars or euros. Many graphic designers made a virtue out of necessity by using hand-rendered lettering – either drawn freehand or constructed using compass and ruler.

Letraset and Mecanorma

To many designers, the advent of dry transfer (or rub on) lettering meant a true liberation. No longer were they dependent on the typesetter's limited collection, or his opening hours. Moreover, the major producers, such as Letraset (UK), Mecanorma (France) and Chartpak (USA), wisely ordered designs from young type specialists who managed to translate the trends of the moment – from geometric via nostalgic to psychedelic – into original letterforms which were issued as dry transfer sheets alongside the classics.

The system was an invention of the Londoner Dai Davies, who in 1961 released his first Letraset series. A surprisingly home-baked process was developed for the production. The forms were cut manually from red Ulano masking film, with no other tools than self-made scalpel-like knives. Letraset set up a studio with a master-apprentice system to perfect the method and pass it on. Well-known British type designers such as Freda Sack (The Foundry) and Dave Farey started their careers at Letraset.

On the European continent, Mecanorma was particularly popular. Besides many famous classic and modern typefaces, the French manufacturer also had its own collection of exclusive designs, made mostly by freelancers. Letraset and Mecanorma released digital versions of their fonts in the 1980s and 1990s.

↓ During the twentieth century, ever new systems hit the market that were to allow designers to typeset their own titles and slogans – usually with little success.

↓ Amsterdam designer Max Kisman, too, cut self-designed letters from Ulano masking film in the 1980. Not for Letraset, but for his own posters and magazines.

The pros and cons of progress

For the printing world, the 1970s and 1980s were a confusing and often frustrating period. New techniques followed one another in rapid succession, and many companies found new, digital technologies knocking on their doors years before their considerable investments in photo-composition had been recovered. Printing and typesetting shops decided to acquire digital systems the size of a car (and more expensive than that) – only to find, a few years later, that they were being overtaken by self-employed youngsters with a Mac.

Initially, typesetting produced with the new techniques was often of questionable quality. Proponents of progress shouted in unison that people had to get used to the fact that type made with new technologies simply looked different. But the shortcomings of these technologies were real and objective. Photographic typesetting was often blurry because the glare of light beams rounded off the letterforms; very small sizes, which were based on the same negatives as larger body text and headings, looked too spindly. Letters produced with (very fast) cathode ray tube technology had jagged edges that were visible to the naked eye. Only after the resolution of scanners and printers was increased by using laser beams, did the printed page obtain a sharpness comparable to that of the old analogue technology.

The end of the typesetting office

Around 1990 desktop computers became common; Apple, especially, invested in typographically sophisticated solutions. Fonts rapidly decreased in price. For design and advertising agencies it became easier and cheaper to set their own type, and one typesetting shop after another folded.

It was inevitable, but together with the old technology, much expertise and professional criteria were discarded that might have been useful to us today. Typesetting by graphic designers is often quite a bit sloppier than that of the exacting fusspots at the typesetting office, and the proofreading rounds that used to be part and parcel of the production process (at a time when manuscripts had to be retyped by the typesetter) have in many cases been reduced to a quick glance, out of economy or nonchalance.

There is a task for design schools here: today's designers need to learn how to perform the tasks of the professional typesetter and proofreader – nobody else is doing it.

Versmalling 20%

Het begin van de loopbaan van Jan van der Heyden als schilder is nogal duister: bij zijn huwelijk in 1661 noemde hij zichzelf als zodanig, terwijl de vroegst bekende datum op een schilderij 1664 is. Hij was vooral uitvinder. In 1668 ontwierp hij een nieuw plan voor de stadsverlichting van Amsterdam (die met 2556 lampen in functie bleef tot 1840). In 1672 bouwde hij de eerste slangen-brandspuit, die hij vanaf 1681 in fabrieksmatige produktie bracht en

Cursivering –20°

Het begin van de loopbaan van Jan van der Heyden als schilder is nogal duister: bij zijn huwelijk in 1661 noemde hij zichzelf als zodanig, terwijl de vroegst bekende datum op een schilderij 1664 is. Hij was vooral uitvinder. In 1668 ontwierp hij een nieuw plan voor de stadsverlichting van Amsterdam (die met 2556 lampen in functie bleef tot 1840). In 1672

Cursivering 20°

Het begin van de loopbaan van Jan van der Heyden als schilder is nogal duister: bij zijn huwelijk in 1661 noemde hij zichzelf als zodanig, terwijl de vroegst bekende datum op een schilderij 1664 is. Hij was vooral uitvinder. In 1668 ontwierp hij een nieuw plan voor de stadsverlichting van Amsterdam (die met 2556 lampen in functie bleef tot 1840). In 1672

← Details of a type specimen from Bloem 'layout compositors' in Amsterdam, who offered complete pages set on a Berthold digital system. The possibilities for electronic letters to be condensed or tilted forward and backward were presented as major advantages. Now these deformations are considered in very bad taste.

↓ The 'a' from the original version of Gerard Unger's Demos typeface. It was designed for Hell Digiset equipment, which worked with bitmap fonts

↘ The drawings for Digiset typefaces were sometimes hand-pixelated by their designers.

Type in the digital age: do we need more fonts?

Until the mid-1980s the world of type design was an exclusive club. To enter it, one had to submit a typeface design (on paper) to a type publisher such as Linotype, ITC or Berthold. If they decided to take you on board, the design would go through a costly production process involving numerous tests, redrawings and meetings. Understandably, foundries published just a handful of new faces each year.

In the mid-1980s a company called Altsys released the first font editors for the Macintosh – Fontastic (a bitmap editor) and Fontographer. Adobe contributed to the democratisation of font production by making its PostScript specifications public in 1990. That same year, FontShop started up the FontFont collection and actively began looking for fresh typefaces to release. Within a few years the type world would be completely reshuffled.

150,000 fonts

Fast forward twenty years. According to a recent estimate there are over 150,000 fonts available for direct download. A large part of these fonts are quick-and-dirty display fonts: not very original and of mediocre quality. This is partly because making and publishing fonts has become so easy. Many designers publish their own fonts, so quality control is often minimal.

The good news is that the production of high-quality, original typefaces has also increased considerably. Ambitious type designers seek peer critiques, online and in real life. Young graphic designers who discover a penchant for type and lettering decide to become students again and enrol in one of the highly professional type design programmes in Reading, The Hague, Buenos Aires, or elsewhere. Being perfectionists, they may hone their first type family for years until arriving at a mature, top-quality product.

The question of whether we need more typefaces comes up often: if an existing typeface does the job, then what's the use of making a new one? Some people argue that type designers should concentrate on clearly perceivable prob-

lems and needs – make more and better fonts for Asian languages, for instance. This is a complex discussion. What does 'doing the job' mean? Typefaces lend character to a text in ways that are almost subliminal. Many users who work exclusively within the Latin script are sincerely interested in new flavours. That alone is a legitimate function of type design: adding subtly new colours to the typographic palette. For instance, the two main typefaces that lend a specific atmosphere to the pages of this book, Rooney and Agile, did not exist three years ago.

Typographic diversity

There are thousands of similar wines, chocolates, textile designs or lamps. Every user has reasons for preferring one particular kind over others at a given point in time. For certain occasions, a simpler and more affordable wine is more appropriate, and it is not so very different with fonts. Diversity in type is a good thing. It is up to the users – especially the professional ones – to develop a taste and some intuition about what works best in which circumstances, or even go all the way and become connoisseurs.

It is true that with so many fonts available, choosing just the right typeface for the job is *not* a no-brainer. But are no-brainers what you should be looking for? Being a (typo-)graphic designer is a job that involves working with a rich world of ingredients, just like fashion design, cooking or DJ-ing. Learning to love and be curious about the ingredients available for shaping text should be part and parcel of a designer's education; it can also make professional life more rewarding.

↑ EcoChallenge is a free iPhone app developed by the Berlin interface design company Raureif in collaboration with Potsdam Technical University. For this 'companion app to a more sustainable lifestyle,' Raureif chose Rooney Pro (also the text face of the present book) as main typeface. This recent type family offered just the right combination of humanist seriousness and a friendly feel; in addition, its open shapes and rounded strokes make it a good choice for small screens. In September 2011 EcoChallenge won a CleanTech Media Award in the Communication category.

Sources and further reading

Below is a selection of books and articles that were used as sources for this book and/or are recommended for those interested in specific subjects. The Dutch-language books I have used are not included here. I did include a few recent books in German that are unsurpassed in their thoroughness.

Ways of reading

Peter Enneson, Kevin Larson, Hrant Papazian et al., *Typo* 13 (Legibility issue), Prague 2005

Thomas Huot-Marchand, *Minuscule/ Émile Javal*, 256tm.com

Émile Javal, *Physiologie de la lecture et de l'écriture.* Cambridge University Press, Cambridge 2010 (or. 1905)

Kevin Larson, *The science of word recognition*, microsoft.com/typography/ ctfonts/wordrecognition.aspx

Gerard Unger, *While You're Reading.* Mark Batty Publisher, New York 2007

Graphic design and typography

Phil Baines & Andrew Haslam, *Type & typography.* Laurence King, London 2005[2]

Eric Gill, *An essay on typography.* J.M. Dent & Sons, London 1960[4] (or. 1931)

David Jury, *About Face: Reviving the Rules of Typography.* Rockport, *2002*

David Jury, *What is typography?* RotoVision, Mies/Hove 2006

Ellen Lupton, *Thinking with type.* Princeton Architectural Press, New York 2004

Theodore Rosendorf, *The typographic desk reference.* Oak Knoll Press, New Castle 2009

Michael Bierut, Steven Heller e.a. (red.), *Looking closer*, Vol. 1–5, Allworth Press, New York 1994-2006

Book design and microtypography

Robert Bringhurst, *The elements of typographic style.* Hartley and Marks, Vancouver 1992 (2005, v. 3.2)

Geoffrey Dowding, *Finer points in the spacing & arrangement of type.* Hartley and Marks, Vancouver 1995 (or. 1966)

Friedrich Forssman & Ralf de Jong, *Detailtypografie*, Hermann Schmidt, Mainz 2002

Friedrich Forssman & Hans Peter Willberg, *Lesetypografie*, Hermann Schmidt, Mainz 20105

Andrew Haslam, *Book design.* Laurence King, London 2006

Will Hill, *The complete typographer; A foundation course for graphic designers working with type.* Thames & Hudson, London 2010[3]

Jost Hochuli & Robin Kinross, *Designing books: Practice and theory.* Hyphen Press, London 2003

Michael Mitchell & Susan Wightman, *Book typography: A designer's manual.* Libanus Press, Marlborough 2005

Gerrit Noordzij, 'Rule or law'. hyphenpress.co.uk/journal/2007/09/15/ rule_or_law. Originally in Paul Barnes (ed.), *Reflections and reappraisals*, Typoscope, New York 1995

Visual organisation, grids

Allen Hurlburt, *The grid: A modular system for the design and production of newpapers magazines and books.* John Wiley & Sons, New York 1978

Josef Müller-Brockmann, *Grid systems in graphic design.* Niggli, Sulgen/Zürich 1981 (2008[4])

Lucienne Roberts, Studio Ink et al., *Grids. Creative solutions for graphic designers.* RotoVision, Mies/Hove 2007

Lucienne Roberts & Julia Thrift, *The designer and the grid.* RotoVision, Mies/ Hove 2005

Jan Tschichold, *The new typography.* Translated by Ruari McLean. University of California Press, Berkeley/Los Angeles 1995

Type and lettering design

Phil Baines & Catherine Dixon, *Signs: Lettering in the environment.* Laurence King, London 2003

Sebastian Carter, *Twentieth century type designers.* W. W. Norton & Company, New York 1995 (new edition)

Karen Cheng, *Designing type.* Laurence King, London 2006

Simon Loxley, *Type: The Secret History of Letters.* I.B. Tauris, London/New York 2004

Jan Middendorp, *Dutch type.* 010 Publishers, Rotterdam 2004

Jan Middendorp & TwoPoints.Net, *Type Navigator.* Gestalten, Berlin 2011

Gerrit Noordzij, *The stroke: Theory of writing.* Van de Garde, Zaltbommel 1985

Walter Tracy, *Letters of credit: a view of type design.* David R. Godine Publishers, Boston 2003

Bruce Willen & Nolen Strals, *Lettering & type.* Princeton Architectural Press, New York 2009

History of writing

Timothy Donaldson, *Shapes for Sounds.* Mark Batty Publisher, New York 2008

Johanna Drucker, *The alphabetic labyrinth: The letters in history and imagination.* Thames and Hudson, 1995

Marc-Alain Ouaknin, *Mysteries of the Alphabet*, Abbeville Press, New York 1999

[John Boardley] *The origins of abc*, ilovetypography.com/where-does-the-alphabet-come-from, 2010

Screen typography, webfonts

Matthias Hillner, *Virtual typography*, AVA Publishing, Lausanne 2009

Stephen Coles, Frank Chimero e.a., 'Cure for the Common Font.' typographica.org

Typographic technology

Johannes Bergerhausen & Siri Poarangan *Decodeunicode: Die Schriftzeichen der Welt.* Hermann Schmidt, Mainz 2011

John D. Berry (ed.), *Language culture type: International type design in the age of Unicode.* ATypI–Graphis, New York 2002

David Jury, *Letterpress: The allure of the handmade.* RotoVision, Mies/Hove 2004

Robert Klanten, Hendrik Hellige, Sonja Commentz, *Impressive: Printmaking, letterpress and graphic deisgn.* Gestalten, Berlin 2010

Fred Smeijers, *Counterpunch: Making type in the sixteenth century, designing typefaces now.* Hyphen Press, London 1996 (2011[2])

Information design

Paul Mijksenaar, Piet Westendorp, Petra Hoving, *Open here: The Art of Instructional Design.* Thames and Hudson; New York/London 1999

Edo Smitshuijzen, *Signage design manual.* Lars Müller, Baden 2007

Edward Tufte, *The visual display of quantitative information*, Graphics Press, Cheshire 2001 (or. 1983)

Edward Tufte, *Envisioning information*, Graphics Press, Cheshire 2005 (or. 1990)

TwoPoints.Net (ed.), *Left, right, up, down: New directions in signage and wayfinding.* Gestalten, Berlin 2010

Jenn Visocky O'Grady & Ken Visocky O'Grady, *The information design handbook.* RotoVision, Mies/Hove 2008

Recommended magazines and blogs

Baseline (UK, irregular) baselinemagazine.com

Codex (Int. English, 2 issues per year) codexmag.com
See also: ilovetypography.com

Eye (UK, 4 issues per year) blog.eyemagazine.com

Items (Dutch, 6 issues per year) http://www.items.nl

Typo (English/Czech, 4 issues per year) http://www.typo.cz/en

Ralf Herrmann, Wayfinding & Typography. opentype.info/blog/

Paul Shaw, Shaw blog & Blue Pencil paulshawletterdesign.com

jasonsantamaria.com/articles

Image index by designer

Tim Ahrens **98, 102, 110, 130**
Barbara Alves **144**
Philippe Apeloig **93, 106, 156**
Apfel Zet (Roman Bittner) **8**
Area 17 **57**

Marian Bantjes **4, 125, 149**
Luca Barcellona **83**
Sofie Beier **78**
Johannes Bergerhausen **131**
Peter Biľak **69, 150**
Blotto Design (Andreas Trogisch) **53**
Erik van Blokland **89**
Irma Boom **121**
Camille Boulouis **106**
Laurent Bourcellier **68**
Alexander Branczyk **155**
Jos Buivenga **111, 114, 135**

Cadson Demak (A. Wongsunkakon) **154**
Oz Cooper **90**
Wim Crouwel **54, 92**

Dalton Maag **111**
Joshua Darden **101, 105**
Jo De Baerdemaeker **153**
Sara De Bondt **153**
Bram de Does **85, 170**
Peter De Roy **92**
Stéphane De Schrevel **161**
Fortunato Depero **154**
Catherine Dixon **31**
Gert Dooreman **18, 58**
DS Type (Dino dos Santos) **99**
Susanna Dulkinys **29, 33**
Studio Dumbar **32, 152**
Christoph Dunst **99**
Rebeca Durán **147**
W.A. Dwiggins **98**

Edenspiekermann **29, 33**
Emery Studio **157**
Experimental Jetset **95**
Felix Ewers **156**

Faydherbe/de Vringer **40–41**
Feltron (Nicholas Felton) **17**
FF3300 (Alessandro Tartaglia) **150**
Freitag **10–11**
Adrian Frutiger **69**

Victor Gaultney **111**
Piet Gerards **48**
Mieke Gerritzen **61**
Christine Gertsch **28**
Armina Ghazaryan **161**
GOOD/corps **115**
Gray 318 (Jonathan Gray) **30, 109**
Luc(as) de Groot **65–67, 94, 140**

Nina Hardwig **95**
John Heartfield **156**
Jarrett Heather **158**
Saku Heinänen **150**
Ralf Herrmann **140**
Klaus Hesse **142**
Cyrus Highsmith **87, 99**
Jessica Hische **109**
Hoefler & Frere-Jones **89, 139**
House Industries **38**
Thomas Huot-Marchand **101**
Vilmos Huszár **90**

Helen Ingham **160**
Boudewijn Ietswaart **109, 122**

Jardí+Utensil (Enric Jardí, Marcus
    Villaça) **25**
Charles Jongejans **124**

Kaune & Hardwig **102, 139**
Max Kisman **77, 171**
Kitchen Sink Studios **37**

Paul van der Laan **91**
Lava **13, 93**
Thomas Lehner **28**
Anette Lenz **19, 55**
Seb Lester **39, 150**
Letman (Job Wouters) **106**
Zuzana Licko **79, 112**

Martin Majoor **68, 85, 99**
Fanette Mellier **23**
Laura Meseguer **137**
Otmar Motter **171**

Moshik Nadav **147**
Gerrit Noordzij **76**
Peter Matthias Noordzij **99**

David Pearson **31, 83**
Axel Peemöller **157**
Vincent Perrottet **19**
Jean François Porchez **111**
Mark Porter **105**

Raureif **173**
Franco Maria Ricci **87**
R2 (Lizá Ramalho, Artur Rebelo)
    endpapers, 155
Nadine Roßa **134**

Judith Schalansky **83, 103**
Ingeborg Scheffers **145**
Alex Scholing **13, 16**
Nick Sherman **148, 160**
Fred Smeijers **62, 165**
Spunk United (Max Hancock) **36**
František Štorm **58, 79, 86**
Andreas Stötzner **80**
Stuntbox (David Sleight) **56**
Sudtipos (Alejandro Paul) **28, 108, 130**
Superscript² (Pierre Delmas Bouly,
    Patrick Lallemand) **151**

Jeremy Tankard **89, 96**
Andrea Tinnes **60**
Mark Thomson **21, 116**
Three Steps Ahead (Josh Korwin) **91**
Alex Trochut **107**
Andreas Trogisch **53**
Trollbäck + Company **159**
TypeTogether (Veronika Burian,
    José Scaglione) **69, 99, 114**
Typejockeys **24**

Ludwig Übele **99**
Büro Uebele **35**
Underware **69, 83, 108, 147**
Gerard Unger **21, 172**

Peter Verheul **152**
Massimo Vignelli **45, 87**
Pierre Vincent **121, 146**

Edgar Walthert **64**
Weiss-Heiten Design Berlin (Birgit
    Hoelzer, Tobias Kohlhaas) **60**
Wim Westerveld **62**
Benno Wissing **26–27**

xplixit **9, 155**

Yanone (Jan Gerner) **111**

Many thanks to Emigre, Font Bureau, Heike Grebin, Annette C. Dißlin (bleiklötzle Buchdruckatelier), Niggli Verlag, Anna Ietswaart, D. Martijn Oostra, Penguin Books Ltd, Nick Shinn *and* Jannie Wissing *for providing images and granting permission for use.*

Thanks to the foundries and distributors who provided fonts: FSI FontShop International, Lucasfonts, Jan Fromm, Incubator/Village, Hoefler & Frere-Jones, Mota Italic, MyFonts, OurType, Jeremy Tankard, 265TM.

← → **Endpapers, front and back:** *Walking.* **Poster designed by Portuguese studio R2 (Lizá Ramalho and Artur Rebelo) for an exhibition at the Paris airports, curated in 2008 by Philippe Apeloig. The posters measuring 4 × 3 m were created by designers from all countries of the European Union.**

About the author

Jan Middendorp is an independent Dutch writer and graphic designer working in Berlin, Germany. He has contributed articles to many international design magazines such as *Eye, Baseline, Items, Swiss Typographic Magazine, tipoGrafica* and *Typo*. He has been an editor and consultant to typographic companies including FontShop, LucasFonts, Linotype and MyFonts. He was a guest teacher of Visual Communication in Belgium, Dubai and Venezuela and currently teaches at the Plantin Institute, Antwerp and at Weißensee College of Art in Berlin.

Other books by Jan Middendorp

Lettered. Typefaces and alphabets by Clotilde Olyff. Self-published, Ghent-Brussels 2000

'Ha, daar gaat er een van mij!' Kroniek van het grafisch ontwerpen in Den Haag, 1945–2000. 010 Publishers, Rotterdam 2002

Dutch type. 010 Publishers, Rotterdam 2004

Made with FontFont. Type for Independent Minds (with Erik Spiekermann). BIS Publishers, Amsterdam 2006 / Mark Batty Publisher, New York 2007

A line of type (with Alessio Leonardi). Linotype / Mergenthaler Edition, Bad Homburg 2006. Korean translation by Seonil Yun: Ahn Graphics, Seoul 2010

Creative Characters. The MyFonts interviews, vol. 1. BIS Publishers, Amsterdam 2010

Type Navigator. The Independent Foundries Handbook (with TwoPoints.Net). Gestalten, Berlin 2011